I0044117

Philippe Davidson
Democratizing Innovation in Organizations

Philippe Davidson

Democratizing Innovation in Organizations

How to Unleash the Power of Collaboration

DE GRUYTER

ISBN 978-3-11-068378-3
e-ISBN (PDF) 978-3-11-068383-7
e-ISBN (EPUB) 978-3-11-068403-2

Library of Congress Control Number: 2021945804

Bibliographic information published by the Deutsche Nationalbibliothek
The Deutsche Nationalbibliothek lists this publication in the Deutsche Nationalbibliografie;
detailed bibliographic data are available on the internet at http://dnb.dnb.de.

© 2022 Walter de Gruyter GmbH, Berlin/Boston
Cover image: gremlin/E+/Getty Images
Typesetting: Integra Software Services Pvt. Ltd
Printing and binding: CPI books GmbH, Leck

www.degruyter.com

Contents

Part 3: **The Training**

Introduction

Organizations operate in ever-changing environments. All too often, established organizations are caught off guard by unexpected changes in market demand or disruptions occurring in the competitive landscape. They stumble because they get insufficient forewarning of these impending market changes; they fail to identify let alone anticipate the impacts that these changes may have on their organizations in time to devise appropriate measures to adjust to them. They find themselves unable to transform themselves quickly enough to remain current and competitive on the markets that they serve. In extreme cases their market power declines, and their viability wanes. The causes are wide-ranging. Global demographics change. Trends shift suddenly. Nimble start-ups quickly convert scientific discoveries and new technologies into marketable products and services that render an established organization's competencies outdated. Some start-ups remain in stealth mode for as long as they can, launching only when their innovations are ready for market which deprives the established firms from sufficient lead time to react. New types of challengers from non-traditional sources take the incumbents off guard; they are just as difficult to track. These unconventional challengers include incumbents from other industrial sectors with technologies that suddenly become relevant in another market. New "champions" from emerging nations propelled by the high rate of growth of their home markets and leveraging unbeatable comparative advantages appear just as unexpectedly on the markets and quickly capture market share. Not only do these unconventional challengers have competitive advantages, but they also innovate differently (Davidson and Ivanova 2011). In fact, there are so many factors of change that one should consider change to be a certainty and a perpetual concern. The pace of change has also increased to such an extent that it increases the risks involved in launching innovation projects. Adapting to these changes shouldn't be reactively and hurriedly undertaken in response to market events, but rather proactively and purposely carried out. The impulse for change should come from within the organization to a far greater extent than it currently does; change should be planned and implemented on the organization's own agenda to support its own goals at its own pace.

Markets should be viewed as being ephemeral. They are too hard to read to justify basing one's organization's strategy and sustainability on them. Organizations serve these markets on what may end up being a temporary basis. Winner one day; loser the next. It is a new reality. This uncertainty in which the organizations navigate gives a new meaning to the expression "playing the markets". Innovation strategizing based on sensing the markets represents a gamble. We contend that organizations should rather manage their capabilities to better protect themselves from an excessive exposure to the serious risks that markets represent. Well-planned, powerful and up-to-date capabilities will cultivate a wide range of opportunities and options on several markets that can better shield organizations from market risks. Thus, the guiding principle should be to make competencies

https://doi.org/10.1515/9783110683837-001

and capabilities evolve for the organization's self-defined purposes, not necessarily to respond to market events. Resources must be updated proactively for the organization to remain true to its development strategy. Therefore, innovation is a relative concept that should be set according to an organization's unique situation, requirements and goals. It represents a progression from its current situation to where it wants to be. Novelty should be gauged according to the organization's own progression. We believe that this organizational resource-based view should be the driving focus of innovation for established organization; their long-term sustainability depends on it.

"How about challengers?", one may feel prompted to ask. They thrive on change. New challengers need to pay attention to innovation as well otherwise they may be ill-equipped to reorient their tentative offers quickly enough on the circuitous path towards finding a demand for their capabilities. They need to find attractive market conditions that they can strive to transform into profitable opportunities supporting their growth. Pivoting should remain in their strategy beyond their initial successes. They need to be ready to move from one opportunity to the next. When they reach the incumbent position themselves, they need to maintain their nimble innovation-driven culture. Therefore, innovation and innovativeness are keys to an organization's success regardless of its position or size.

Some organizations apply a project-driven approach to innovation. They launch occasional innovation projects that they view as being on the cutting edge and transformative. In addition, it is commonly believed that innovation requires "fresh thinking" that can only be found externally. Moreover, it is often assumed that an organization's 'regular workers', who have been conditioned by the traditional corporate culture for an extended time, would be unable to break from their deeply engrained thought patterns to produce something innovative. We believe, on the contrary, that there is already considerable innovativeness amongst an organization's regular workers that is unrecognized and underused possibly even stifled. This group of workers is normally assigned to work on one's organization's regular production and is purposely excluded from innovation initiatives to avoid disruptions. We believe that this approach is wasteful and that the said disruptions that innovation may cause to an organization may occur anyway possibly with more intensity if the regular workers weren't involved from the start. We contend that they should be allowed to innovate in a self-determining manner, both collectively and responsibly, that is to say to contribute to the exploration of novelties and the continuous improvement of their work processes. Regular workers should not be viewed as obstacles to change, but rather as agents of change. Therefore, in order to make an organization more innovative as a whole, its senior managers should start by engaging all the regular workers in innovation. This involves unleashing, supporting and managing the workers' collective and collaborative energies and imagination. They should be trusted to work in their organization's best interest. Validation will come from the wisdom of the group. In other words, innovation is a process that shouldn't simply be top-down, but on the contrary, it should be bottom up, lateral, interdepartmental, open, consultative, and mutually supporting. The regular workers form a knowledge-based community that shadows the organization's current organization structure. It enhances the organization inventiveness by bridging areas of expertise that are often siloed. Thanks to these connections, an organic, collaborative and networked innovation capability is revealed and enabled. In addition, groups innovate better than isolated workers ever could. The clash of ideas and their search for clarity leads to more appropriate solutions being found. Group activities, especially discussions, go beyond the apparent initial dissonance of diverging views; they eventually produce the consonance of shared understanding, and even an amplification of resonance resulting in sounder outcomes. Furthermore, the traditional boundaries of organizations become increasingly blurred; the definition of an organization's workforce must be extended to include external contributors and partnerships, which may even include one's customers when working with them is mutually advantageous.

Market demand also has evolved in another way. Current demand has become so specialized, and markets are so fragmented that organizations pain to address by themselves every variation in demand for every market segment and sub-segment. Most innovation projects require a diverse set of skills. As a result, the teams involved in innovative projects need to adapt their team memberships to their evolving needs as the exploratory process unfolds. Even the original project premises and objectives may change as new information is collected or uncovered. The innovation projects are tentative endeavors; they may morph, shift, pivot, get integrated to other projects or be discontinued. Innovation is a dynamic process of exploration with several parallel paths and likely quite a few failures along the way to success. An innovation project is anything but straightforward; it is venturing into the unknown, developing new knowledge along the way and making discoveries in a process leading to valuable novelties. Organizations must allow for spontaneous team assignments in response to the innovation projects' evolving needs in a flexible process of 'spreading activation.' This involves team members joining and leaving the innovation project teams as the need for expertise change. First and foremost, the workers need to be allowed to help out colleagues who reach out for their expertise on an ad-hoc basis. Far from being a distraction from their regular work, it should be a recognized and rewarded; it should even be a celebrated activity that is part of every worker's regular duties.

We contend that to carry out innovation that is both ambitious and sustainable, one clearly needs to draw on the expertise of several people who must collaboratively work together. The lone inventor is, to a great extent, a myth; this is because there are simply too many considerations to take into account and such an extensive body of knowledge that comes into play that no single person can manage the challenges of innovation alone. Simply put, it takes several minds to get it right. Therefore, we set as a premise that collaboration is the single most important activity in making innovation happen.

This book is structured in three parts of three chapters. The three parts guide the reader through the overall subject of this book which investigates how a ubiquitous capability in democratized innovation may be established amongst an organization's workers. In Part 1, we review the principles and practice of democratized innovation from which the reader will acquire an understanding of the democratized-innovation framework (to which we shall refer henceforth as 'the Framework') that we devised to support it. In Part 2, we investigate the concept of innovation as a domain of knowledge through which the democratized innovators will navigate. Enticing them to innovate in their daily activities is one of the purposes of the Framework. Finally, in Part 3, we review how trainers should provide instruction in democratized innovation to an organization's regular workers. Therefore, this three-component structure follows what we believe to be a natural exploratory process through a new domain which includes 'understanding' (in the sense of situating the subject), 'knowledge' (which is a deeper dive into the subject) and 'wisdom' (that elevates the perspective with advanced topics). This structure is also applied within each part of the book. In Part 1 (the Framework), Chapter 1, reviews the justifications and principles of democratized innovation, while in Chapter 2, we focus our attention on knowledge points related to decision-making in the Framework featuring a set of deliberation thinkLets. In Chapter 3, we investigate advanced considerations, namely, how to establish the Framework in a particular organization while the workers get acquainted with its inner workings and how to integrate external contributors. In Part 2's (the Domain Knowledge) Chapter 4, we seek to clarify the ambiguity surrounding the concept of innovation. A straightforward typology of innovation centered on learning is proposed. Chapter 5 relates typical considerations that workers may have as segues into the subject of innovation. It is designed to be a catalyst for discussions about the principles of innovation. Chapter 6 presents advanced conceptual models that address key considerations in innovation, namely managing the risks of innovation projects, managing organizational capabilities and defining an innovation project's strategy. In Part 3 (the Training), Chapter 7 presents an innovative approach to worker training that is both participatory and experiential. It features the rediscovery of the subject matter by the learners. Chapter 8 covers a set of practical points that come into play when conducting workshops in democratized innovation. Finally, Chapter 9 describes how trainers may address and resolve the learners' common propensity to resist change. In addition, it describes the concept of exploratory and creative dialectics that are used in guiding the exploratory discussions leading the learners to rediscover the workshop's study points. They also come into play when conducting co-creative deliberations and when exercising critical thinking.

The text is written both for sequential reading and for reading sections nonconsecutively. Because of the latter mode of reading, some key points are repeated in several sections to ensure that they are conveyed to the reader who picks and chooses the sections to read.

The Framework is flexible and inclusive. It brings out the innovativeness that is already present in an organization. It establishes a knowledge network from which the workers' creativity will rise which inspired the design of the book's cover. The Framework is designed as an addition to any existing organizational structure, not as a replacement. Let us now discover democratized innovation.

Part 1: **The Framework**

We start by examining how to develop a democratized-innovation capability throughout an organization. Innovation should become a natural reflex and a skill that is readily exercised by all the workers in their day-to-day activities. They should constantly be on the lookout for opportunities to innovate. Democratized innovation increases the chances that they will enthusiastically engage in innovation. Then we investigate how decision-making should be carried out to maximize the value created from the collaborative team effort. Negotiation techniques that apply in the context of group creativity are investigated. We examine how collaborative innovation can be scripted to induce repeatability and reliability while maintaining the flexibility required for free-flowing exchanges. These scripts once modelled can guide the regular workers turned into democratized innovators through the complexity of carrying out collaborative deliberations about their innovation initiatives. They produce more predictability in the otherwise ambiguous innovation process. We review a step-by-step process to establish an organization's particular implementation of 'the Framework' (which is the abbreviation for "democratized-innovation framework" that we will be using henceforth). Since organizations increasingly need to reach out to external associates to carry out their innovation projects, the extension of the Framework beyond the traditional delimitations of an organization is examined with a particular attention to the control of the organization's sensitive information.

https://doi.org/10.1515/9783110683837-002

Chapter 1
Democratized Innovation

Before investigating how innovation can be democratized in organizations, let us review why traditional top-down decision-making in innovation no longer produces the best results in an increasingly challenging business context.

How can communications on innovation strategy foster innovation?

An organization's strategy should include a description of how it plans to innovate. This innovation strategy will guide the decisions made, the resources deployed, and the actions applied to materialize the innovation. All these considerations need to be diligently organized and managed to create the value that the organization's customers or its internal stakeholders want. Thus, defining the innovation strategy as part of the organization's strategic planning is a mandatory starting point. With the traditional approach, this task is the exclusive responsibility and prerogative of the organization's senior managers. Because of the disconnection with the regular workers, the strategy then needs to be communicated to them. This must be done with the utmost care because the strategy may adversely impact them. The release of information is tightly controlled; it may be disclosed only to the affected workers, but it is usually easier to communicate it to all the workers at the same time to project coherence. Communicating one's strategy means selling the underlying vision and inspiring the workers. Also, the workers need to understand its practical implications. The workers are the ones who will make it happen despite their not having been consulted about it beforehand; their enthusiastic engagement is important but often hard to obtain. Their concerns must be alleviated. Allowing the ambiguity to linger on may be disconcerting and possibly damaging. The strategy may be of limited scope or on the contrary represent a significant reorientation of the organization's priorities and activities. In the latter case, it could also be disclosed as a grandiose revelation orchestrated in a way that inspires and even mesmerizes the workers to imagine a "new bold future" for the organization possibly even one that would be a little daunting but that would instill an awe-inspiring sense of purpose and pride. Such an ambitious goal would have the effect of boosting the workers' motivation by allowing them to transcend the humdrum of their daily routines.

However, let us not forget the dark side of any organizational change which all too often translates into lay offs when the required new skills don't perfectly align with the ones that the workers currently master. Selling a vision to a small and targeted group is certainly more effective, since a common set of motivations and interests are easier to identify and to excite than to a larger audience that may

https://doi.org/10.1515/9783110683837-003

comprise several departmental affiliations with their own agendas and special interests. However, with an incremental approach, word of a planned reorientation may come out anyway and spread to the wider audience in an uncontrolled manner which could foster misinformation and mistrust especially if workers suspect that their jobs and livelihoods may be at stake. Rumours of up-coming reorientations of the business' activities will be interpreted as being restructuring that will inevitably raise concerns and cause turmoil in the organization. It goes without saying that a primary consideration that will inevitably be on every worker's mind is whether the strategy involves them at all, which may understandably foster anxieties. Mishandling this announcement may cause issues and concerns with rumors distorting reality which could hinder the later attempts to win over the workers' support. For all these reasons, worker buy-in is essential to implement the innovation strategy successfully. Is there a better way? Despite upfront efforts and costs, there are significant advantages in engaging the organization's regular workers early in the innovation process. Soliciting input and feedback can go a long way towards fostering the trust and the engagement necessary to ensure an innovation strategy's ultimate success; they won't argue against something that they took part in creating. This should be done not only to secure the workers' support, but because they can usefully contribute to the reflections about innovation. These upfront consultations should be viewed as being early preparations that will facilitate the later integration of the changes in the mainstream operations with the benefits of reducing the typical surprises, anxieties, and resistance to change. In addition, it allows to undertake any required staff training early on. Obviously, not every worker can be removed from his or her regular assignments to work on innovation projects, but all workers can acquire a feeling of involvement even if it is simply being aware of the innovation initiatives and a feeling that they are part of a forward-thinking organization. In practice, they need to be encouraged to continuously be on the lookout for ways to innovate by improving on their regular tasks and making and reporting unusual observations that could lead to discoveries.

Overall, the corporate culture needs to be adapted to ensure that change isn't viewed as inauspicious, but rather as an innocuous process that occurs regularly, if not continuously, and that one can expect. Change, whether it is evolutionary or revolutionary, must become the norm; being on the standstill should be what is perceived as being an abnormality. Faced with continuous change, a responsive organization should actively retrain its staff whenever possible, which may provide many opportunities for worker self-actualization and professional fulfillment.

Hence, we contend that innovating in a way that is disassociated from the organization's workers is a misguided approach because it ignores the importance of the numerous considerations relating to the integration of novelties which may compromise the value that is sought. Furthermore, in doing so the organizations' senior managers ignore an invaluable source of ideas, experience and feedback, that is readily available amongst their regular workers. Rather than communicating strategic decisions after the fact, informing and consulting regular workers early on is more effective in the long run. Moreover, innovativeness is more than the simple sum of each worker's individual inventiveness; it is a holistic function within an organization. A vibrant culture of innovation should involve all workers as active participants.

How can regular operations and exploratory activities be balanced?

Performing regular operations that apply current know-how and techniques is what is referred to as exploitation. Traditionally, separating a team mandated with the development of a novelty from the regular workers was a common practice. This approach addressed the most common concerns, such as avoiding any disruptions to the current business processes and production, and preventing the stakeholders associated with regular operations from unwittingly stifling the development of new ideas by resisting change because it could affect their ability to produce. For these reasons, separate organizational entities are created to house the innovation initiatives or distinctive new brands are inaugurated. They are established to clearly distinguish them from regular production. An innovation strategy that involves emerging technologies or new business paradigms usually means ambiguity and risk. Many components underpinning the innovation strategy may first need to be worked out, perfected, developed, and tested before it is ready to be integrated into the organization's regular operations. On occasion, the novelty may even cannibalize existing products or services establishing an uneasy form of internal competition. This concern is often used as an excuse to justify delaying the disclosure of the novelty to other parts of the organization or to its customers. Its implementation in its regular operations may be postponed until the uncertainties surrounding it are fully resolved. Its opportunity and value must be confirmed beyond any doubt. The rationale for doing so is easy to understand; change can cause disruption, possibly even turmoil, that could interfere with the proper performance of the production processes involved in the exploitation of the organization's current assets both tangible and intangible; these processes are the very livelihood of the organization. The mismanagement of the novelty's integration may interfere with the proper operations of the organization's activities and have a detrimental impact. Therefore, engaging in change must be carefully planned out before it is executed; dithering and worse backtracking could be even more disruptive than the originally planned integration process; it should be avoided.

Organizations often exhibit a negative bias against projects that are perceived as being risky or prone to long delays before reaching profitability. Planning projects that involve emerging technologies is also challenging because their feasibility and their impacts are harder to predict. More often than not, decision-makers naturally shy away from the uncertainties of exploration which means that innovative projects are often systematically ranked unfavorably compared to projects that involve familiar technologies or techniques for which the outcomes and returns can be estimated more accurately and more reliably. In addition, novelties may at first temporarily underperform while the quirks are worked out and while related supporting processes are being established – a weakness which may be derided by some critical workers. Indeed, they may resist, defy, and even disparage a novelty that they perceive as being a threat. Interestingly, resistance to change may also foster a form of defensive innovation based on incremental improvements of the current technology that may extend its lifespan for a little while longer. This is a source of innovation that may prove useful when unforeseen issues with a novelty cause delays in its deployment. In addition, customers may hold off purchasing an organization's products if it is rumoured that a better version is in the works. Word of improved upcoming versions may stall the sales of current versions. To avoid these situations from occurring when the novelty is still at an early stage, organizations often elect to keep the exploration of novelties separated from the rest of the organization, possibly even conducting the exploration covertly that is to say without the regular workers nor even its customers being aware of it. In addition, exploration teams are often shielded from what may be viewed as being tedious constraints of production because it is feared that they could restrain the innovation team's creativity. Simplifying the problem is often a useful tactic when experimenting with a novelty but scaling of a proof of concept later may create a difficult hurdle over which to jump; it could even compromise the innovation project's success in case the initial approach doesn't scale.

Ambidexterity in the context of an organization refers to its ability to balance its exploitative and the exploratory activities. Ambidexterity is sequential when the innovation team is temporarily removed from the rest of the organization while it conducts exploratory work and reintegrated in the organization when it has completed it. When the organization's workers are allowed to exercise their own judgement in deciding whether to engage in exploitation tasks or in exploratory ones, it is said to be 'contextual' (Birkinshaw and Gibson 2004). 'Harmonic ambidexterity' involves the concurrent pursuit of exploitation and exploration. Allowing workers to deviate from standard operating procedures as they develop their proficiency at a new task and as they find better ways to carry it out are examples of this type of ambidexterity. Generally, involving regular workers who instigate, launch and undertake innovation initiatives makes the balance between exploration and exploitation contextual since they implicitly adapt novelties to their reality and to their evolving needs. There are other typologies of ambidexterity that reflect when exploration is carried out in the workers' schedules and whether the resources involved are permanently dedicated to research and development. Staff members who work part-time on innovation projects exercise temporal ambidexterity, while a permanent research and development department is a structural one.

In designing the Framework, we were guided by the goal of establishing an environment in which innovation initiatives coming from the organization's ranks can flourish. Regular workers who identify an opportunity for innovation become the instigators and owners of their projects; also, they are accountable for them. To realize their projects, they may work part-time on them or draw on other internal resources in a matrix organizational structure to undertake larger ones; these consultations are an application of temporal ambidexterity. The project may require competencies that are foreign to the organization; in which case it will need to call on external contributors. Thus, blending several perspectives together one may end up with a hybrid form of ambidexterity, which reflects the fact that the Framework is flexible enough to be added to any existing organizational structure.

The Framework is mostly an application of contextual and harmonic ambidexterity with workers instigating innovation projects and remaining on the lookout for opportunities to improve on their work. They keep their eyes open for any observations and information that could trigger discoveries and inventions. These could be the result of purposeful inquiries and experimentation or mere chance. In addition, we believe that they should have an active role in setting the orientation of innovation in their organizations. They should be invited to bring their ideas forward and to freely, albeit respectfully, critique the other workers' ideas. Also, workers should seek advice from others in a casual manner. Operations teams that find efficiencies relating to the activities that they perform together should share their insights with other groups. There must be an allowance for them to participate in other workers' innovation projects when invited to do so. This participative, collaborative and networked framework means that *all* regular workers are de-facto democratized innovators.

How does collaboration come into play in democratized innovation?

A novelty is more than a technology, a technique, a procedure or a mechanism. It is a blend of its intrinsic features with special-purpose know-how, practices and processes developed especially for the context in which it will be used. Some of these supporting assets may be codified; others are tacit which means that they are difficult to transfer from one worker to another by any other means than by coaching and mentoring. Developing these complementary knowledge assets usually takes extensive time. This justifies consulting and integrating an organization's regular workers who know the ins and outs of its operations and business processes when developing innovation initiatives. They are the one's who make a novelty work in an organization's operations by adapting its generic features to the organization's needs. This integration is critically important for the ultimate success of an innovation project because it is at that stage that the novelty is converted into a value-generating innovation for real users. Furthermore, the regular workers may improve on it as they use it in effect exercising harmonic ambidexterity without necessarily being aware that they are doing so. Hence, the regular workers should be active participants in the innovation process. They should be engaged as early as possible to provide the insights into the business and operational processes, and to develop the complementary assets as early as possible. Managing knowledge assets shouldn't be confused with intellectual property (IP) management that simply formalizes knowledge ownership.

It is widely recognized that groups are more creative than individuals working in isolation (Davidson 2019a, 2019b). Furthermore, rather than sporadically isolating innovators and innovation teams only to reintegrate them with the novelty in the organization at a later date, all the organization should be proactively engaged in innovation as a regular preoccupation and activity. Senior management must establish a global culture of innovativeness, which means developing a capability to recognize, to capture, to trace, to relate, to prioritize, to diffuse and, especially, to reward the contributions to innovation made throughout the worker community. Innovativeness must be elevated to the level of a sought-after ability that every worker aspires to attain, and that the organization recognizes and even celebrates as one of the principal factors of its success.

A team of people can bring insights beyond the imagination of individuals. A greater number of minds, each with different backgrounds, experiences and viewpoints will generate a larger number of ideas and, generally, more creative ones. The exploratory group discussions challenge its participants to formulate their ideas and their thoughts clearly to communicate them effectively to others. The group works its way through incremental refinements and improvements by means of an exchange of proposals and arguments. The discussions are creative and even vibrant to eventually reach what Sawyer (2007) calls "in-flow improvisation". In turn, the participants may express their doubts phrasing them as open probing questions. Questioning and challenging one another's ideas force their proponents to clarify them; the exchange brings out issues that they may not have considered which further develops ideas that may have been initially vague. The search for multiple solutions avoids fixating on a single approach. Blending several ideas together, making compromises and finally reaching a mutual agreement will ensure that the focus remains on creating value for the innovation's stakeholders. All these group deliberations will result in superior and more valuable outcomes than individuals trying to be creative by themselves ever could. Diversity in all of its forms is a key ingredient of a group's creativeness. It avoids falling in the trap of uniform thinking that inevitably leads to solutions that lack originality. Breaking the mold, straying from what is the norm or what is common, daring to be different, these are the imagination-enhancing behaviors that an organization should develop amongst its workers. Purposely hiring diversity can also fosters out-of-the-box thinking.

Projects aiming at developing novelties are becoming increasingly complex. As a result, they require an expanding range of skills. Identifying who may have the knowledge that one needs at a particular time for a given project can be challenging in a large organization. Moreover, being allowed to pull this person away from his or her regular work often raises administrative issues. This process should be dynamic with team members being casually approached and engaged to contribute their expertise on innovation projects on an ad-hoc and temporary basis. The spreading-activation mechanism associates a worker with a set of competencies which may each be represented by a node in the virtual knowledge network. They should have the latitude to reach out to other workers, when need be, and the workers who are approached must be able to help without needing to deal with administrative impediments. Moreover, assisting democratized innovators should be part of any worker's standard duties. Their participation should be documented and recorded, and their contributions evaluated. Thus, there needs to be a formal trace of the spreading activation as it takes place despite it being flexible and casual. Workers' contributions should be rewarded, which means that a formal record should be added to their yearly performance evaluations.

Nowadays, the customary organizational boundaries are less delineated that they were before. Making an organization organic also involves reaching out to external expertise when need be. Special rules must apply to ensure that the organization's sensitive information remains protected. Performing tasks in general and innovation in particular is not only the production of an outcome; it is also a continuous learning experience. When the work is carried out by a group of people with diverse domains of expertise, the knowledge is shared and often internalized by the participants. There is what one might call a "cross-pollination" of knowledge that takes place. Therefore, collaborating with external knowledge contributors is both a risk and an opportunity. Organizations need to manage the risks of external collaborations while taking advantage of their benefits. This means that sensitive knowledge must be tagged as such; topical exchanges may be reframed in a generic manner to avoid disclosing their sensitive aspects. When project teams reach out to external expertise it should be clear to them which knowledge is sensitive and, therefore, shouldn't be shared and which subject matter is open for discussion. Preclearing external contributors relieves this constraint to some extent. Despite these risks of sensitive information leaking out, working beyond the traditional boundaries of an organization can give the organization the flexibility that it needs to expand beyond its core competencies; this may naturally come into play when taking on complex customer projects. It is an important step towards making one's organization more organic. Moreover, the internalization of knowledge by external workers may not end up being durable; indeed, knowledge that came into pay for a project may naturally fade if it isn't later reused. Thus, there is a loss of remembrance in external partners which is also an important part in shaping an organization's own evolving knowledge base.

Barriers of all types, whether administrative or functional, within organizations need to be broken down to allow for free-flowing exchanges and casual consultations. All too often, workers carry out their tasks in isolation. Group affiliation certainly helps develop fruitful working relationships and mutual reliance amongst workers, but unfortunately, it may go wrong if the excessive group focus distorts the workers' motivations. Democratized innovation builds on a community spirit. Organizational silos may stifle network-enabled exchanges. They are static and closed while networks need to be dynamic and open by constantly adapting to shifting needs. Workers need to be encouraged to reach out to one another and to consult people in the know in an unrestrained manner. Enhancing connectedness is more than setting up communications technologies. The organization may be structured in any number of ways, but the organization's competency structure should be networked to foster these exchanges and maximize the reuse of the knowledge. Moreover, new learning amongst workers makes this network ever changing. It cannot be rigidly set; it will be in continuous fluctuation.

Risk-taking is an important part of innovation. Refraining from taking risks maintains a status quo that may itself eventually be rendered obsolete. Therefore, there is risk in experimentation and change, but there is also a significant risk involved in ignoring the need to change only to find oneself unprepared when it occurs. A risk-taking mindset should be cultivated, especially in organizations that find it difficult to break through the rigidity of standard processes and practices to carry out innovation. Businesses in industries that are traditionally more conservative may require more attention in this regard than others. Generally, people avoid taking risks because they fear failure, especially if they anticipate that failures could be career affecting. To avoid this incapacitating propensity from occurring, failures should be reframed as useful learning opportunities. In fact, people and organizations can learn more from their failures than from their successes.

It is generally recognized that groups make riskier decisions than individual decision-makers because the responsibility is diffused amongst several people (Wallach et al. 1964; Dion et al. 1970). Allowance for alternative scenarios as the unknowns of ambiguous projects are cleared and project-type quotas, that force a minimum proportion of exploratory projects in project portfolios, can make risk-taking more systematic. However, on the downside, groups may sometimes engage in excessive risk-taking which is a phenomenon that is called "risk-shift". Risk in innovation is a delicate balance to manage. To alleviate the drawbacks of this phenomenon, Kirkman (2017) recommends that developing alternative solutions should be a standard practice to provides a catalyst for dissenting views. Members of a group who may silently disagree with a solution may more readily and openly express their concerns in the context of discussions in which several design options are compared. Also, he recommends naming a devil's advocate or inquisitor. If being the criticizer is a standard role, making unsettling remarks will come across as the person carrying out the duties of the role, making them less personal. Finally, Kirkman recommends avoiding making decisions under time pressures. The pressure of a deadline could preclude properly thinking things through which could result in disproportionate risk-taking. Another phenomenon that can undermine group creativity is 'groupthink'; it could be defined as a tendency to seek premature concurrence, or in other words team members avoiding conflict or feeling under pressure or enticed to conform with an emerging consensus or with the opinion of a vocal or influential participant. When this situation occurs, the group members cease to exercise critical thinking appropriately and hold back from expressing the dissenting views that they may hold. They may be inhibiting their own power of expression sometimes without even realizing it. It may also be a form of social loafing when participants prefer a comfortable position of a complacent agreement rather than engaging in the effort and possible anguish of contradicting another member's views. Groupthink may be the result of misguided leadership and deference to it by group members acting like followers, as the case described by Houghton (2015) suggests. Although groupthink might result from overpowering leadership, it could also more subtly be a side-effect of charisma, seniority or even exceptional expertise. Leaders in democratized innovation should cultivate their humbleness to avoid this phenomenon from occurring. Although democratized innovation should mostly be self-managed, organizations may choose to create coordination roles to ensure that it operates smoothly. These coordinators will need to hone their negotiation skills to ensure that the democratized innovators participate willingly and work efficiently towards common goals.

Granting the freedom to experiment to the workers allows them to find ways to improve on their work sometimes even intuitively. Indeed, running one's organization like a proverbial "tight ship" may sound efficient but will inevitably hinder innovation by depriving the workers of the time to reflect on their work and to experiment with new techniques. Senior managers need to keep in mind that implementing procedures too rigidly will stifle the opportunity to learn and to gain efficiencies from this learning; there are useful learnings to be extracted from failures as well. Time should be allotted for a systematic analysis to figure out what went wrong; valuable learnings may be extracted from them. This latitude to experiment could be granted as a general policy relying on the workers to apply it when they need to. It should be granted on a discretionary basis or made official with time on the workers' schedules dedicated to exploratory tasks. Progressing on the learning curve is very much an operational consideration that ties into the organization's efficiency and profitability. It involves finding often minute efficiency gains that speed up a process. Improving on one's skill may also improve the quality of production which also creates value. Workers – individually or as groups – intuitively develop meta-routines as they repeatedly work through sequences of sub-tasks; the meta-routines are valuable improvements albeit often tacit and, thus, difficult to capture and to diffuse to other groups. Innovation of this type should also be encouraged, periodically reviewed, acknowledged, adopted, shared, diffused, recognized and rewarded.

Regular workers should be reassured that their jobs will not be jeopardized by the introduction of a novelty within their organization. It should be made clear that they remain part of the organization's evolution plan with appropriate retraining. Moving workers from one department to another or from one project to another should be commonplace to widen the range of their experiences and knowledge; it should be carried out in a way that doesn't distress them. However, this needs to be carried out with proactive organizational support that helps connect the workers with innovation projects that require their skills. Project teams that draw on the expertise of workers from several functional groups in a matrixed organization will also ensure the diversity of perspectives and competencies that can foster unformal learning. In addition, as they move from one project to the next, the new knowledge will naturally diffuse to other parts of the organization. Any formal training should include domain-specific instruction, mentoring and coaching as well as training on innovation principles and practices. Of course, familiarity with the principles and inner workings of democratized innovation should become ubiquitous. Mentoring programs should pair up new workers with tenured ones, especially those who need retraining. A win-win situation should develop with the new worker acquiring the tacit knowledge about the organization's practices while the senior worker gets exposed to new techniques.

Knowledge is increasingly becoming *the* preponderant resource in organizations; it is crucial for their success. Exploiting knowledge and processing it takes an increasingly central role in a wide range of industrial sectors, even in those that don't primarily sell their knowledge or their expertise per se. Traditionally, observing one's competitors' moves and customer feedback were the principal signals to update one's knowledge base. But learning should rather be proactive. Knowledge includes a domain's fundamental principles, practical know-how, lessons learned from failures, problem solving, knowledge about when a piece of knowledge is applicable or not, and knowledge about who has or may have the expertise to help in any given situation relating to the organization's line of business. Knowledge can be collected from scientific publications, trade journals and conferences or many other sources over which an organization doesn't have direct control. It could be acquired or developed internally or created through external collaborations. We set as a premise that collaboration is an important catalyst in the elicitation, production or acquisition of knowledge that is new to the organization. Organizations need to become more cognizant of what knowledge they possess and process, and how they need to enhance it. Generally, they need to make far better use of it to remain competitive.

An innovation project work team develops the information that is specific to a project. In doing so, it may uncover or develop new knowledge that could be applicable to other similar projects, which then becomes new accepted working learnings or lessons learned if the project failed to produce the expected results. This type of project is focused on problem-solving or on producing a specific innovative outcome in a limited amount of time. Once the projects completed, the team members are redeployed on other projects. At that point, the communities of practice need to take charge of the newly acquired knowledge to prevent it from being lost. They will evaluate it and if it is convenable to do so, they may diffuse it to other groups within the organization. Innovation project teams represent the convergence of knowledge and competencies to tackle problems that single workers would be unable to address on their own either because of their complexity or because they are multi-disciplinary. There is usually a core team that owns the project and that is accountable for it with expert advisors who join and leave as it progresses.

How can democratized innovation be exercised in organizations?

Democratized innovation aims at making an entire organization innovative, which means involving the regular workers in innovation endeavors. We advocate focusing on innovation that comes from within the organization rather than responding to external events. However, reaching out to external help is included despite this internal focus; it must be orchestrated by the organization to achieve its own purposes. Therefore, this Framework is designed to benefit one's organization, which of course shouldn't go against caring for other external stakeholders' interests as well, especially the organization's customers and suppliers, since they are often partners in creating value.

The Framework is more of an organizational enhancement than a change per se; it is about adding a knowledge network, enabling greater collaboration amongst workers and a knowledgeable management of the organization's capabilities. However, it must be clearly supported by senior management to be successful. There are four principal management policies that need to be established: (i) giving the regular workers the latitude to develop improvements on their own work, (ii) allowing them to develop their innovative ideas in an environment that fosters collaboration, (iii) proactively managing the organization's knowledge assets (i.e., competencies and capabilities) by knowledgeable workers, and (iv) consulting the community of workers for its recommendations on the orientations of innovation. These policies relate to four organizational groupings of workers, namely: the production workers or production units, (ii) the innovation project teams, (iii) the communities of practice and (iv) the organization's worker community at large; workers may belong to one or more of these groupings. These groupings and their related practices form the four cornerstones of the Framework as illustrated in Fig. 1.1. The cornerstones of the Framework are distinguished on the horizontal axis between those that focus on the enhancements and management of the organization's accumulated knowledge (i.e., improvement and validation) and those that involve the development of new knowledge (i.e., orientation and prospection). On the vertical axis, they are differentiated according to either their action-focus (i.e., improvement and prospection) or their reflection-focus (validation and orientation). An organization's implementation of democratized innovation (to which we will refer as its 'manifestation') is represented as a square in the center of this figure with a typical team of three democratized innovators; it will apply its principles and practices in a way that is adapted to a specific work context. We shall review the other components of the Framework as our investigation into democratized innovation proceeds.

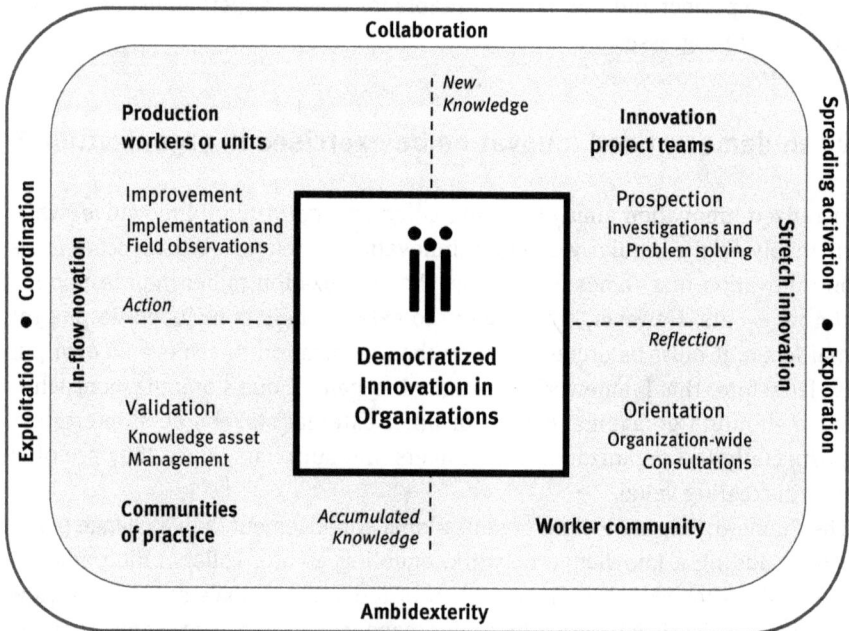

Fig. 1.1: The four cornerstones of the democratized-innovation framework.

Let us take a closer look at the functions and the implications of each cornerstone. While practising their daily activities, production workers or production units may find ways to improve on their work (see Fig. 1.1 top left). As these individual initiatives accumulate, the organization as a whole progresses on its learning curve; it becomes increasingly efficient and effective. The recognition and enablement of this natural process involves a transfer of responsibility to the individual workers or groups of workers forming the ranks of the organization. This responsibility comes with a certain degree of independence and autonomy which is part of the concept of democratization. Innovation occurs as workers incrementally find what are sometimes hardly noticeable efficiency gains as they carry out their tasks; yet these incremental improvements accumulate and eventually produce significant value gains. This process occurs because the human mind naturally reduces its cognitive workload by amalgamating sequences of tasks into single composite meta-routines as it becomes increasingly familiar with them. In this manner, the mind develops ways to carry out the meta-routines almost intuitively and automatically which frees up mental resources for other thought processes. The tasks may also be more skillfully performed which could improve on the quality of the output. In addition, the human mind seeks regularity. As a result, workers may stumble upon observations of anomalies that represent deviations from the familiar circumstances. Being on the front line, these observations are far more visible to them than they would be to any manager. These anomalies could form the basis of inventions; they should be noted and reported for further examination. The same processes may occur for teams working closely together for extended periods of time. As a cohesive production unit, they experience the same kind of cognitive phenomena as individual workers do; they coordinate their actions and develop team-based meta-routines. Some organizations may have implemented standardized operating procedures that inhibit this natural learning process. In this situation, workers should be allowed to lodge transformation requests in order to schedule the three-step change process identified by Kurt Lewin (1958) namely unfreezing, changing and refreezing; this process allows for an orderly change with all the necessary safeguards. These improvements are valuable; organizations should strive to capture them. The learnings derived from these improvements should be shared and diffused throughout the organization which further multiplies the value gains. Finally, production workers or production units should be allowed to experiment with new techniques that improve on their work on a discretionary basis as long as the quality of the output and their overall efficiency at their tasks aren't negatively impacted. They should be allowed to make use of any free time in their regular work schedules to do so. This allowance can stimulate their overall motivation when faced with the monotony of repetitive tasks.

The spreading activation mechanism comes into play throughout the Framework, but particularly in the innovation project teams' work (see Fig. 1.1 top right). They reach out to their peers for advice when they need help. The workers consulted should be allowed to allocate some of their time to respond to these requests on a discretionary basis and, moreover, they should be recognized for their contributions. This form of networking should be self-organizing. Furthermore, these teams carry out creative activities in groups. They challenge one another's ideas and arguments with probing open questions that stimulate other members to articulate their thoughts or to expand on them. As the discussions proceed, the protagonists edge closer to a state of shared understanding. Eventually, they devise the best possible outcome together. They use their diverse skill sets to look at a problem from different angles that a single mind may not have otherwise considered. Together, they better anticipate the many issues that could come about. They debate their innovation endeavors intensely and creatively expressing their opinions candidly without avoiding engaging in respectful disagreements. Indeed, disagreements are opportunities to clarify what is unclear and to get to the bottom of issues; they should be perceived as part of a positive process that can be carried out without distressing confrontation. In addition, new ideas rise from this collective dynamic exchange; it is a catalyst for creativity. They explore multiple ideas in parallel to compare with the options already presented. The differences between the ideas draw out unexpected insights and stimulate critical thinking. Ultimately, they allow the debating group to find the best possible outcome more knowledgeably. The task is exploratory; it is part investigation, part problem-solving. Ideas clash; compromises and decisions are made by the team members with extensive use of astute negotiation techniques to find optimal outcomes that satisfy all the stakeholders.

Nowadays, knowledge is increasingly recognized as an asset for organizations irrespective of their line of business. The management of knowledge assets includes the validation, adoption, incorporation, and diffusion of new knowledge, such as improvements developed internally, novelties developed by the organization's innovation teams and industry updates, such as best practices, technologies, procedures and techniques. The establishment of the communities of practice is a recognition that the organization's sustainability depends on this knowledge being proactively managed. The knowledge could have been generated internally or acquired from external sources to be integrated in the organization's operations. Managing knowledge is a key organizational function; failure to do so can (and will) undermine its competitiveness and sustainability. Managing knowledge includes removing what is obsolete, which is the organizational equivalent of forgetting. Moreover, too little effort is applied to transfer the knowledge detained by workers who are about to leave their organizations. This knowledge may be of critical importance, and their leaving without properly transferring their knowledge may have a profound and detrimental effect; one could view this event as a loss of organizational memory.

Contrary to innovation project teams that are assembled on a temporary basis for specific projects, the communities of practice are enduring and they are mandated with the oversight on a particular domain (see Fig. 1.1. lower left). Their membership may change over time, but often their members remain despite their moving from one functional group to another; they transcend functional groups. The communities of practice are longer lasting than market-focused teams. Knowledgeable workers should be invited to participate in communities of practice in disciplines relevant to the organization's competencies and lines of business. They are groups of people, knowledgeable in a particular field, who collaborate in developing more efficient processes or techniques for their area of expertise; these communities often include expert advisors who are external to the organization. The members of these communities contribute to the advancement of the organization's knowledge base and to updating it. One should think of them as part knowledge-keepers part competency and capability managers who maintain the relevancy of the knowledge assets used in the organization. They diffuse new updates throughout the organization. Generally, the knowledge will be action-oriented and grounded in practicality; it will be converted into competencies and capabilities that define how the organization produces value for its stakeholders. The communities of practice validate the improvements and novelties proposed by other stakeholder groups in the Framework. Overall, they engage in critical reflection on how knowledge is used or how it should be used in their organization. This cornerstone highlights that, for democratization to occur, data, information and knowledge must be freely available to all and authentic; for knowledge assets to be recognized and applied, they must have been validated by knowledgeable people.

Therefore, communities of practice play an important role in ensuring that an organization remains current in its field. They are knowledgeable about the implications of novelties on their organizations; they assess the opportunity to apply them. They strive to monitor or even to anticipate advancements in the domain and to understand their relevance to their organization. They may entertain ties with research institutions or professional associations to identify scientific discoveries that may forewarn of upcoming paradigm changes that could affect the domain's practices. They assess the impacts and the risks; they make extensive use of benchmarking data to gauge the organization's performance in their domain. They should be established for each domain of knowledge in which the organization operates. Their members share a common interest; they have extensive experience and knowledge in their domain. They may proactively put their minds together to solve common domain-specific problems or enforce new standards. If this problem-solving goes beyond simple investigations, they launch special innovation team projects to be handled by a designated team of qualified workers.

The orientation of innovation (see Fig. 1.1 lower right) in an organization relates to the notion of democratization in a more literal sense, that is to say, in giving a say to all stakeholders in the decision-making process, usually as organization-wide consultations. The community of workers at large is engaged; it participates in group reflections. They make joint recommendations on how innovation should be conducted within the organization. This function touches on the notion of self-determination of the concept of democratization. This cornerstone highlights the fact that regular workers may have insightful ideas and that they should be viewed as being agents of change; as stakeholders affected by the changes, they should indeed have a say. The mode of thinking applied in this cornerstone is prospective; worker ideas are brought out through a range of means, such as challenges, idea boxes and even crowdsourcing for large organizations. It is important for organizations to foster an entrepreneurial spirit to capture the ideas that its workers may have. Many workers may secretly cultivate the idea of launching their own start-up to develop their own ideas, often without realizing the huge challenges that it involves. Provided with favorable support, many might find it more attractive to develop their ideas internally that is to say in a familiar environment. Defining and developing an idea requires a range of skills from the outset. Intrapreneurs should be encouraged to work in small teams from the outset rather than by themselves to draw on this range of expertise.

Exercising democratization involves extensive free-flowing exchanges with advanced networking and consultations in a general spirit of trust and knowledge sharing that takes place throughout the organization at all levels. The more people depend on one another in conditions that are favorable for all, the more they will be inclined to cooperate for the greater good of the collectivity.

The greater autonomy of the Framework begs the question about how it relates to the existing organizational structure. Essentially, the existing organizational and reporting structures remain unaffected; the Framework simply adds a knowledge network to the organization that draws out the innovation capabilities of its regular workers. The Framework integrates validation and safeguards while preserving its intended flexibility that is key to its success.

How does the Framework relate to other models?

Pervasive social networks (PSN) are established by social activities, such as gaming and interpersonal exchanges, taking place over networking platforms (Dingli et Tanti 2015). The democratized-innovation Framework relates to the interconnectedness of PSNs (although not necessarily over electronic means) with the pursuit of a specific purpose which is analogous to "distributed problem-solving networks" (DPSN) (Chui et al 2009; Chamberlain 2014). DPSNs leverage the power of groups to resolve specific problems. In the Framework, we extended the concept of problem solving to include the investigations leading to the development of new knowledge and new capabilities and the enhancement of existing ones that enable innovation. Putting the two together suggests combining the power of technology-enabled networking if it is available in an organization with the problem-solving capabilities of an extensive group of people.

A significant amount of research has been conducted into interorganizational collaboration. The democratized-innovation Framework relates to the concept of "pervasive collaboration networks" (PCN) that are self-organizing and include a large number of cells (Muller et al., 2008). Drawing on the analogy of wireless telecommunications infrastructures that extend their range by drawing on cells that are outside of their base networks, the PCN paradigm in a management sense involves seamlessly reaching out to expert individuals – outside one's immediate work group – who are each viewed as a distinctive "competency cell"; it is pervasive in the sense that all of the organizations' members de-facto participate and contribute to the network as part of pre-established agreements and commitments. Dutton (2008), in his analysis of PCNs, points out that their formation isn't made with explicit managerial knowledge or explicit top-down approval. Our Framework relies on similar ad-hoc consultations. We believe that democratized innovation should be allowed to just happen by letting knowledgeable people interact with one another. In addition, the knowledge network should shadow the existing reporting structure – giving it the depth of knowledge – but not challenge it. The modus operandi should be to leave the workers in the know figure things out by themselves rather than being instructed on how to do so; initiative needs to be cultivated amongst the workers. Dutton also notes that PCNs don't necessarily follow the strict boundaries of an organization's work teams, departments or business units. Similarly, we contend that organizations need to develop the ability to attract the creativity of external PCNs to it by signaling that they offer a preferential way to channel external inventions in a way that enables value-bearing innovations; thus, being well connected to these external PCNs can foster co-creation. We assimilated the PCN's notion of a cell to the concept of knowledge enabled by a group of experts of a community of practice, as we called it in our Framework, and which is responsible for overseeing a competency in a given domain. Let us note that we blended the notion of a knowledge community in the concept of community of practice. Hence, the combined knowledge of the members of a given organizational group may become a distinctive competency cell that carries a holistically value dependent on the cross-dependencies and the interactions amongst the competencies that come into play in a complex and often specialized domain of expertise. The PCN paradigm relates to the spreading activation amongst the nodes of the knowledge network that is part of our Framework.

Caminhenos-Matos and Afsarmanesh (2006) described 'collaborative networks' that provide a framework for several organizations to collaborate and to jointly learn through their collaboration. They draw on socio-organizational mechanisms supported by advanced information and communications technologies to bring together people who through the diversity of their competencies and backgrounds help produce more ideas and more efficient solutions in a co-creation model. These concepts relate to the innovation project teams in our Framework; we emphasize that collaboration should support the creation of competencies and especially capabilities that underpin the organization's innovation endeavors. Davidson (2019a, 2019b) suggested that the knowledge-based collaborative networks working in the background of the regular organization will establish a de-facto organic quality to the organization that may be exercised when the need for flexibility arises without it needing to be explicitly engineered and managed; it just happens, and it self-adjusts. There is also a work-culture change that needs to be carried out to support it. Workers should be recognized not only for the work their accomplish, but also for the knowledge that they hold and that they contribute to the organization.

Peter Senge (1990) introduced the notion of a "learning organization". It emphasizes that an organization's race against obsolescence requires agility; in order to face rapid changes, this model promotes not only supporting self-improvement and self-learning towards the goal of "personal mastery", but also team learning, that is to say learning that is mostly the result of staff members working together, thus often incidental. The development of what he calls "mental models" conditions the workers' abilities to process and to reason about the information that comes into play in the performance of their tasks. Mental models combined with "systems thinking", that emphasize the interrelationships existing between a system's components, allow fundamental knowledge to be put in practice in a specific workplace. Knowledge sharing is also an important part of Senge's model, like in our Framework. In addition, his model includes the collective development of a "shared vision" to build staff motivation with a decentralized approach. In our Framework, this notion of decentralization supports the pertinence of involving regular workers in the reflections about the orientation of an organization's innovation strategy rather than simply communicating to them the decisions that were made by the executive team working in isolation. Such consultations allow for a more adapted balance between exploration and exploitation activities by introducing through the workers contextual considerations from the outset. It is through this process that an organization makes fundamental knowledge its own. Our Framework also shares the focus on learning, especially group learning; in our view, learning is an innovation enabler. In addition, we contend that the speed of change can be better managed with a resource-based approach that emphasizes preparation than by reacting to market and competitive contingencies often too late. Learning is a supporting organizational capability that fits well in this resource-based approach. Davidson (2019a) also argued that the regular workers' learning and mastery of the principles of innovation gives them the legitimacy to participate in innovation-related activities.

The development of a novelty involves an investigation into the unknown through practice which, in a way, relates to action research. The aim is obviously imminently practical, which suggests that the action-research methodologies are particularly relevant to the creative investigations that take place in the Framework. These methodologies involve simultaneously taking action while conducting research which can also be called "practitioner-based research". Critical reflection on the actions carried out is a key process in conducting the research analysis. In other words, one investigates how to uncover new knowledge by working on a specific development project. John Heron (1971) talks about "research 'with' the people rather than 'on' the people" in sociological contexts; all participants become co-researchers in developing what Argyris and Schon (1974) call "action science" that we view as relating to co-creation. Amongst the action research methodologies, the "cooperative inquiry method" proposed by Peter Reason and John Heron (1995) stands out because of its highly participative approach; it advocates balancing autonomy and collaboration, that is to say the ability to self-create and to transfigure one's work in a creative and corrective feedback loop. Interestingly, the cooperative inquiry approach involved four types of knowing (Reason and Heron 1997), namely propositional knowing (i.e., delineating the subject of the research that we related to the determination of the orientation), practical knowing (i.e., a first-level action phase), experimental knowing (i.e., a second-level action phase that we related to advancing through the learning curve in a production setting) and presentational knowing (that we related to validation and codification). Coincidentally, these stages fit well in the Framework's four cornerstones. Furthermore, the cooperative-inquiry methodology involves several iterative cycles, which may alter the definition of the original goals of a research project as a better understanding of the issues is gained. This phenomenon often applies when discoveries are made on the basis of the observations of unexpected side-effects which end up generating more value than the original objective sought. Also, problem-solving teams often realize that there is a more important underlying problem to solve and that they may have been investigating the mere symptoms of it. Design Thinking's Empathize activities are especially conceived to ensure that the design team is indeed solving a real user problem. Finally, as Kurt Lewin (1958) pointed out, people are more likely to adopt new ways when they are involved in the decisions affecting them, which ties into our argument in favor of contextual ambidexterity. However, he stresses that the results of action research cannot be generalized, because they are highly contextual. In our Framework, we address this concern about generalization by assigning a validation function to the communities of practice; their members evaluate the self-improvements and assess their potential for reuse in other contexts in the organization; thus, in doing so, they investigate the potential for generalization. Also, we advocate that the manifestation of the Framework should be adapted to the specific needs of each organization.

"How about the concept of democratization?", one may ask. Increasingly, one hears and reads the term 'democratizing' referring to the popularization of a given field that was previously reserved for an elite or for the initiated. Popularizing a field means making it widely understandable and accessible to a broad uninitiated audience; it is bringing them to a point at which they know enough to get started and to be motivated to continue learning more. This interpretation applies to the subject matter of this book, but with the added notions of autonomy (in the sense of decision-making being decentralized and innovation endeavors being mostly self-directed). Furthermore, democratization involves a population that has a say (in the sense of being consulted) on matters that affect its members. Let us note that the expression "democratizing innovation" was originally introduced by Eric von Hippel (2005). He referred to a co-creation model in which end users of goods are provided the means to design and to produce them by themselves. He argued that end users can better meet their specific needs than the designers of manufactured goods ever could. Von Hippel's concept also includes co-creation partnerships between lead users and manufacturers especially for new product uses that are poorly understood; these lead users help the manufacturers to better understand ambiguous requirements and provide a rich source of creativity. Our conception of democratized innovation is distinctive from von Hippel's because it focuses on organizations.

These models emphasize collaboration, connectedness, and learning. The vision of democratizing innovation in organizations draws on all these concepts to get everyone in one's organization engaged in innovation. Our Framework provides a practical way to make all of one's organization innovative not just a small portion of it. The creative resource, that is to say one's regular workers, is already present in one's organization and likely eager to participate; it is simply a matter of empowering these workers to do so to get things started.

Summation

Traditional approaches to innovation lack the nimbleness that today's dynamic market conditions require. The democratized-innovation framework offers flexibility, resiliency and sustainability. It involves collaboration, exploration, improvements, knowledge creation and learning with the aim of creating the value that is one of the defining principles of innovation. It overlays the existing organizational structure by adding organic qualities to it which are essential in increasingly challenging market conditions due to augmenting complexity, shifting trends, game-changing novelties and ever-disruptive competition. An organization flourishes because it has expertise that allows it to effectively and efficiently respond to a need. The organization is defined by its competencies that are leveraged by its workers to generate value. Balancing exploration and exploitation appropriately is important to ensure that the organization captures the value of the knowledge that it creates in a sustainable manner.

Chapter 2
Decision-Making in Democratized Innovation

Collaboration in innovation necessarily means that several people have a say in the innovation endeavor that is under development. Their interventions both contribute to the project and constrain it. These stakeholders could include customers or the people defending their interests in their name, managers at all levels, team members, suppliers and partners in the value chain, government regulatory agency officials and often several more. All these people either participate in the novelty development process or influence how it is conducted. They may also be affected in one way or another by its execution or by its outcome. To maximize the creative potential of collaboration, their preferences and ideas should be put to good use. But they may also have diverging priorities and interests. Their points of view must be integrated into the project. In the end, a novelty must have catered to every stakeholder's interest and needs in a way that is satisfactory to all for it to be declared a success as an innovation. Optimizing the value generated by innovation means finding a happy balance between all these interests. Therefore, innovation carried out by groups of people involves two key considerations: (i) that the ideas be developed and refined through thought-provoking discussions, and (ii) that group decisions be made through discerning deliberations which may involve negotiations. Hence, to carry out these activities effectively and efficiently, innovators must become skilled deliberators and negotiators.

How can deliberations stimulate creativity?

Sawyer (2007) related creative discussions amongst the members of a team to improvisation in jazz. He calls it "the purest form of collaboration". He emphasises that one improvises on the basis of something not in a void. Seeding is indeed a well-known technique to stimulate brainstorming. Sawyer adds that ideas are gradually developed in a sequence of what he calls sparks. In our concept of collaborative deliberations, sparks could be embryonic ideas, merely clever thoughts, or insightful observations in a discussion, that don't in themselves completely solve a problem or represent a terminally conclusive "Eureka!" moment. They build on what others have already said and on the accumulated information and arguments made. As the discussion unfolds, the ideas are refined with the participation of others until something of value emerges. Since the outcome of a collaborative effort occurred through a process that may have been convoluted, the final idea or the final version of the idea truly belongs to all participants not only to the individual who launched the discussion on that track. The process is tentative; when a given line of discussion doesn't lead anywhere, it is time to reframe or to reset it by

https://doi.org/10.1515/9783110683837-004

seeding the discussion again. A lull in the discussion may simply be caused by fatigue, in which case the best thing to do is to pause to resume later. The participants may still keep the points discussed in the back of their minds and find new ideas related to them while they are in a relaxed state of mind. Therefore, even a pause in the group discussions may be productive as the participants ponder over what was said during the discussion. There are no failures in group creativity; creative discussions are a continuous exploration through possible conceptual avenues and an information gathering activity. Generally, more information means better outcomes, but only up to a point. Too much information may overload the participants minds, in which case, it is necessary to summarize and reorganize to make the amount of information manageable again.

It is interesting to expand on Sawyer's jazz improvisation example, since there are more learnings that may be inferred from it. The musicians initiate a well-known melody and then together they extend and expand on it using a mix of experience and imagination to produce a new musical composition which is a unique ephemeral event. Like a team of specialists, each musician pitches in with his or her instrument until a peak in creative band performance is attained. This is what Sawyer called a "state of flow". One musician plays a few notes that are picked up by the other musicians as creative prompts; they play along with the developing musical creation while exchanging the lead, adding their original contributions to it which provide even more creative avenues on which the other musicians may elaborate and so on and so forth; nobody presides over the exchanges: they follow a natural flow. Similarly, the innovation deliberation team is self-directed; it is guided only by the pursuit of shared understanding and discovery. Nobody knows precisely how one got to a given point nor where one is going, but one thing is for sure, creative talent finds in a mix of curiosity and action a fertile ground for imagination developing in a state of collaborative creative elation. It is a unique performance; it is original, like a creative happening.

Let us examine more closely the composition of the participants by considering once again, the jazz band analogy. Each musician is like a specialist of a particular instrument and is essential to the band's capability and identity. It is implicitly understood by all that if any given musician didn't participate or wasn't allowed to participate fully and freely, the band wouldn't perform as well. Everyone receives the other musicians' contributions with enthusiasm and open-minded interest. All members of the band must be cognizant of this interdependency, which is fundamental to the band's originality, cohesion and sustainability. Creative debating is a similar process; like the so-called "cool cats" in jazz, all the participants contribute their unique knowledge, experience and perspective to a common thread of discussion. Each one of them is recognized and respected for his or her distinctive skills and for the original knowledge-based perspective that they can bring to the team. It is a celebration of diversity. Experts in a given field may be invited for a consultation-style intervention joining and leaving the discussion group like an external soloist invited now and then to participate in a jam session with a home band.

The discussion must be transformational in the sense that it advances towards a commonly shared understanding of a given topic progressing towards a common goal even if there are disagreements along the way. The process must be flexible and may even at times be disorganized, with the participants remaining cognizant of the overall objective and edging or rather meandering towards it. The thinking should be profound although it is expressed through spontaneous exchanges. The proponents should always seek to be discombobulating because the very purpose of these deliberations is to challenge the status quo and to find new patterns of thought. Although relaxed, it cannot be a mere social discussion; the participants are discussing tangible subjects for a purpose, even though they can be highly conceptual at times. In this type of discussion, it is as important to think aloud as it is to be an active listener seeking clarifications when required without interrupting the flow of a current line of reasoning and encouraging the person expressing his or her thoughts. Participants should help the speaker clarify an idea that he or she is developing on the fly. Thinking as one speaks is often a confused and unclear process. Participants need to go along with other participants' lines of thought; they must consider their ideas with as much interest as if they were their own. Doing so should be a common courtesy. In addition, they should strive to spark ideas in their colleagues' minds through their comments. It is a group conversation but also an exploration into shared understanding and collective imagination. As much as someone should help the speaker, one must also respectfully challenge the speakers not to make them shut up, but to make them expand on their thinking. Challenging ideas is not only alright, it is necessary since the goal of such discussions is to find enlightenment. One shouldn't be complacent to avoid unsettling anyone. Disagreements should be viewed as opportunities and prompts to better explain one thought; they don't signal impending conflicts. Group members should also periodically ask themselves whether they are working on the right problem. More often than not, there may be an underlying issue to resolve with a reported problem being a mere symptom of it.

Communications involves an emitter and a receptor. Human language is often vague, ambiguous, marked by short-cuts and hanging sentences. There are assumptions implicitly made about the listener's knowledge of a field or about the subject being discussed that lead to implied meanings that may be lost on the receptor. Different interpretations of words result in misconceptions and misunderstandings that make one's comments unclear. However, this lack of clarity isn't all bad, since it can prompt creativity in the listeners' minds as they try to decipher what the speaker is trying to express; they try to associate the unclear speech with their own thought patterns which may generate original insights. Furthermore, what can be obvious for someone trained in a given field may not be so for people who have another background; professional assumptions condition the way people formulate their thoughts and the way they interpret the vocalisations that they hear. The emitter must be cognizant of the limitations of verbal communications by making one's discourse as clear as possible to all. Thus, to ensure that the points came across accurately, the emitter should welcome being challenged to clarify his or her thoughts and the receptor needs to be comfortable expressing that he or she hasn't grasped what has been said. Open questions, tentative statements and rebuttals will force back-and-forth verbal exchanges to clarify, to reword and to adapt what the speaker has said. It is often useful to articulate one's thoughts in different ways or to purposely choose a way that is most likely to be understood – which often means avoiding specialized technical jargon or acronyms. One shouldn't simply be talking about something; one should be communicating with the aim of helping one's colleagues build an accurate mental model of one's conceptualizations. Ambiguous wording is often a clue that there are aspects of an idea that aren't fully thought through. In doing so, the speaker is implicitly asking to be assisted in clarifying concepts that may still be vague in his or her mind; one needs to play along by being their sounding board. One must keep in mind that opponents in a debate are not adversaries; they are partners in exploration.

The clash of ideas and opinions, deliberations and negotiation stimulate group creativity. De Bono (1994) formalized these confrontations with debating roles that participants are randomly assigned to play. It allows participants the opportunity to be critical without making it personal when needing to deal with colleagues who could easily take offense. It brings out the multiple aspects of a problem. However, the process flows more naturally when the debating group members becomes comfortable enough with one another to allow for uncontrived discussions in which participants move from one role to another in a free-flowing yet balanced manner as the debate unfolds. Finally, participants must avoid monopolizing the air waves; being brief is a prized quality and sometimes even a courtesy. If excessive verbosity becomes an issue, the group could challenge the participants to one-minute interventions; a chess clock could help keep track of each participants total speaking time, all in a good spirit of course.

Let us now consider the power of open questions. Conversations easily stray away from the topic. Although, it can be divergent thinking taking place, more often than not, this reflects that some participants consciously or subconsciously avoid addressing ambiguities or flaws in their arguments. Probing open questions are a powerful way to elicit information, since they invite expansive answers without restricting their orientations. These questions reframe or refocus the deliberations and bring to light areas that remain unclear. They require participants being comfortable enough with one another to express aloud what they are wondering about. Humbleness and a genuine interest in what others think are useful attitudes to display since it gives others the opportunity to express themselves. Questions also represent what could be viewed as being 'micro-challenges' prompting one's teammates to reflect on a specific aspect of a problem. Mastery of question formulation is a useful skill to develop to facilitate a debate and to ensure that the conversation remains on topic while stimulating the generation of ideas.

How do group deliberations come into play in the Framework?

Collaborative innovation involves communications, inquisitive questioning, deliberations and ultimately negotiation between stakeholders. The Framework implies autonomy and empowerment of the workers, which also means some decision making which could be progressively increased as trust is built. Decisions will undergo the scrutiny of collective wisdom as a natural validation process. senior management may keep a final approval privilege at least until they are reassured that sound decisions are being made; delegation of decision-making authority could be made selectively for certain types of decisions.

The Framework, as illustrated in Fig. 1.1, is function agnostic in the sense that its structure, goals and processes can be applied anywhere and everywhere in the organization. Its precepts should be ubiquitous to make all the organization innovative; all workers should have acquired skills in democratized innovation. Production workers and production teams will need to convince the communities of practice of the validity of their improvements which members, in turn, will need to negotiate amongst themselves whether to incorporate them in the organization's official processes and the extent to which they should be diffused. The worker community at large will be called on to argue in favor, to justify and possibly to defend the innovation orientation ideas that they bring forward. Innovation project teams will need to agree amongst themselves on the best ways to address problems. And so on as so forth. In every activity and at every step there are ideas that compete, proponents who disagree, opinions that diverge and interests that divide. Negotiation comes into play frequently in democratized innovation. It shouldn't become a destructive chaos of passionate negativity. On the contrary, negotiation should be viewed as an effective way to stimulate creativity through purposely destabilizing exchanges. It ensures that the best of several ideas is retained that satisfy all the stakeholders. One should learn to appreciate one's opponents in negotiation because they will help bring out the inspiration that extended exposure to conformity may have kept subdued.

Democratized innovators are likely to be involved in any of the four cornerstones of the Framework. They may simultaneously participate in several of the Framework's cornerstones and in different roles as described in Davidson (2019a) on which we expanded. These are: (i) advising other workers on an ad-hoc basis, (ii) improving one's work processes individually or as a team, (iii) taking part in innovation project teams, (iv) partaking in extended-group or organization-wide consultations, (v) validating other workers' innovations, (vi) keeping an eye open for new practices and technologies, and (vii) managing the organizations competencies and capabilities.

All these activities involve decision-making. Managers are encouraged to delegate decision-making as much as possible. Negotiation is the primary decision-validation mechanism in the Framework.

How should decision-making be carried out in the Framework?

The democratized innovators, who strive to collaborate effectively and efficiently will need to develop collaborative and knowledge-driven decision-making. They need to embrace a distributed decision-making model. Creative innovators are likely to be passionate about their ideas and to hold strong opinions about them. Furthermore, decision-making discussions amongst a multidisciplinary team are likely to involve several parties holding opposing interests that need to be reconciled; the various solutions proposed need to be made congruent. Since there are no ranks amongst the democratized innovators, decision-making must be based on negotiated agreements leading to outcomes that are clear, well thought out and satisfactory to the stakeholders involved and to the organization at large.

A collaborative approach to decision-making suggests seeking consensuses. Consensus-seeking implies that participants involved in deliberations challenge themselves by striving for a consensus, while keeping the option of settling for a high majority that approximates a consensus as a fall-back option. Each organization may set the thresh-hold that works best for it, but generally we recommend seeking two thirds of the total votes. This means that in a group of three, two favorable votes will suffice to win. This approach reduces the risks of a minority of participants, such as workers who resist change no matter what arguments are presented to them, from blocking the decision-making process with unreasonable demands. This would establish an undesirable situation in which the power of a few increases as the deliberating group works towards a consensus.

The solution that will be considered as being optimal is the one that satisfies a high majority of the stakeholders with compromises and trade-offs. Thus, negotiation skills are important to work through this process successfully. Negotiators in innovation must seek to maximize the value of a novelty for all stakeholders.

How can negotiations for optimizing an innovation's value be carried out?

Productive deliberations thrive on facts; fact-finding is a non-partisan process that can bring opponents to start working together. Setting decision-making criteria upfront will help reduce later disagreements because it dissociates the agreement on the criteria from the options to be debated later. However, the weights attributed to criteria may also be subjective. Data from credible external sources, reference to precedents and applicable theoretical principles and practices help to reframe the disagreements with objective arguments. However, a rational and quantitative approach, even with the referent power brought about by the consultation of an independent expert, may still not be sufficient to bring a group of people to agree.

Unsurprisingly, collaborative innovation requires negotiation techniques that produce collective value. Opponents in a disagreement often engage in the deliberations with a single option in mind, when in fact, disagreements could be resolved in several different ways. Focusing on a rigidly set position is self-limiting and often even self-defeating if it prevents any agreement from being reached. The opposing parties must set aside their respective positions to focus instead on uncovering their respective interests. These interests may not have been explicitly declared in the original position statements which means that some artful probing may be required to get the opposing parties to reveal them. Volunteering something about one's own interests and asking seemingly innocuous open questions can build trust and get the candid exchange started. For example, opponents who are insisting prematurely on using a particular technique could be asked to describe their previous experiences with it. It is a process of collaborative discovery. Parties who value their on-going mutual relationship will more readily engage in this exercise. Indeed, revealing one's deepest motivations and interests requires trust and respect; without it the opposing parties may never open up in fear of losing an advantage. In practice, one needs to uncover and understand the other parties' underlying needs, wants and concerns to transcend the specific stumbling blocks causing the disagreement. This understanding can provide useful clues on what really matters to them, which may not be what one may have originally thought. This approach moves the opposing parties away from a closed frame of mind to a mental space where there are alternative possibilities. This means persistently inquiring with successive amicable yet still resolutely probing questions to genuinely understand the other party's motivations. Reflective listening confirms that one has understood and signals that any points made have been noted and taken seriously; they can be integrated in the statement of the next questions that probe even deeper. It converts the dispute into a constructive candid discussion.

Integrative negotiation, that is also known as win-win negotiation, involves finding complementary interests or relative differences in how much the opposing parties value one aspect or another of a matter at issue. Unsuspected value can be found, sometimes with little respective loss or pain, and on which the opponents can readily agree. One could view this process as finding the free value in a deal. This approach relates to the logrolling technique that involves making concessions in areas more valued by the opposite party in exchange for making gains in areas that one values more. The respective preferences shouldn't be on the same register otherwise the negotiation deliberations will quickly become distributive, which means that whatever one party gains is made at the expense of the other. These complementary value perceptions are highly contextual and temporal in the sense that they are dependant on circumstantial conditions that apply at a specific conjunction in time. They may quickly disappear if the parties involved don't quickly capitalize on them.

Integrative negotiation is a value-discovery technique that is, in fact, compatible with the value-creation process of innovation. Therefore, the concept of 'innovation negotiation' energizes the innovation discussions through deliberations focusing on value. Respectful disagreements are not necessarily bad. Lencioni (2002) goes so far as to identify the fear of conflict as one of the dysfunctions of a team. Several researchers have integrated "constructive conflicts" as a key concept in their research on team shared mental models (Van den Bossche et al. 2011) and "shared understanding" (Bittner and Leimeister 2014). We prefer to use the term disagreement rather than conflict because we believe that dissention in the business and professional context should focus on the merits or the disadvantages of the competing ideas at play rather than on any possible antagonism between the opposing parties. Mutual respect and civility should be the premises of collaborative work. Disagreement stimulates people's minds to move away from what may be complacently considered as being normal; it brings out new patterns of thought. Counterintuitively, it allows the proponents to make their case and the protagonists to express their concerns. Through the clash of ideas, and the alternating exchange of arguments and rebuttals, the team will be far more likely to uncover original ideas. Therefore, let us celebrate the disagreement as a catalyst for creativity. A 'negotiated innovation' could be defined as a novelty that has undergone the test of a negotiation. The stakeholders sought deeper for value in seeking areas of agreement which means that through persuasion or compromises, the areas of dissention were resolved, and the novelty optimized. Negotiating one's innovation should be regularly exercised.

Let us have a closer look at the drivers of value involved in negotiation for innovation.

How can value be created when innovating?

Before investigating how value may be created in innovation, let us have a closer look at the concept of 'value' in this context. A classical interpretation of value relates to what a good, a service or an option may be worth, that may be expressed in terms of a quantifiable measure produced by the quotient 'benefits/costs', or an exchange value on a marketplace that is determined by principles of supply and demand. In the field of value-based pricing, the value of a product or a service for which a price is being sought is the sum of the price of the alternative option plus the differentiation value. This may be difficult to assess for novelties that are so new that there is nothing comparable; however, substitutes could be used even if the comparison is imperfect. Often, the novelty provides the value of convenience over other traditional options. Furthermore, if the novelty is yet to be developed, its quantifiable value may need to be discounted according to the risk involved in its development. However, the risks once understood can be mitigated, which may once again boost the novelty's value. Functional value may determine how well a good or a service fulfils a set of user needs or contractual requirements. A novelty's monetary value may be tied to its future expected performance discounted in proportion to the risk involved in its early adoption, which means that the novelty's promoter assumes at least part of the risk. However, the hopeful adopters of a promised, but yet to be delivered, novelty may bear the cost of opportunities that were lost in waiting for a speculative option that never materialized. Assessment of value may also be based on the cost incurred if one were to be deprived of it. Hence, quantifying value isn't always straightforward.

Value may be assessed qualitatively in terms of how desirable, important, appreciated, or useful something may be to someone. The beneficiary may have an intuitive ability or the skill to assess the value that a novelty may bring. Sometimes people don't have this ability and, as a result, they use comparative product pricing as a proxy for value which can end up being an imperfect measure of it. Popularity of a novelty represents a similar reference, assuming that its adoption by a group reflects genuine group wisdom rather than simply a fashion. However, on the contrary, sometimes value may be in how uncommon (and exclusive) something may be. Normally a declining price increases the value that it represents for the buyers. Counterintuitively, the Veblen effect will establish a positive correlation between price and demand for products that show off social status (Leibenstein 1950). Rarity may also increase value. Therefore, there may be extrinsic derived value resulting from the underlying affective connection between a product and its owner or user, such as projecting a social standing, an image or a sense of belonging, for example. Product or service adoption may also signal a commitment to a standard or a technology, triggering positive or negative network externalities that affect the value enjoyed by other people who made the same choices. But simultaneous choices for the same option may result in loss of value for other stakeholders who compete for the same resources.

Value may be intrinsic and measured on a scale or monetary reference or classified according to a rating system – sometimes related to quality level, feature set, target-user skill level or functional power. Let us note that Dewey (1939) challenged the notion of intrinsic value arguing that it may only exist if there is someone to recognize it. In other words, he argues that in a vacuum, intrinsic value disappears. Value may be contextual. Something may be coveted in a given context may be irrelevant in another; for example, a ship-wreck survivor marooned on a deserted island might find gold to be of little value compared to coconuts that are critical to his or her survival. Value may be amplified when it is obtained beyond one's original expectations leading to delight; this is a principle that is often exploited in negotiation by cunningly reducing the other party's expectations early in a negotiation which sets the stage for making limited concessions made later appear more valuable. Value may be instrumental when it enables something else that in turn creates value. It may have little value on its own, while contributing to an amalgamated value created when it is combined with other elements or components. Ironically, the value of an insignificant component may come to the forefront when it ceases to function. For example, few people think much about the extent to which their lives depend on electrical power until a power outage disables all their cherished electronic devices.

All these notions of value, that are sometimes contradictory, highlight how value assessment may differ from one individual to another and how difficult it is to establish. In a negotiation, although quantifiable value assessments may be helpful in setting what is at play, at the end of the day, value is a rather personal and subjective notion, which, moreover, is relative, contextual and temporal. Interestingly, it is this subjectivity that is the key to unlocking mutually beneficial agreements in a constructive give-and-take process.

Innovation deliberations should focus on exploring the positive and the negative aspects of a novelty including the side-effects of its development and implementation. These considerations make something, relatively speaking, more or less desirable for one party or another (or even for those who may not be present or explicitly represented in the deliberations). Moreover, the extent to which these aspects are sought after or rejected may be a matter of personal perception, cultural or professional bias, or even circumstances pertaining to one of the parties' current situation. To paraphrase a popular saying, value is very much in the eye of the beholder. Exploring and understanding the multiple aspects and intricacies of the perception and the recognition of value by the full range of stakeholders may be a very involved exercise. They are the drivers in converting a novelty into an innovation. Therefore, democratized innovators must become skillful negotiators as they strive to maximize collective value collaboratively.

Value may be elevated for deceptive reasons; an illusion of value can be artificially created. Mark Twain (2010) described, in his acclaimed 1876 novel, how Tom Sawyer, who was tasked with the whitewashing of Aunt Polly's fence, feigned to enjoy the work simply to cultivate feelings of envy in his buddies who happened to be passing by. Cunningly, he artificially elevated the value of the task to entice them to implore him to let them do the work in his place. However, the negotiated-innovation process requires authenticity and benevolence; only factual arguments should be put forward with commendable intentions. Doing otherwise should be clearly rejected. Not only is it disingenuous, but it also undermines the objective of reaching mutual understanding.

Finally, let us consider that a novelty's value will dwindle down as time goes by and as it progresses on its life cycle or as it is disrupted by competing novelties entering the market. Value is ephemeral; it needs to be constantly renewed. A novelty's value is necessarily a limited-time benefit. However, despite being obsolete, it may acquire value once again as a vintage item that is representative of a long gone yet still cherished past era.

How can collaborative creativity be scripted?

Schank and Abelson (1975) described how social interactions can be modelled as scripts. Similarly, customary creativity techniques can be made to be more flexible and effective by breaking them down into individual scripts. They can be assembled as required by the natural flow of a group creativity session. Therefore, the most effective way to develop a flexible capability for collaborative creativity is in the following steps: (i) identifying reproduceable modes of interaction that are known to alter the flow of discussions in ways that advance the creative process, (ii) codifying them, and (iii) reusing them as they are or with some adaptation. Moreover, once codified, they become artifacts that may be analyzed, manipulated, and adapted. They materialize interpersonal interactions that are otherwise inherently abstract. Once scripted, they can purposely be applied. Indeed, calling on the muses to bring ideas is a viable option when the goal isn't critical and time-sensitive, but applying mechanisms to stimulate imagination consistently is preferable in a work setting. The scripts are generic and reusable. They can be assembled into more elaborate suites to model more elaborate creative group interactions.

Hence, the codification of the interactions should be viewed not as being contrived or constraining, but rather as a way to guide improvised discussions towards predictable outcomes. In keeping with Sawyer's (2007) principle of creative group improvisation, the scripts need to orientate the innovators' thinking and guide them towards novel ways of conceptualizing design problems and deliberating on them, but in a manner that still remains flexible and natural enough to support the meandering thought processes of creative minds at work. Even improvisation in jazz is based on well-defined musical principles that ensure that improvisation sound pleasing. Thus, jazz improvisation isn't literally fully spontaneous either. It is guided by principles that have proven to be effective, but still the creative possibilities remain boundless. Similarly, creative discussions are more effective when guided by recognized modes of interactions.

De Vreede and Briggs (2005) developed reproduceable patterns of collaborative interactions that they called 'thinkLets'. As described by Kolfschoten et al. (2006), they support different aspects of collaborative deliberations, namely: (i) widening the range of the options to consider (i.e., divergence), (ii) narrowing down the number of options or elaborating on the ones already identified (i.e., convergence), (iii) classifying, filtering and organizing the options identified, (iv) evaluating these options and (v) building agreement (i.e., what they call consensus). Comprehensive complex processes can be assembled by aggregating the thinkLets that they identified to form 'compound thinkLets'. In practice, the outcome of one thinkLet, such as a list of brainstormed ideas, a filtered and prioritized list of ideas, ideas related to others, etc., will become the input for the next thinkLet.

De Vreede and Briggs (2005) describe thinkLets with the following fields: (i) a mnemonic name, (ii) the reasons to choose the thinkLet or to pass over it, (iii) an overview of the thinkLet, (iv) inputs, (v) outputs, (vi) setups and configurations, (vii) steps, (viii) usage insights and finally, (ix) success stories. ThinkLets come into play as operational group interaction scripts to support a creative process (Kolfschoten et al. 2004). Faced with a rising number of thinkLets being developed by research teams, de Vreede, Kolfschoten and Briggs (2006) proposed a consolidated hierarchy of thinkLets including classes and modifiers that can be shared across several think-Lets. For example, the 'OneUp' thinkLet described by de Vreede and Briggs (2005) constrains the participants to propose new ideas only if they are arguably better than the ones already presented. This restriction was later converted as a modifier that can be added to several other thinkLets (Kolfschoten et al. 2006). Also, they realized that the concept of a thinkLet script was too rigid. They devised the concept of a rule that provides more flexibility than scripts. We derived a similar rule-based approach to defining new thinkLet-like interaction patterns for a set of negotiation-deliberation thinkLets. Rules specify the way in which free (i.e., spontaneous) discussion may be constrained to make it more conducive to producing a creative outcome. They define how a creative dialogue may be conducted to stimulate or to restrain certain behaviors. Gradually, participants become conditioned to make use of these thinkLet-rules without explicitly being aware that they are.

To illustrate this approach, let us consider the following tale that a good friend of ours once told us; here is how it goes: a monk who regularly sang in a monastery's choir complained to the choirmaster about another monk who recently joined the choir. The newcomer's constant sniffing is annoying; he explained, adding that he couldn't stand it anymore. The choir master astutely instructed him to go chat with the sniffing monk for at least one hour. However, he applied an important constraint (that corresponds to an interaction rule in our thinkLet-like model): they could talk about any subject that they pleased, he instructed, except about the sniffing issue. The complaining monk complied and engaged in an amiable conversation with his sniffing colleague. As the choirmaster shrewdly anticipated, the casual conversation allowed both monks to get better acquainted and to develop a benevolent predisposition towards one another; mutual understanding and camaraderie ensued. As a result, the complaining monk now felt compelled to disregard the sniffing previously considered to be aggravating; in other words, he subconsciously realized that in the overall scheme of things, the sniffing wasn't really as serious an issue as he originally thought. He never brought up the matter again; the problem was implicitly resolved. The approach exercised in this fable could be transposed as a thinkLet designed to increase each protagonist's tolerance for the other participant's singularities that may otherwise needlessly increase tensions between them. A greater tolerance for people makes it easier to find a mutually agreeable compromises on a divisive issue. This thinkLet-like interaction could be called 'KnowThyOtherParty' with a one-on-one conversation setting and a rule stipulating to engage in small talk for one hour or more while avoiding any known contentious subjects or in pseudo-code: 'free discussion' of length ≥ 1 hr, of type 'informal discourse', with topics ≠ contentious subject(s). Similarly in innovation deliberations, free – yet hopefully enlightened – discussions are considered as the basic precondition for group creativity to take place with constraints added to produce a stimulatory effect. We applied conciseness in the definition of the thinkLets; in keeping with this objective, we limit our presentation of the specialized thinkLet-like interaction patterns to the definition of the rules that condition or that constrain a group's exchanges, since the other details are straightforward.

ThinkLet modifier rules can be designed to prevent unproductive interactions. For example, to neutralize a long-winded participant from dominating the discussions, one could add the "RoundRobin" modifier to several of the thinkLets that ensures that all the participants are given the opportunity to express themselves or to explicitly pass on their turns before any other members who already expressed themselves in a 'round' can speak again. Similarly, the "ElevatorPitch" modifier forces the participants to make their points in one minute or less before being cut off.

The "Echo" modifier reinforces active listening and shared understanding by requiring a designated participant to briefly summarize the point made by a previous speaker; this will prompt the original speaker to correct any misinterpretations early on. The Echo modifier also forces a point to be reformulated in different ways which helps clarify vague concepts, because no two people express themselves exactly in the same way.

Some thinkLets relate to the way that meetings are conducted to stimulate creativity. Pausing a discussion session in an impasse suggests an "Incub8" thinkLet that would simply interrupt a work session in the hope that illumination will occur upon resuming it later. As Simon (1979) suggests, the process of forgetting that occurs during incubation allows for illumination when the mind returns to the task but at a higher level of reflection while still benefiting from all the information gleaned up to the previous blockage point, but while disregarding the sticking point that led to the impasse.

There are endless possibilities; it is a good practice to derive one's own set of thinkLet rules or modifiers from observations of what works or not in one's specific situation. The points presented above are simply intended to illustrate the types of thinkLets and modifiers. They are but no means intended to be definitive.

How can negotiated innovation be scripted?

The creative-negotiation process brings out arguments, clarifications and rebuttals which overall help a team move (or rather zigzag) towards a convergence of their thinking that enables what Van den Bossche et al. (2011) call "shared mental models". A more colloquial expression could be that everyone is on the same page – a state that all should reach acquiescently rather than grudgingly. Van den Bossche et al. frame this process as "team learning". Consensus thinkLets (de Vreed and Briggs 2005) bring to light areas of agreement and disagreement amongst the participants by examining their voting patterns, tracking the opinion-changing arguments and seeking clarifications about the motivations underpinning previously defined option rankings obtained through a voting thinkLet. Expanding on the Van den Bossche et al. (2011) team-learning behaviors model, Bittner and Leimeister (2014) propose a compound thinkLet that they called the "MindMerger" which is designed to help discussion groups reach a state of "shared understanding" on a discussion topic and to build commitment. They identify a three-step process comprising what we paraphrase as (i) individual interpretation leading to the initial construction of a set of mental models, (ii) one-on-one team discussions and clarifications of these mental models towards co-construction, and (iii) constructive group-wide conflicts aiming at reaching mutual agreement. Contrary to these researchers, we believe that all of these steps are more effectively performed as a part of a group or a team effort rather than individually or through one-on-one subgroups. We adapted the model that they proposed by identifying the following three collaborative steps, namely (i) disambiguation, (ii) conceptualization and (iii) concurrence. Disambiguation involves clarifying the problem – in a way that is similar to the empathizing in Design Thinking that leads to a better understanding of the user needs and a clearer definition of the problem to solve. Conceptualization relates to the co-creation of solution options through several iterative divergent and convergent activities, or the Ideation domain (i.e., step) in Design Thinking. Finally, the team deliberates and argues the pros and the cons of the set of options to prioritize them or to narrow them down to only one. Thus, it takes a process to go from a cacophony of misunderstandings and diverging views to a state of shared understanding and general agreement (i.e., concurrence).

We derived a set of thinkLets that apply the principles of value-driven negotiation in innovation. As the thinkLet examples provided by de Vreed and Briggs (2005) suggest to do, they are identified by a short mnemonic name, often compounding several words. We only included their short descriptions, because their full forms are straightforward. Let us review them:

'OpenUp' thinkLet: this models the interest-based negotiation technique that involves setting aside the respective positions and probing into the other parties' underlying needs, preferences, interests and personal situations. It is a preparatory component thinkLet for ensuing value-seeking ones. One should ask open questions to bring the other party to reveal their motivations and to expand on them. Revealing something about one's own preferences helps to get the conversation started.

'LogRolling' thinkLet: this is a common integrative negotiation tactic that is easily translated to a thinkLet. It is a composite thinkLet that comprises an OpenUp thinkLet first being carried out. The protagonists investigate ways to satisfy their respective underlying interests by exchanging reciprocal concessions on points that they care less about against gains on points that they respectively value more.

'SpoilSport' thinkLet: Some participants may be over-confident about the sustainability of a current comfortable situation and use this situation as an argument to block any novelty. They may not realize that success is often ephemeral. "Why change what isn't broken?"; they typically say. This point of view has led to some of the most striking business failures in modern history; it is often called the "incumbent's curse" (Chandy and Tellis 2000). This thinkLet forces the participants to consider the hidden risks of the status quo that are typically obsolescence, unexpected competition or paradigm changes or even looming catastrophic events. Stories of unprepared leading organizations that found a sudden demise may help engage the conversation in this direction. However, one should expect to be labelled as a defeatist. Getting people to realize their vulnerabilities will motivate them to more readily agree to novelties that represent contingency plans against them.

'RiskOnUs' thinkLet: since there is always an element of risk in any innovation proposal, this is a thinkLet that may be used if an OpenUp thinkLet previously revealed that one of the parties' has concerns about its risks. Indeed, different people may have different degrees of tolerance to risk. Some may be highly risk averse while others may be more comfortable with risk or may have the means to assume any of its detrimental consequences. The more risk-tolerant party may offer to take on more if not all of a debated proposal's risk.

'SelfDisruption' thinkLet: the objective is to put oneself in the shoes of a competitor concocting ways to disrupt the participants' own organization. Keep in mind that the participants, as regular workers, are better able to figure out how to disrupt their own organization than any of their competitors would be. Indeed, they have insights on any of the possible weaknesses that are usually common knowledge within the organization. This thinkLet may convince previously reluctant participants to agree to a proposed novelty. They may even agree to new lines of products or services that cannibalize the organization's existing ones once they have been brought to realize that these lines may be at risk anyways.

'SwitchingCosts' thinkLet: one party assumes all of the costs that a novelty proposal incurs, whether direct or indirect. These may include the proposer covering the direct costs, such as the cost of new equipment or the cost of relocating a disrupted work group during implementation, or indirect costs, such as alleviating any consequential detrimental impacts, with retraining for example.

'PieceMeal' thinkLet: an ambitious proposal involving a significant cost and risk is likely to trigger reservations. This thinkLet explores the opponent's willingness to engage in a first incremental step with the understanding that the project could be discontinued if any issues arise, if milestones are missed or if pre-determined intermediate objectives aren't met. It is a piece-meal tactic designed to get the other parties to commit to a first step around which they can better wrap their head than they could with the original full plan. Getting later approvals for the following incremental steps is usually easier to obtain once the merits of the initial step have been demonstrated. Also, people generally dislike writing off their investments. The challenge is on the proposer to make this first step compelling; this suggests selecting a step that produces the most tangible outcome.

'ReferentPower' thinkLet: getting the other party to accept prior case examples, a standard or the advice of an expert, is a known tactic to bring a reluctant party on board. This thinkLet may entice a reluctant opponent to accept an option that has been directly or indirectly validated by people in the know.

'SwissArmyKnife' thinkLet: involves bringing forward secondary benefits that make the original value proposition even more appealing. What is proposed is not only effective for an original use, it could also be used for other value-bearing purposes.

'Reframing' thinkLet: when the cost of a project is expensive, it may become more appealing to the other party viewed from another the frame of reference. For example, a capital-intensive innovation may become more attractive by comparing its total cost of ownership with other less ambitious options. Alternatively, an expensive full cost could be spread over a longer period of time or simply broken down into a lesser incremental cost over a shorter time period. However, the latter case is simply obscuring the real cost to make it more palatable, which goes against the principle of shared understanding that we advocate. Therefore, it should be applied with a genuine argumentation that highlights the affordability of the options that one promotes.

'Means2anEnd' thinkLet: corresponds to an innovation being an enabler for future accomplishments or capabilities. It represents instrumental value as opposed to intrinsic value on its own. An instrumental novelty should be transformational for the organization; it should typically prepare it for the future.

'TurnTheTable' thinkLet: when the other party persistently maintains an adversarial position no matter what arguments and compromises are brought forward, as an ultimate tactic, one may challenge him or her to tell you what it would take to get their agreement; this approach forces the other party to take the role of proposer in the deliberations.

'One4All-All4One' thinkLet: this is a thinkLet that is designed to establish a cooperative mood amongst the deliberation team. It involves emphasizing the shared goal that all the parties may have, reminding them that there is common ground achieved up to that point in the deliberations or a common challenge that affects everyone, such as the expression "we're all in it together!" would convey. This brings the opponents to realize that there are higher-level common interests or a greater good, before moving into the discussions on more granular points of contention.

'GoodOrBadFirst' thinkLet: Researchers Legg and Sweeny (2014) investigated the optimal order in which to present good news and bad news when engaging in challenging discussions. As they recommended, when the other party has the power to change the bad-news situation, it is preferable to engage the discussion with the good news. This raises up the opponent's spirit which motivates him or her to make the necessary efforts to remedy the bad news situation which is a point of contention in the negotiated-innovation process. The thinkLet concludes on the expectation that the other party will address the bad new.

'EducateThyOpponents' thinkLet: any decision may involve theoretical principles, best practices or heuristics with which the other party may not be familiar. This thinkLet involves educating the opponent on the underlying precepts that may justify a proposal. It is essential to avoid coming across as patronizing the other party. We recommend calling on a neutral third party to deliver the knowledge free of any influences and any affiliations with the protagonists. Ideally, the expert should be known and respected by the opponent as an authority in the field. The opponent should be free to ask any follow-on questions directly to the expert.

'BeautyContest' thinkLet: faced with an opponent who is adamantly defending an option over another, launching an exploratory challenge into both options may be compelling. Rules must be set in advance to evaluate the outcomes fairly. Also, since budgets are always tight, the challenge should involve limited proof of concepts that highlight each competing proposal's distinguishing features. The proposal that best demonstrates its benefits prevails.

We presented a set of thinkLets that demonstrate in practical terms how value-based negotiation may translate to negotiated innovation. Negotiation is a domain that comprises many more tactics. In particular, there are tactics designed to influence or even to manipulate the opponent often subconsciously, such as "this is a proposal that only someone with your extensive experience will appreciate to its full extent" (i.e., flattery designed to manipulate someone into agreeing to something), artificially limiting the number of options from which to choose (which in the author's mind triggers the search for the other option that the opponents is trying to conceal) or the infamous 'Pull-rank' tactic in which one opponent claims to have precedence over another in one way or another – a tactic which is guaranteed to create rancor. The objective of negotiated innovation is to reveal any reservations that stakeholders may have about proposals as early as possible in the innovation process. The arguments point towards ways in which they may be revised to maximise overall stakeholder value, or to bring to light options that otherwise may not have been considered. Thus, it should be viewed as being an exercise of revelation, not one of confrontation per se. We advocate that the democratized innovators should strive for frankness in their intent and genuineness in the information that they convey to the other parties in the deliberations. One should be open to the notion that there may be a better way than what one originally identified. The search for illumination is the goal; negotiation is simply a way to dig deeper for value than through other more commonly known creativity techniques. That being said, there is value in being aware of manipulative tactics if only to spot them when they are attempted.

The set of thinkLets presented above is by no means finite. Codifying interactions into thinkLets makes them reproduceable. Whatever works in one's particular work environment could be defined as an in-house thinkLet. Moreover, thinkLets aren't rigidly defined; they can also become the focus of creativity in themselves. They can and should be adapted to one's team's preferences or to practices in one's industry. In addition, there will be learning taking place as they are applied.

Summation

In this chapter, we examined how decision-making should be carried out to maximise the creative potential of workgroups. A consensus-seeking decision making process forces the participants in creative deliberations to try harder to convince their colleagues; as a result they apply more effort in articulating their proposals. This generates more creativity. We related the search for value that is at the center of innovation to value-based negotiation. We argued that such negotiation allows to uncover additional value in the innovation process; the outcome is a negotiated innovation. Turning to the relatively new field of collaboration engineering, we investigated how the patterns of interactions that characterize value-driven negotiation could be defined as a set of thinkLets or thinkLet modifiers. They come into play when negotiating agreements in deliberations about novelties in a way that can stimulate group creativity. The thinkLet descriptions were reduced to the way that they constrain free speech or orientate the discussions. Some thinkLets can be assembled into composite ones; other modes of interaction may modify thinkLets that one may have already selected. They determine the terms and conditions of the deliberations.

In addition, thinkLets may capture how people deliberate about their innovation initiatives; this knowledge is often tacit and therefore challenging for organizations to identify, to capture and to reproduce for lack of a representation. Codifying collaborative and innovative interactions is an effective way to make the process more reliable and reproduceable; they may be adapted to better suit particular cases or assembled as composite thinkLets for commonly encountered situations. A record could be kept of which thinkLets were applied to derive new learnings in creative negotiation. Expressed in the form of codified scripts, rules or modifiers they can become part of an organization's knowledge assets. They could be kept for an organization's exclusive use if they are deemed to support its competitiveness but sharing them will enrich the field of collaboration engineering and the community of democratized innovators at large. This sharing would represent a form of 'open democratized innovation'.

Collaboration engineering is a new developing field. Democratized-innovation teams should include a collaboration engineering specialist who is knowledgeable in adapting existing thinkLets to specific needs or situations. Alternatively, this specialist may create entirely new thinkLets especially designed for novel approaches to collaboration; this person could also take on the role of facilitating the group-creativity sessions. However, the end goal should be to gradually develop the democratized innovators' abilities up to a point at which they can carry out collaborative creativity sessions on their own.

Finally, let us conclude this chapter with a word about the delegation of decision-making to workers. The democratized-innovation framework doesn't imply that managers relinquish their decision-making prerogatives. At an early stage, these worker-group decisions may be framed as recommendations subject to official confirmation. As the trust is built, more autonomy may be granted. It is efficient to do so. Eventually, managers may elect to dedicate more time to the setting of the policies that frame the democratized-innovation decision-making than carrying out the day-to-day decision-making themselves. Managing may become to a greater extent a policy-making activity leaving processes and resources to manage themselves according to these policies. Indeed, the management function is also an organizational capability to manage.

Chapter 3
Internalizing and Externalizing the Framework

In this chapter, we describe how an organization may adopt the democratized-innovation framework. We refer to this process as the internalization of the Framework rather than its establishment to emphasize the fact that it is an enablement of a knowledge network comprising existing workers. It is a matter of establishing the connections, developing their knowledge, adopting the Framework's practices and enticing them to start innovating. As already mentioned in Chapter 1, we emphasize the fact that the Framework isn't designed to replace an existing organizational structure, but rather to support it with greater worker engagement in innovation. Thanks to the Framework, an organization will enable the knowledge to flow more freely throughout its ranks. Attaining this goal requires that the regular workers embrace its precepts, acquire knowledge in innovation, and make innovativeness a common reflex. The regular workers must think of themselves as democratized innovators. Each organization will need to adapt the Framework to its own circumstances. Moreover, the knowledge network itself will self-adapt as time goes by; it will evolve naturally, continuously, and dynamically to the organization's evolving needs. We refer to this customization process as the revelation of the organization's manifestation of the Framework because, to a great extent, it occurs automatically by building on existing components and motivations that are already present but mostly overlooked. It is a matter of establishing favorable conditions and, with some guidance, letting the manifestation develop naturally. This is one of the principal advantages of the Framework: once seeded, it self-propagates and evolves according to the organization's shifting needs for expertise; it morphs in a way that maintains its pertinence. We distinguish the process that should be applied to establish democratized innovation from the regular operation of the Framework once it has been established. The former situation involves setting up the components of the Framework in a way that ensures that it establishes itself on a steady footing. The latter one requires continuously self-adjusting processes that run infinitely.

It is increasingly challenging for organizations to handle the complexities, the scale, the speed, or the risk of change by drawing exclusively on their own resources. They need to reach out to external associates and partnering organizations who have the expertise that they need to carry out challenging innovation endeavors. Openness and cooperation are key principles. In the Framework, this means allowing some branches of the knowledge network to grow beyond the boundaries of one's organization; accordingly, information and knowledge may flow outside the organization. We call this extension the 'externalization' of the Framework in the sense that the internal knowledge network must interface with the external contributors, suppliers and partnering organizations. Since the Framework is organization-centric, it seeks to maximise the inbound flows of knowledge (i.e., flows of

https://doi.org/10.1515/9783110683837-005

information from the outside contributors to the internal network). Outbound flows of information are designed to enable the inbound flows. However, it is important to control the outbound flows of information and knowledge to external participants in a way that prevents the inadvertent disclosure of sensitive information. External resources should be used for non-core competencies as much as possible. Establishing a rich external knowledge network as an extension to the internal one will contribute to the organization's success by providing agility, depth and extended scope. External contributors may participate on an ad-hoc and short-term basis or with medium-to-long term agreements.

Although the principles of the Framework are domain agnostic, knowledge is subject to industry-specific practices, to the accumulated effect of path dependencies tied to an organization's history and to contextual circumstances, all of which give the manifestation of the Framework in a particular organization a special if not unique character.

How can the democratized-innovation framework be internalized?

The goal is to establish the organization's own manifestation of the Framework. The first time through the process involves setting up the resources while executing the tasks in the Framework's cornerstones. Naturally, the process requires learning and possibly trial and error as the workers gain familiarity with it. Thus, the first consideration is determining with which cornerstone to start. The steps described in this section are illustrated in Fig. 3.1 that is an abstraction of Fig. 1.1 to bring the process to light. In this figure, the central vertical axis distinguishes the reasoning processes that draw on past experience (i.e., accumulated knowledge), such as the management of capabilities and operational improvements, from those that involve the development of new knowledge, such as defining the orientations of innovation, and conducting investigations and problem-solving related to the development of novelties. To launch the manifestation of the Framework, we recommend first focusing on the cornerstones that involve accumulated knowledge that defines the organization's current competencies. The workers' familiarity with these areas will facilitate the initiation of the manifestation. It is important to gain an understanding of one's organization from the point of view of the knowledge and competencies that come into play. It is recommended to start on the side of current expertise because, more often than not, the regular workers' impulse is to propose improvements that relate to their current activities.

In the first step (see Fig. 3.1 step 1a), a list of current competencies that characterizes one's organization is established by senior managers. "What are we good at?" is the very simple question that one should ask oneself when drafting this list. The perspective should be inward-looking in that the competencies shouldn't reflect market successes but rather those that are exercised to accomplish them.

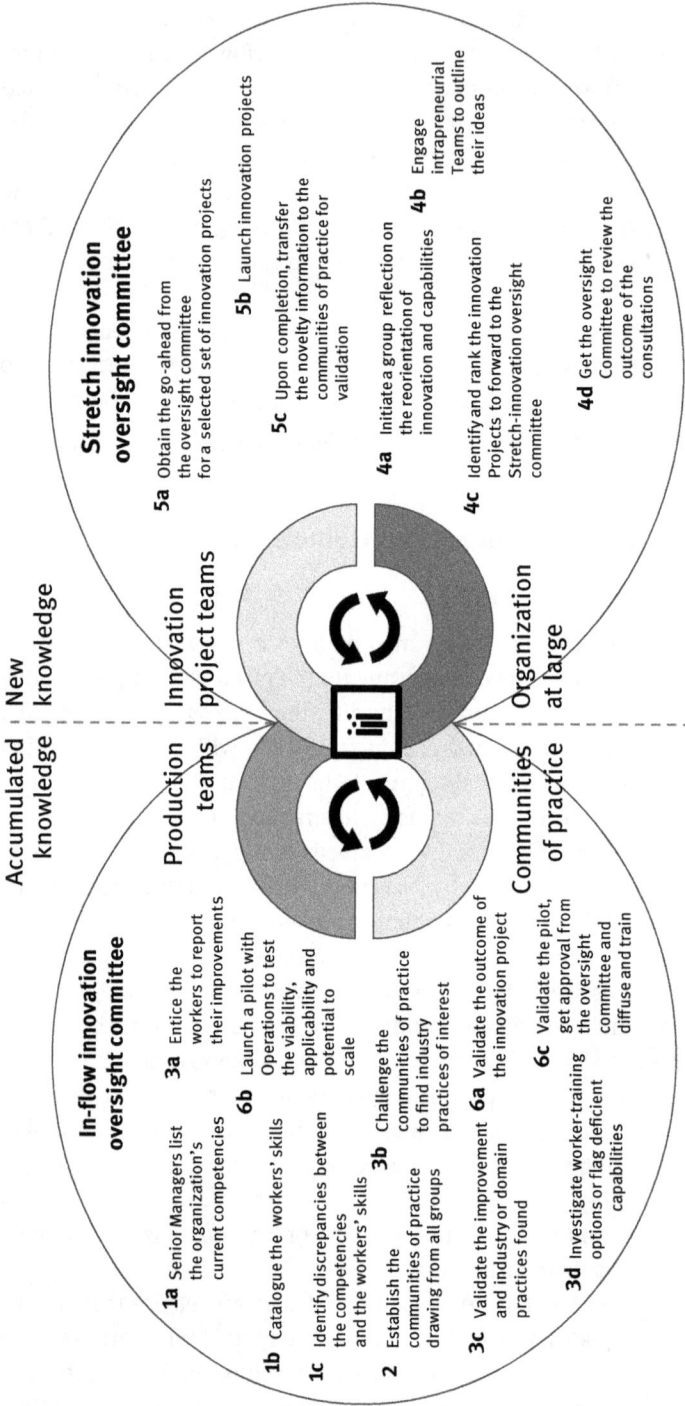

Fig. 3.1: Democratized-innovation integration process.

Stretch innovation oversight committee

5a Obtain the go-ahead from the oversight committee for a selected set of innovation projects

5b Launch innovation projects

5c Upon completion, transfer the novelty information to the communities of practice for validation

4a Initiate a group reflection on the reorientation of innovation and capabilities

4b Engage intrapreneurial Teams to outline their ideas

4c Identify and rank the innovation Projects to forward to the Stretch-innovation oversight committee

4d Get the oversight Committee to review the outcome of the consultations

In-flow innovation oversight committee

1a Senior Managers list the organization's current competencies

1b Catalogue the workers' skills

1c Identify discrepancies between the competencies and the workers' skills

2 Establish the communities of practice drawing from all groups

3a Entice the workers to report their improvements

3b Challenge the communities of practice to find industry practices of interest

3c Validate the improvement and industry or domain practices found

3d Investigate worker-training options or flag deficient capabilities

6a Validate the outcome of the innovation project

6b Launch a pilot with Operations to test the viability, applicability and potential to scale

6c Validate the pilot, get approval from the oversight committee and diffuse and train

Accumulated : New
knowledge : knowledge

Production : Innovation
teams : project teams

Communities : Organization
of practice : at large

Detailed competencies may be organized as a hierarchy of competencies. For large organizations that comprise multiple lines of business, business units and departments, this exercise could be carried out at the level that represents a distinctive center of expertise. If there are overlaps in the competencies present in several organizational entities, they should be considered together. The second step (see Fig. 3.1 step 1b) involves cataloguing and classifying each worker's skills – preferably supported by academic degrees and other official certifications, refereed publications, past participations in projects, professional-association memberships, years of experience in each skill, etc. The claims to expertise should obviously be as genuine as possible; the assessment criteria should be uniform. The assessment shouldn't be guided by a worker's title, because workers' often have more competencies than those required for their current occupations. At the very least, one should attempt to draw out the workers' hidden skills by asking them which skills they would like to exercise more often. Ideally, a short list of primary skills that are deemed to be truly current should be drafted. Indeed, because memories fade, skills that were not exercised for a long time may no longer be as sharp. They may be consigned on a list of secondary skills to reactivate with refresher training if need be. To carry this out, we recommend asking the workers to draft a list of their skills with the justifications for each one entered. A human-resource (HR) specialist should then meet each worker individually to review his or her skills list to enforce consistency across the board. For later updates to these lists once the Framework's manifestation will have been established, this validation could be left to a manager in charge of worker training. It is preferable to avoid assigning this task to the managers to whom the workers regularly report because they may subconsciously align the workers' lists with their respective group's functions or with the worker's role. This natural reflex could prevent hidden talents that the workers may have from being identified. Alternatively, functional managers could be asked to carry out this process by swapping their respective groups of workers. Moreover, these managers shouldn't have been previously involved in the identification of the organization's competencies to avoid any distortion from occurring. Indeed, the intent is that both examinations provide an accurate and unbiased picture of the situation. The lists must then be compiled in a central location; statistics for the unit of analysis (i.e., the organization, business unit, department or other organizational entity) should be derived from them. This exercise should reveal a picture of the organization's current competencies. It may also provide hints on possible intergroup synergies.

The compilation of the workers' declared skills and the managers' perception of the organization's competencies should then be compared. The comparison of the lists is likely to highlight competency gaps and discrepancies (see Fig. 3.1 step 1c). If any are found, they should trigger either of two actions: (i) registering the areas in which the workers need to be trained or in which new workers with the required skills should be hired, or (ii) feeding this information to the initial collective consultation on the orientation of innovation in the organization. Skill redundancies provide clues that suggest the possibility of their being grouped together. The groups requiring these skills could then access these workers on a matrix-team basis. Regrouping resources in the same areas of expertise generally enhances the capabilities. In the spirit of the Framework that strives to leave the organization as it is, these workers could be virtually grouped.

The second step (see Fig. 3.1 step 2) involves establishing the communities of practice for the organization's most important competencies; they don't necessarily overlap the organization's functions. These communities of practice should span across several functional groups and assemble the most experienced workers in each respective area. These communities should comprise quite a few members, since all the members may not always be available to participate at every meeting. The purpose of the communities of practice is to proactively manage the knowledge assets related to specific domains of knowledge. They relate the organization's procedures to industry or domain practices. They react to proposed updates, that are prompted either by an improvement proposed by internal production workers or by the novelties submitted by innovation project teams. They enforce quality and compatibility standards and harmonize the new practices with the existing ones. There needs to be sufficient breath and depth of expertise amongst their ranks to engage constructively in critical reflection.

The third step involves enticing the workers to bring forward the improvements that they may have uncovered in the performance of their work (see Fig. 3.1 step 3a). These improvements are likely to be closely related to their regular occupations. They will then need to be reviewed by the corresponding community of practice that will validate them and check their compliance with the organization's policies (see Fig. 3.1 step 3c). The communities of practice will make recommendations about which improvements should be formally incorporated in the organization's operations, and if they should be diffused to other groups in the organization.

The communities of practice may also instigate innovation by keeping track of any external innovations occurring in their respective domains that may be relevant to the organization (see Fig. 3.1 step 3b); they will evaluate them (see Fig. 3.1 step 3c). They are responsible for ensuring that the organization's capabilities remain current and flag any deficiencies identified (see Fig. 3.1 step 3d). They may reach out to external industry experts and participate in industry events, trade shows and conferences. Communities of practice embody the knowledge-domain perspective. They are not intended to replace any existing organizational functions, such as marketing or business intelligence. Through these communities of practice, the Framework enables another channel for creativity that all too often is ignored in favor of customer requirements often at the expense of long-term sustainability. For example, so-called "technology debt" may fail to be appropriately addressed, or the organizations may fail to get with the times.

In their capability management role, the communities of practice may need to organize targeted training initiatives to upgrade some of the workers' skills (see

Fig. 3.1 step 3d). They should be allocated a budget for that purpose. Training initiatives enable innovation because they develop the workers' expertise that will likely translate to novelties. Training can kick start an organization's efforts to explore the potential of a new domain with the goal of developing a new organizational capability if the training and experimentation related to it prove to be conclusive. Indeed, to recognize the value of a new domain of knowledge, one must first gain some degree of understanding of it before even considering assimilating it and putting it to use in one's organization. Initial formal training may be followed by experimentation to develop the competency and eventually the capability organically. This process may be accelerated by the acquisition of tools or by hiring new workers who are already proficient in the new skills. The communities of practice should report on their investigations to share their reflections and to seek feedback from the oversight committees. Indeed, their observations may trigger new rounds of reflection on the orientation of innovation in the organization, that is to say the step-four sequence in our Framework integration process.

At this point, the reader may be wondering whether the communities of practice have a far-reaching influencing role. In effect, they do, but this influence must be strictly guided by their mandate to oversee a specific domain of knowledge. Any power that they develop must be strictly derived from knowledge-based considerations. Their validation rulings must be supported by a rigorous knowledge-driven evaluation process; they must be prepared to explain their decisions.

In Step-four, a community of practice will typically have flagged a shift in its domain of knowledge that is so significant that it warrants a new round of reflection on the orientations of innovation in the organization (see Fig. 3.1 step 4a). In some cases, these shifts could put the organization at risk of obsolescence. These changes will require the development of competencies that are new to the organization. Thus, a key question to address is whether the organization engages in the development of these new competencies or rather seeks new markets for its current ones. Engaging the regular workers in the consultations on the directions in which to develop innovation broadens this reflection with a wide range of perspectives. Also, they are important stakeholders. Developing new skills requires a great deal of commitment and effort on their part; they are likely to be affected either way. There are several techniques that can be applied to support these consultations, such as challenges, idea boxes, hackathons and crowdsourcing depending on the scope and the scale of the collective reflection that is engaged. Organizations should encourage workers to form intrapreneurial teams to sketch out their ideas (see Fig. 3.1. step 4b). In doing so, they will have a range of skills to investigate their ideas from several angles. The ideas should be outlined to be presented to the other participants. They should be sketched out, but not fully investigated yet, since this activity will come later. Once the ideas have been presented, the group votes on the ideas to rank them (see Fig. 3.1. step 4c). This ranking represents the group's recommendation to the stretch-innovation oversight committee that, in this first run, will need to have previously been established. The members of this committee will include senior managers and possibly internal or external experts. They review the ranked proposals (see Fig. 3.1 step 4d).

As a fifth step, upon having previously reviewed the recommendations resulting from the consultations, the stretch-innovation oversight committee selects the ones that can proceed (Fig. 3.1 step 5a). The ideas that aren't retained must be kept in a repository for possible later use; it should be periodically revisited. The newly identified innovation orientations may require new competencies that will be developed through the novelty development projects. The innovation projects are launched (see Fig. 3.1 step 5b). Core innovation projects teams are formed; they usually include the members of the original intrapreneurial teams. Additional members may be added to complete the required skill set for the project as well as any other required resources in equipment, facilities or other. Transient consultants, internal or external, may be invited for specialized expertise as the project progresses. Once an innovation project is completed, a transfer of project information and knowledge occurs from the innovation project team to the relevant community of practice before the innovation team that has completed its mandate is dissolved (5c).

In Step-six, the communities of practice validate the outcomes of a completed innovation project (see Fig. 3.1 step 6a). They assess its potential and viability for integration in the organization's regular operations. To do so, they may reach out to a functional group from the organization's operations to test the practicality of the proposed novelty. A pilot project to validate the novelty's potential in real-world operations may be launched. It could involve an assessment of the viability of the approach and whether it scales (see Fig. 3.1. step 6b). In case scaling requires further development, the novelty may require an extra-cycle of development that could be handled through the organization's regular requirements and project management processes. Indeed, at that point the uncertainties surrounding the novelty should have been significantly reduced or at least much better understood. Once the pilot project completed, the community of practice reports its findings to the in-flow innovation oversight committee to seek its approval before integrating the novelty in the organization's practices and diffusing it (see Fig. 3.1 step 6c). It will also arrange for any required worker training related to it.

As part of their on-going responsibilities, the communities of practice provide feedback to all the other functions in the Framework. In doing so, they support the other functions of the Framework, but the other functions need to support them as well to ensure that the investigations of innovations that are in the process of being validated are swiftly carried out. The communities of practice and the resources from the Production (i.e., Operations) function dedicated to support them report to the in-flow innovation oversight committee; it is composed of members of the organization's senior management team.

Especially in the initial set-up cycle, senior management must express its support for the Framework. This support must include tangible incentives for the workers to participate, such as their being credited for their support of the communities of practice and their consultations to the innovation teams. These measures should be established before the first run through the Framework is initiated. It goes without saying that all these activities must be appropriately financed. Project codes must be set up for the workers to register the time that they apply on the activities related to democratized innovation. Separating the in-flow and stretch oversight committees prevents from the exploitation-related activities stifling the exploratory ones, which is often the case in organizations when customer requirements take precedence over long-term capability-sustaining ones.

Eventually, as democratized innovation will have been exercised by an increasing number of workers for several cycles, its principles and inner workings will become widely mastered; its activities will occur concurrently, and its components will become increasingly intertwined. Its functional parts will come closer together in a process running infinitely as illustrated in Fig. 3.2.

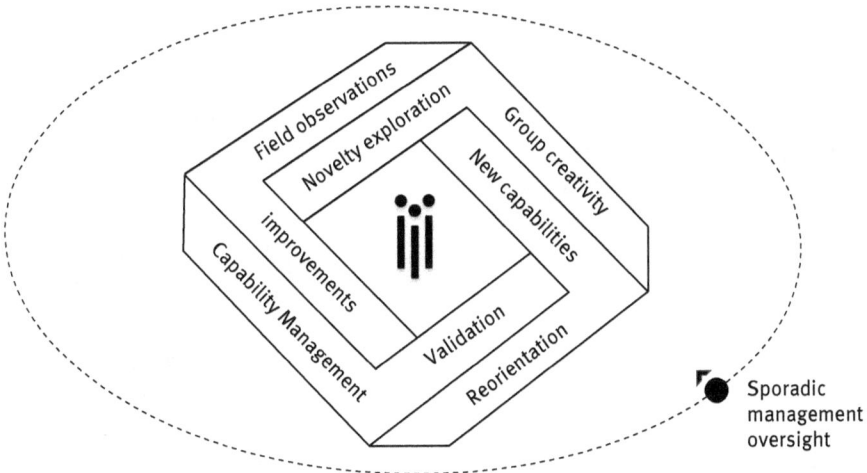

Fig. 3.2: Fully operational Framework manifestation with intertwined activities.

At that point, information and knowledge flow seamlessly throughout the Framework. It becomes a mesh of interactions between workers who are highly networked. The Framework becomes a virtual organizational entity supporting the regular organization through the depth of its knowledge and the creativity of the ideas that flow out of it. In addition, as positive outcomes are recorded and trust develops, management oversight could be reduced. The two oversight committees could eventually merge into one; the concerns that justified keeping them separate may eventually diminish as the managers get better acquainted with the principles of resource-based management as they are applied in the Framework. The merged committee could then focus its attention on major events as they occur in any area of the Framework. Its supervision becomes sporadic and event driven. Figure 3.2 illustrates this arm's-length oversight as an orbiting entity circling around the now highly integrated Framework manifestation. This oversight is based on need, and it is flexible; it is agile management at work. Managers in charge of this supervision could then focus their attention on setting policies that maximize the benefits of the Framework, and that safeguard against any possible missteps. Being more removed from day-to-day supervision allows them to focus on strategic considerations relating to high-level goal attainment while being confident that the manifestation of the Framework takes care of the operational details. At its optimal level of activity, the Framework operates with a high degree of autonomy. Workers are trusted to do the right thing; most of them will rise to seize the opportunities of this empowerment and to take on its challenges in earnest.

How can democratized innovation integrate external participants?

Nowadays, user needs are more and more specialized forming smaller niche markets; markets are increasingly fragmented. This is the hyper-specialization of markets; this phenomenon makes it harder to achieve economies of scale. The trends shift quickly; the windows of opportunity open and close abruptly. Research and development costs have increased dramatically. As a result, organizations find it increasingly difficult to understand these specialized markets and to cater to their needs by making use of only their own resources. In a networked production model, organizations reach out to external organizations to be more agile; collaboration makes it possible to share the risks of innovation and to improve the cost-effectiveness of innovation projects. The outcome of collaborative work is usually of higher quality because the partners are more specialized and therefore more experienced at their respective trades. The ability to find the right partner for the right opportunity will increasingly become a key success factor, that is to say a factor that an organization must satisfy in order to be a player on a market. The concept of partnering that involves participants from several organizations working together as if they were a fully integrated team is commonly applied on major engineering projects that are too large and complex to be addressed with the resources and expertise of a single firm. Consortia of organizations are usually assembled to provide an organizational framework for several distinctive organizations intending to work together to fulfill a common goal. However, let us note that on such projects, the ownership of the outcome – whether material such as a civil-engineering infrastructure or intangible such as a new technology custom developed for a specific purpose – remains with the customer. The consortium partners usually neither seek nor claim any rights to the intellectual property (IP) that is produced unless the customer explicitly transfers it back to them. For example, this situation could occur when a government agency sees an opportunity for economic development in this transfer. Other than the financial proceeds of the contract, the participants gain the experience that can help them bid more successfully on future projects since experience is usually an important consideration among the tendering selection criteria. Organizations may become more ambitious as they gain experience by bidding on tenders of increasing size, scope or complexity. Naturally, the consortium members may harbor concerns that their partners may learn from their collaboration and eventually become their competitors. However, Loss et al. (2008) point out that the knowledge developed through joint learning within a short-term alliance working as a virtual organization may in fact only be truly functional within the context of the alliance; for the competencies to be persistently internalized by the alliance partners, the collaboration would need to have been a long-term one. In other words, the alliance, in itself, becomes an enabling contextual consideration; once this context is removed after the alliance is disbanded, the value of the learned knowledge diminishes considerably. Furthermore, this transfer and internalization of one another's competitive knowledge may also be controlled through the following means. Each project has its particularities that make the generalization of the information or of the pieces of knowledge exchanged amongst the partners difficult to achieve. Without this generalization process, the learning allowing lasting operational competencies being internalized by a partnering organization would be unlikely; simply put, it couldn't credibly compete without broader knowledge and more depth of experience. This concern may be further alleviated by purposely focusing the exchanges between consortium members on project-specific information for unique deliverables. In other words, one should work with one's project partners, not train them.

The management of the collaborations becomes, of course, more problematic when there is IP at play that holds value beyond the completion of the collaborative project and that may provide a competitive advantage to whoever makes use of it. However, despite the complexities of the considerations related to the IP, the rising costs of research and development still justifies engaging in external collaborations. The concept of "open innovation" (Chesbrough 2004) was introduced in response to this realization; it provides a framework for large organizations to cooperate with other ones on selected projects. It allows for the flows of knowledge across an organization's traditional boundaries to be explicitly managed and controlled, possibly even limited to specific subjects and areas. The open innovation activities are specifically defined by memoranda of understanding and contracts that explicitly describe the way that the information will be exchanged and how the rights to the produced IP will be shared. Joint ventures may be created to house this joint ownership of the IP which can then be licenced out to each participating organization that wishes to make use of it. In this way, the shared value is housed in the joint venture that benefits to both of its original founding members. The open innovation framework also allows for an organization's unused IP that no longer involves any competitive value to be sold rather than shelved. The open innovation framework usually involves clearly defined communication channels and dedicated workers who are seconded from each organization for the period of the collaboration project. Nothing is improvised in this model; the exchanges are carefully planned, arranged and formally managed. Similar considerations apply to interorganizational alliances; they have a strategic purpose, and their scope is wider. Typically, the alliance partners strive to leverage one another's strengths to improve their positions on their markets (Doz and Hamel 1998).

Democratized innovation is different because it should be allowed to occur without it needing to be planned in advance; it is driven by ad-hoc circumstances. Project-related requests for expertise must turn around very quickly. It is a networked organizational model that activates its functional components and reconfigures itself in response to dynamic project needs – even if it coexists within other formal organizational structures. The communications and exchanges cannot, practically speaking, be as easily framed ahead of time in contractual agreements and statements of work as is the case with the open innovation framework. Thus, the safeguards against unwanted transfers of competitive information and knowledge must be directly associated with the project information and knowledge, not the use that is made of them. Hence, they must be tagged with information sensitivity levels.

How should information sensitivity classifications be used?

The information that an organization produces should be tagged according to its sensitivity irrespective of its intended readership. Indeed, it would be impractical to define in advance which projects could involve external participants and which couldn't. Spreading activation reaching outside the organization's boundaries should just happen with the same flexibility as it does inside the organization. One should avoid having to tag the sensitivity levels of information after the fact because it would become a tremendous barrier to the sharing of project information. Default sensitivity levels may be set to facilitate the process. Furthermore, re-use of prior project information is also something to encourage in democratized innovation; two projects could involve different classifications. Hence, it is safer to assume that all project information could potentially be viewed by contributors who aren't covered by the usual contractual confidentiality clauses that are part of the regular workers' standard work contracts. The sensitivity levels associated with specific pieces of information and knowledge are subject to change as time advances. Indeed, information that is highly sensitive at one time may become less so at a later date. Therefore, the sensitivity tags must be periodically revised; they may eventually be downgraded or even declassified. A specific moment in time for this re-evaluation should be set when applying a classification which may be a date, a set period of time or a trigger that could be tied to the occurrence of other events, such as the completion of a project, the release of the novelty on the market, the retirement of a product line, etc. The organization should establish a classification guide or decision aid to ensure that it is applied consistently throughout the organization. This classification expertise may also become one of the organization's communities of practice serving other functions in the organization. The critically important consideration is that these sensitivity levels must not hinder the spirit of free-flowing information that characterizes democratized innovation.

The information and knowledge sensitivity classification levels may be original or derivative. The original classification of a document is set by a person or an authority that is accredited for that level. A derivative classification applies when classified information is used to create new informational material; in this case, the sensitivity level is inherited from the source documents' levels. A classification level is set based on the damage caused if it is inappropriately released. Generally, there is a trend to simplify classification levels to facilitate their processing; more levels mean more administration, more complexity and more risks of mistakes being made. The Framework shouldn't involve accessing sensitive personal information or personal identification information about the workers, its external contributors, its suppliers or its customers. Sensitive data may be anonymized, but it is often harder to achieve in practice, since the human mind has an uncanny ability to fill in the gaps in the information through simple inferencing. Also, let us set aside the situations in which information security is already regulated by authoritative bodies. In these cases, suffice to say that the information in the Framework would simply need to comply with whatever principles apply, such privacy-by-design (i.e., with proactive and preventative measures built-in), rules, such as data minimization (i.e., collecting only the data that is strictly necessary for a particular use), retention limitations (i.e., retaining information only for as long as necessary), data life-cycle protection (i.e., protecting the information from its collection to its destruction), and information access tracking (i.e., the logging of who accesses the information and at what time). Alternatively, the people authorized to access the data whether internal or external could all be required to hold the appropriate accreditations or clearances; once these are obtained, all the participants would be on the same footing as far as their access to information is concerned.

Since the healthcare or defense situations are already highly regulated, let us rather focus on the cases that could cause business disruptions. A critical piece of information may be lost, or its integrity compromised when the information is inadvertently deleted or modified by someone who didn't have the authority to do so. The altered information could cause a commercial loss or the loss of proprietary information (such as customer lists, research and development project lists, lists of employees, research results and findings, etc.). The proprietary information could be even more sensitive if it relates to IP, such as discoveries not yet officially disclosed or made public, or not yet protected. The organization's reputation may be tarnished if some types of information leak out, such as product or service deficiencies not yet addressed nor communicated to the affected customers. Any confidential or restricted information should be handled through the regular organizational structure rather than in the Framework.

Classifying information into four levels is generally the norm, namely (from higher to lower levels of sensitivity): 'Restricted', 'Confidential', 'Internal' and 'Public' (or equivalent terminology). The lesser the number of levels which can easily be understood and managed, the better it is. Information that is created and circulated within the Framework should belong to either the 'Internal' or the 'Public' data-sensitivity classification levels. This means that for most of the activities taking place in the Framework, external participants should be cleared for access and consultation of documents tagged 'internal'. This usually means their signing simple non-disclosure agreements (NDA) upon joining. When reaching out to an external expert for a specific, one-time and non-recurring consultation, the consulting members could choose to share only public information to avoid introducing needless complexities and awkward signing requirements. Information belonging to the 'Confidential' level, such as unreleased clinical research data, for example, should be accessed on a need-to-know basis. However, any information that requires special authorization to access slows down the information exchanges which goes against the Framework's free-flowing information principle; therefore, it should be used sparingly. Documents at that level should have their classification reviewed and, if possible, downgraded or screened versions with the confidential parts removed or blacked/whited out should be produced for use in the Framework at lower levels of classification. Training in this regard should be provided to the workers as part of their preparation for democratized innovation.

Contrary to the privacy-by-design approach to systems engineering in which a high level of privacy is the default setting, it should be assumed that a document in the Framework is by-default accessible and sharable among all NDA-covered participants, that is to say classified as being 'internal', unless otherwise indicated. A report produced by an expert who wasn't cleared to avoid unnecessary administrative hassles, as mentioned previously, would be labelled 'public' since it was written without any knowledge of internal information. If a new document involves both public and internal information, the public parts should be handled through rigorous and explicit references to the original sources rather than simply being blended into internal informational material. Indeed, unreferenced, or improperly referenced information from the public domain may incorrectly imply organizational ownership over it.

The Framework is very compatible with open-source and open-design movements. Indeed, when the end-goal is to make one's organization's novelties public, one becomes far less preoccupied about information leaking out. Traditional IP protection may hinder collaborative innovation because it discourages third-party use. Moreover, obtaining a patent doesn't guarantee commercial success by any means.

To sum up, integrating external partners boils down to a great extent to managing the sensitivity of the information that is exchanged amongst the participants of an innovation project to prevent unwanted disclosures about the organization's knowledge assets and business. Defining the innovation projects in a way that keeps their information either at the internal level or, even better, at the public one avoids much of the concerns about involving external participants. In cases in which sensitive or proprietary information needs to be used, democratized innovators will need to keep track of it as it is shared which is troublesome. Even if one's organization embraces an open-source or an open-design approach, that is to say even if the outcome of the democratized innovation process is ultimately publicly shared, the timing of a novelty's release may still be a preoccupation that justifies exercising some control over the information related to it.

Summation

In this chapter, we described a step-by-step implementation process for the democratized-innovation framework. We recommended starting with the cornerstones that involve accumulated knowledge. This approach allows the participants to focus on what they known best while they gain familiarity with the Framework. In addition, establishing the processes related to the current practices sets the Framework on a firm footing from the start. An inventory of skills that are related to the organization's competencies points to which communities of practice should be established. They will be mandated with the on-going management of the organization's competencies and capabilities which are critically important to ensure the organization's sustainability. The subsequent steps involve organization-wide consultations about the orientation of innovation and launching innovation projects to be executed by small teams drawing on other workers' expertise with a flexible spreading activation mechanism. The outcomes of these projects are reviewed by the communities of practice before being incorporated in the organization's standard procedures and diffused. Senior managers oversee the changes through two committees that could eventually be merged into one once they become more familiar with the balancing of exploitation and exploration.

Also, we examined the challenges of involving external participants in the Framework. Project information must be classified according to its sensitivity which determines who may have access to it. We recommended keeping the information exchanged within the Framework at the internal and public sensitivity levels, that is to say levels that don't require any need-to-know justifications. Restrictions on the access to information are contrary to the free-flowing principle that should prevail in the Framework.

Open-source and open-design approaches are gaining in popularity which argues in favor of making project information public; it facilitates the establishment of co-creation agreements with external contributors who are instrumental in to-day's fragmented markets. Making novelties open-sourced means that the organizations must develop their competitiveness by other means that are preferably hard to reproduce, such as their reputation and branding. The Framework lends itself well to unconventional approaches to the management of information and IP such as putting the novelties in the public domain. Since the Framework requires that the participants who work in the cornerstones be tracked for accounting purposes, it makes it easy to identify their respective contributions to innovation initiatives for recognition purposes.

In the idea-to-novelty-in-use process there are many ways to create value all along the innovation process. The value creation may not even stop once the novelty is delivered to its users. Indeed, a novelty may allow for end-user customizations which extend the creativity beyond the producing organization to where it is used to create value in other value streams.

Democratized innovation allows for flexible access to specialized knowledge, which means facilitating interpersonal connections and exchanges between knowledgeable people. Their interactions must be dynamic, flexible, ad-hoc and event driven. Throughout the network, recognition and rewards entice the participants to contribute willingly and enthusiastically. Creativity in a context of complexity needs to draw on an overarching virtual knowledge network that isn't restrained by departmental delimitations nor even by the organization's traditional boundaries. The Framework multiplies the number of creative minds to which an organization's regular workers can reach out and the range of expertise on which they can draw. An inclusive approach to innovation will unleash the creative potential of one's regular workers. The empowerment will entice them to rise to the occasion uncovering value in one's organization that one never expected to be there.

Part 2: **The Domain Knowledge**

We have seen how democratized innovation requires that the workers collaborate, deliberate and negotiate in a process that seeks to maximize the value for all stakeholders. We qualified this process as seeking an optimal outcome. The ensuing consideration is for the workers to master the principles of innovation in order to be able to practice them at their workplaces. We will start this investigation by developing a better understanding the ambiguous concept of innovation. We clarify the reasons which should bring the managers of organizations of different types to integrate people skilled in innovation in their organizations. Then, we relate common preoccupations that workers may have when conducting innovation endeavors as entry points into the subject of innovation as a body of knowledge. Beyond a few classics (such as Utterback 1996, Brandenburger and Nalebuff 1996, Cooper 1999, Moore 2002, von Hippel 2005, Ries 2011, Christensen 2016 and several more that the reader may find in the reference list at the end of this book) there are many innovation primers in the literature, in fact so many that we will let the reader find the one or the ones that works best for his or her needs. We investigate how the risks that innovation involves should be managed. A resource-based approach to managing innovation that relates to the management of capabilities is described. Finally, we present a model that helps to define one's innovation strategy.

https://doi.org/10.1515/9783110683837-006

Chapter 4
Value-creating Exploration

Exploration in the context of organizational management means searching for value through an investigation into the unknown. It is discovering new seeds of value creation and developing them until their benefits, once fully developed, can be harvested. Exploration contrasts with the notion of exploitation in organizational management which involves making something better through knowledge that is currently mastered. Exploration implies proactively seeking to change something that is established or replacing the old; it may be more or less disruptive. It could be construed as being creative replacement or, more dramatically, as creative destruction (Schumpeter 1942). In both cases, the aim is to derive a benefit for someone who may simply be oneself. It is change that is embraced by those who believe in it, adopt it or switchover to it, promote it and remain with it at least long enough to qualify them as adopters. However, as we shall see, there may also be mixed modes in innovation with exploitation in exploration when one applies or improves on other people's ideas, and exploration in exploitation, when previously cast-off solutions are rediscovered, reactivated and reutilized. We purposefully introduced this chapter with the concept of exploration rather than that of innovation because innovation conjures up a wide range of folkloric interpretations that are prone to misconceptions that may deter from looking at the subject from a new angle. However, since innovationess is at the center of value-creating exploration, let us now then turn our discerning attention to the ambiguous concept of innovation.

How could innovation be defined concisely?

A good starting point when approaching any new domain of study is to challenge oneself to define it as clearly and concisely as possible. As Nicolas Boileau (1998) once wrote in 1674: "What you understand well, you enunciate clearly". Thus, one should resist the temptation of including in the definition all the many nuances and subtleties that a domain of knowledge may involve. The definition should reduce the concept to its very essence – an exercise which, admittedly, can be challenging. An indication that the exercise has been successfully completed is when there are no more words that could possibly be removed from it without the definition breaking down completely. "Less is more!" as the architect Ludwig Mies van de Rohe (Eckardt n.d.), who associated form to function, once said, or "Keeping it short goes a long way" as Sir Richard Branson (2014) said, presumably tongue in cheek. Following this principle, Davidson (2019a) suggested that innovation, as an outcome, is "creating value from something new" – a definition that could be

https://doi.org/10.1515/9783110683837-007

further reduced to 'value from novelty' or even further to 'value-creating novelty'. If the word innovation is taken as the action of innovating, one could suggest that it is 'value-creating exploration' which is the title of this chapter. Thus, the concepts of 'novelty' and 'value' are fundamental notions of the approach that we propose. Innovativeness is the capability to produce value-creating novelties. Improvements should also be considered as a form of novelty involving exploration in exploitation.

We contend that democratized innovation boosts an organization's innovativeness. It allows for 'value-creating novelty enabled through ubiquitous collaboration amongst empowered regular workers', or for short: 'collaboratively-developed worker-empowered value-creating novelty'. It is an innovation that involves bringing several minds and domains of expertise together in a holistic manner to solve problems that are either too broad in scope or too complex for anyone to effectively tackle alone. It also involves workers being allowed to innovate on their own work to capture the benefits of their virtual progression along the learning curve as they carry out their tasks time and time again. This is a value-creating improvement which is also a form of innovation.

Since we highlighted the two concepts of 'novelty' and 'value', let us define them in this specific context. A novelty is something that is new and unfamiliar to a worker, a group of workers, an organization, a group of organizations, a population designated as a market or as a user-base, or possibly even, when the novelty is far reaching, society at large. Being unfamiliar means that it hasn't been experienced before and, thus, that it is something about which there is a lack of knowledge and know-how. The newness of a novelty is always relative to the prior experience of the stakeholders for which it is intended or who will make use of it.

We described the concept of value in Part 1 of this book as it relates to integrative negotiations for what we called 'negotiated innovation'. In the context of innovation, the most common meaning is that value is the usefulness that something brings to someone or its utility, that is to say its suitability for a given purpose. However, all the other types of value that we identified in Part 1 may come into play to form innovation.

Let us now consider another method for circumscribing the elusive concept of innovation.

How do common misconceptions provide insights into innovation?

Defining how a concept may be misconceived, in fact, helps to better delineate it. This approach applies the exclusion method, that is to say the successive elimination of false beliefs and statements about innovation to remove from our tenets about it in our search for clarity. Thus, let us consider some of the most common misconceptions about innovation.

Is innovation only about technology and products?

People usually associate innovation with technology and products when, in fact, there are many significant process and service innovations that we experience every day. This mistaken belief takes its roots in the fact that the production processes are invisible to the end-users; similarly, services are intangible. As a result, less attention is drawn to them. Identifying how something can be produced more efficiently, in greater quantities or at a lesser cost, certainly involves considerable ingenuity and will undoubtably create genuine value. Also, since our economies are increasingly service-oriented, there are many opportunities to create value by imagining better ways of providing them. Thus, processes and services are important to keep in mind when looking for ways to innovate. In addition, with the advent of software-as-a-service (SaaS) and subscription-based computing models, functionalities that were previously provided as products are now moving into the realm of services.

Is innovation about leading-edge domain expertise?

Innovation often involves developing leading-edge novelties in a given field. The lead innovator is viewed as a domain guru or a person who knows all the ropes of a business generally thanks to a long tenure in an industry or at an organisation. Thus, one may think: who would be better qualified to lead an organization's innovation initiatives than someone who has expert-level knowledge in the domain? Extensive domain experience or cutting-edge research expertise are certainly useful skills to include on any innovation project team. But skills in managing innovation shouldn't be amalgamated with domain expertise. Innovation management is a discipline in its own right that involves understanding how an organization creates value, how it manages risk, how it fosters collaboration amongst its workers, how it manages its sustainability in ever-changing market conditions, how to continuously learn, how to manage its competencies and capabilities and how to pivot effectively. Moreover, an organization may have mastered the domain of expertise that comes into play in producing its goods, but it may lack the innovativeness to remain on the cutting edge after an initial success and to reinvent itself. Core competencies can become core rigidities as Leonard-Barton (1992) pointed out. However, innovation and innovativeness ensure that one's organization's competencies don't become obsolete and that they don't indeed become rigid barriers that undermine its sustainability. Innovation may relate to a wide range of non-technological considerations, such as social, business and management ones for example.

Does innovation exclusively occur within a single organization?

A common belief is that innovation is inward-looking, that is to say singularly focused on – and carried out within – one organization. In fact, innovation can often be outer-looking by drawing on the innovations developed by one's suppliers or by coaching one's customers as they strive to innovate in their own respective organizations. Value chains in innovation are created by connecting the functions that create value. These organizations each own segments of these value-producing processes; they may also be pursuing several innovation tracks simultaneously working concurrently, jointly, in sequence or implicitly through market mediation. Inventing a novelty isn't a pre-requisite; novelties may be bought from innovative suppliers. Innovating with a purchased novelty is still innovation even if the invention and value-creation steps are separated in space and time. Organizations may adopt the third-party's novelties to improve the efficiencies of their production processes or to integrate into their own products or services which in turn could be adopted as innovations by their customers. As previously mentioned, for innovation to be achieved it must involve a novelty which produces a value; but novelty is a relative notion in that it means that it is new to one's organization and not necessarily new in absolute terms.

Is innovation about making more advanced technologies?

It is often believed that innovation is about making products and services more and more technologically advanced which in turn usually means that they involve increasing complexity. On the contrary, more often than not, innovation is about simplifying an existing technology or its user interface to make it more accessible or more usable. The early versions of a technology may have been exclusively used by a well-to-do tech-savvy elite because it was complicated and expensive. Its simplification makes it more readily usable by the uninitiated. Furthermore, a greater volume of sales may then reduce its production costs, making it less expensive and more accessible to price-sensitive users. Hence, making technologies easier to use by removing complexity may counterintuitively represent a higher level of sophistication and evolution; it creates tremendous value especially if this newly-developed ease of use and this affordability allow the members of a mainstream market to use it. This process unlocks value for a greater number of otherwise uninitiated people who, up to that point, where excluded from using it because of a cost or skill barrier.

Does innovation always involve a brand-new invention?

Tying innovation singularly to invention neglects a rich source of innovation. Indeed, valuable ideas may be found by looking back to the past. Innovation can be about rediscovering an invention that was never adopted because the market conditions weren't right at the time of its original market introduction. It may have failed in a primary use, or it may have been prematurely – and possibly frivolously – abandoned because of a shift in styles, fashions or social habits. Lee, Lee and Lee (2003) underline the bias that inventors often have in favor of exploration – that is to say for seeking new inventions and discoveries while neglecting the potential of existing – yet unused or even forgotten – inventions that could perfectly well fit a current purpose often at a much lesser cost since they are essentially already developed. As the colloquial expression goes, inventors often reinvent the wheel. Hence, it can be beneficial to search for previous inventions before engaging in new development.

Is innovation always adopted quickly?

It is often believed that the benefits of a novelty will be quickly and widely recognized by a user-base eager for change, and that its superior properties will bring users to readily adopt it. It is a naïve view that is often entertained by neophyte entrepreneurs. The reality is that there is usually a considerable resistance to change. In addition, novelties often underperform severely compared to proven current technologies in their early stages of use while the unforeseen implementation and usage issues get resolved. However, once the issues have been fixed and once a given inflection point in the adoption rate has been reached, their superior attributes usually prevail rendering the previous technologies obsolete and more likely to be phased out. The users must then learn how to use them, which represents another barrier.

Is innovation about responding to technological shifts and market trends?

Innovation is often thought to be about reading technological shifts and quickly responding to them. In fact, because the innovation requires time and sometimes even extensive amounts of it, it may be difficult if not impossible to do so. This explains why so many incumbent firms get caught off guard by nimble start-ups introducing novelties that they didn't see coming. It is important for organizations to monitor early discoveries made by research organizations to get the appropriate forewarning; in other words: look at the science before the technology hits you! Similarly, anticipating future market needs and preferences involves considerable uncertainty; it may even be unrealistic to a great extent. Indeed, guessing when market trends will develop, and when they will end may be as unpredictable as gambling because of the wide range of factors that come into play especially those that one expected the least. Trends may not last long enough to allow an organization to adjust appropriately. In some cases, organizational managers may need to simply accept the fact that they cannot compete effectively against a competitor that developed an early lead. In this case, a better alternative might be to find an alternative market for what the organization produces if the shift is persistent or even permanent, or, conversely, to buy into the new market through a merger and acquisition. A trend may only be temporary; missing a trend may not mean that one is permanently excluded from a market. Thus, organizations that are established in their fields and start-ups seeking value need to develop the capability to quickly pivot. For a nimble organization, pivoting may mean temporarily pivoting out of a market only to pivot back onto it when the conditions are more favorable.

Is innovation a form of project management?

Many people believe that innovation is an advanced form of project management. This is a misconception that is commonly reflected in many so-called innovation management software systems. This misconception comes from the fact that a novelty development project is often part of the innovation process. Innovation requires a benefit to be attained for stakeholders; it is the determination of how this value will be achieved that is at the center of innovation. Innovation initiatives necessarily become projects that need to be appropriately managed; once they can be considered to be regular projects, there is hardly anything inherently different about managing them than managing any other types of projects. Any novelties related to the project management interpretation of innovation management represent in fact innovations in the field of project management. In addition, the value unlocked by innovation often has a holistic attribute because its value isn't achieved until all of its constituent parts are in place to provide the benefit sought after. This rationale should guide the design of a minimum viable product (MVP) (Ries 2011) which must deliver complete value albeit in a minimalistic manner. Breaking down the value into incremental value-attributions as is the case for value-based project management may be more of an intellectual exercise than the reflection of a partial worth that could be enjoyed by anyone unless someone takes over a suspended incomplete project to follow through with it.

Is innovation mostly about creativity and having ideas?

It is a long-held belief that innovation is mostly about creativity and ideas. Although inventiveness is always useful and often part of the innovation process, adopting, applying and sometimes improving on other people's ideas or other organization's inventions is also worthwhile and, in fact, the most common way of innovating. Thomas Edison (Morris 2019) is credited for stating – presumably facetiously – that he never had any new ideas; he was expressing the notion that there is more to innovation than having an original idea. There is a lot of hard work involved in bringing it to fruition or, to use the terminology that relates to this chapter, there is a need to carry out exploitation-related activities in the exploration process towards the achievement of value.

Is it essential to be the first on the market?

There is a mystique about being the first on the market with an idea. It is the so-called "first-mover advantage" that paves the way to success. This is a common belief; however, it often makes more sense to wait until others have entered the market only to take the fast-follower role. There are many examples of pioneering companies that consumed huge amounts of their resources and eventually ran out of resources in trying to educate the market on their novelty and to work through the issues that early adopters inevitably encounter. In fact, holding off until the market experimentation has almost finished and until the time that the customer-base will have been made aware of a novelty or will have been educated on it is a sound practice. Utterback (1996) suggests that the most opportune time to enter the market is right before a dominant design in the adopters' collective minds emerges. In addition, if one had to map the attractiveness of a market against the number of competitors operating on wit, the typical curve has an inverted 'U' shape. This means that an early market with few players and few customers who, moreover, aren't aware and cognizant of the novelty will be less attractive than a market with several competitors that implicitly cooperate in growing the awareness of the market (Haveman 1993); this is what Brandenburger and Nalebuff (1996) called "co-opetition". In other words, following a pioneer is a strategy that has often paid off even if it is less glamorous than being in the pioneer role. Start-up entrepreneurs are often dispirited when they learn that a competitor has entered the market that they were stealthily preparing to engage. In fact, they should be comforted that another company will take on the head winds of early introduction of a novelty and implicitly share the cost of educating the market.

Is innovation about market success?

Although market-success stories are always inspiring to read about, market success is extremely hard to predict. The best technology may not end up winning the market; pioneering firms often get overtaken by fast followers as soon as there is market traction. In addition, since innovations may be intended for oneself or for one's fellow co-workers, success isn't always measured in terms of market gains; it can be an increase of a product or service's quality, a performance improvement, or any other attribute that generates value for end users.

All these misconceptions stem from the persistent lack of a common understanding of the concept of innovation. This exercise has allowed us to circumscribe the concept by rectifying these misconceptions, which enriches our pursuit of clarity on the subject.

How can innovation typologies guide our understanding of innovation?

Now that we devised a concise definition for the concept of innovation and reviewed some of the most common misconceptions about it, let us turn our attention to yet another way to gain insight into a new domain, that is to say by identifying and analyzing the typologies that relate to it. To do this, one should ask oneself: 'How can innovation initiatives be classified?' This question remains a favorite topic of discussion at academic and professional innovation gatherings. In fact, identifying typologies is a useful exercise to define innovation because it helps to draw out the fundamental components of the body of knowledge by understanding how they relate to – or differ from – one another. In other words, identifying that an innovation belongs to one category and not to another usually highlights a key difference that is likely to bring to light an important piece of knowledge. One could say that structuring is a way of understanding.

Amongst the types of innovation identified in the literature, one finds those that focus on the degree of novelty of the outcome for the producing organization, namely, at both ends of the spectrum, incremental innovation – which is a simple improvement – and radical innovation – that is more ambitious in that it represents a departure from what is currently done. Other categories focus on the potential disturbances that the innovation is expected to cause once introduced on the market. Depending on the degree of turmoil produced, these types of innovations may be qualified as being disruptive (Christensen, Raynor and MacDonald 2015), breakthrough or even revolutionary. Instigators of innovation look for initiatives that cause disturbances because it is thought that they can redefine the terms of competition and open up opportunities. They seek to challenge and to undermine unprepared competitors to improve their own positions on the market; the novelty must bring a competitive advantage. However, in reality, the disruptive effect is something that one can only safely identify after the fact. Anticipating it in practice relates more to conjecture than to an exact science. For this reason, we believe that market disruption is too unpredictable for practitioners to use reliably. Indeed, predicting the future impacts of innovations on the market is a haphazard exercise. More often than not, the market turmoil doesn't produce the desired effect. Instead of revolutionizing a targeted market, the novelty may flop, fade away or simply create a small niche for itself. For example, originally, two-wheeled self-balancing personal transporters were originally heralded as a technology that would usher in a new era in personal transportation. In reality, they only managed to capture several niche markets. Disruption remains a classification worthy of interest for academic researchers analyzing innovation cases in hindsight. There are other types of innovation that reflect how well-known components of existing solutions may be rearranged forming new solution architectures. A systemic interdependency reflects the existence of considerable coordination amongst the market stakeholders which causes excessive market inertia, long delays before mainstream-market adoption, winner-takes-all market dynamics, and the market being locked for extensive periods of time. They often require collateral material being created by third parties which show-cases the novelty. These types are just a sampling of the many innovation types that are recognized in academic and professional circles, albeit with variations in terminology and with slightly differing interpretations of the terminology that still foster passionate debates. In other words, tongue in cheek, one could say that the "dominant design" (Utterback and Abernathy 1975) of innovation typologies hasn't emerged yet.

This multitude of viewpoints reflected in the range of typologies described above leads us to contend that an organization shouldn't define itself exclusively by the goods or services that it produces and commercializes. The fruit of its production – which generates proceeds – at any given time simply reflects an ad-hoc matching of its capabilities with a temporal market opportunity. Basing one's organizational strategy exclusively on market demand means chasing a constantly moving target. We submit that an organization should define itself by what it knows and what it is able to do, or in other words, by its capability to make its competencies productive in one way or another. As Greek philosopher Seneca is reported to have said that: "luck is what happens when preparation meets opportunity". We interpret the word preparation as the early learning of the competencies that will eventually allow an organization to seize market opportunities when they arise. Sir Francis Bacon (1824) emphasized the importance of knowledge when writing that "knowledge itself is power" in which we interpret the word power as meaning the power to achieve something that has value.

As noted earlier, Leonard-Barton (1992) warned that core competencies may become an undesirable source of rigidity in organizations. This view suggests that an organization constantly needs to respond to market dynamics by adapting its competencies. More often than not this is hard to carry out because of the extensive and inevitably time-consuming learning required to master new competencies and to be able to derive value from them. To alleviate this concern, we believe that core competencies matter more to an organization's sustainability than the vagaries of market demand at any given point in time. In case of market disruption causing an unexpected mismatch between these competencies and the market demand, organizations should be prepared to shift to another market to find a better match elsewhere. Organizations may lose their focus by relentlessly following the whims of market demand.

A resolute commitment to continuous organizational learning and to the sound management of the organization's capability life cycles should alleviate the concern about rigidity. In practice, this organizational learning requires that on the one hand, at a high level, a general orientation to be set and, on the other hand, at a granular level, that the learning takes place when its workers acquire new knowledge and skills and when they share them with their fellow workers. These granular learnings roll up to form comprehensive organizational competencies. This learning occurs as they carry out their work or participate in projects. To support this learning appropriately, organizations must ensure that the workers have ready access to training resources. They will also derive new knowledge from cross-disciplinary interactions. Workers need to be encouraged to embrace life-long learning because exploratory innovation necessarily means that new knowledge and new competencies will need to be acquired. Learning how to learn in the workplace is a skill in itself that organizations need to cultivate.

The key to an organization's sustainability over the long-term is to develop its resiliency to market turmoil and crises caused by any number of reasons, such as

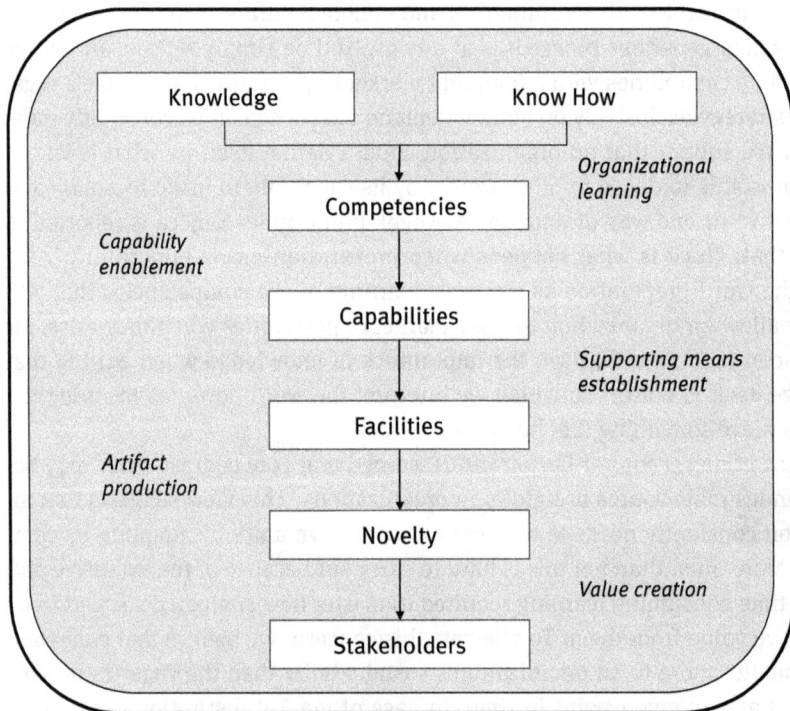

Fig. 4.1: Progression from organizational learning to value creation.

market shifts, new competition, regulations, deregulation, changing environmental conditions to name a few. This can be achieved by astutely managing one's organization's competencies and capabilities. First, let us define a competency as a distinctive area of knowledge with related know-how and supporting practices acquired in context through organizational learning. There are also other dependant knowledge assets that become increasingly specific to a context and a given purpose, as illustrated in Fig. 4.1. Experience in applying a competency will enable a 'capability'.

A capability is an actionable competency that is deployable to carry out a goal; thus, it comes into play to produce value in very practical terms. 'Capability enablement' is the process by which competencies are converted into one or more capabilities. An organization derives a competitive advantage through its distinguishing capabilities. Thus, with sustainability in mind, managing an organization's capabilities, upgrading them, and developing new ones is as critically important for the proper management of an organization's innovation function as the management of its production lines' responses to temporary and possibly even transient market needs. A capability can be applied on several production lines for a range of markets and market segments. A 'facility' is an assembly of tangible means established to support and to enable a capability that allows a productive activity to be carried out, sometimes with additional resources. A novelty can be an artifact produced by a facility developed through its capabilities that creates value for a set of stakeholders; for example, a leading-edge research laboratory produces discoveries that, in turn, enable an innovation process.

To sum up, learning, which enables the development or upgrading of new competencies which translate into capabilities, is at the center of innovation. Thus, for this reason, we propose that there is an alternative typology of innovation, which, in our view, better applies to the goal of democratizing innovation. It focuses on the degree of learning that an innovation initiative involves for an organization. The concept of novelty means that something is new to a given organization; it is a relative concept not an absolute one, as we have already stated. A competency may also be commonplace in one industry but not in another. Distinctive industrial sectors may converge in a way that causes disruptions. This occurs when challengers that are well established on one market enter another market by introducing more efficient means from their original industrial sectors to address a market need that the incumbents previously addressed with traditional means (Davidson and Ivanova 2011). It is a clash of competencies and capabilities. Incumbent firms may not be able to carry out the required learning quickly enough to react. The displacement of chemical photography by digital photography is a classical example of this phenomenon.

An organization interested in an ambiguous market opportunity often struggles to understand it well enough to produce an offer that will be successful; trial and error is common. Von Hippel (2005) emphasized the advantages that manufacturers may gain by reaching out to lead users. These passionate early aficionados (that one could even call 'proto-customers') can help them to better understand a nascent market. Because they are themselves users of the developing novelty, they have the motivation to find solutions that really work. They experiment passionately and tirelessly with fast-paced iterations to satisfy their own needs and to resolve their own early-use issues faster than any manufacturer ever could. Thus, co-creation with lead users represents a tremendous vicarious learning opportunity for organizations that can considerably reduce the design cycle and avoid costly mistakes. This type of learning is more effective (and potentially less expensive in the long run) than the formally validated learning that takes place in the trial-error-pivoting process, which is practiced in the Lean start-up model (Ries 2011). These partnerships are invaluable; in the future, they are likely to increasingly become part of the innovation process.

Thus, our learning and competencies-based approach is squarely focused on creating a competitive advantage by leveraging an organization's resources whether internal or external. This perspective relates to the resource-based view of organizations. We view learning as a key enabler for innovation. For this reason, we focused on a typology that relates to the degree of learning that an innovation initiative involves. Moreover, learning, as a generic skill, is instrumental in that it is an enabler for innovation, both to develop an organization's innovation capabilities and to acquire domain-specific or market-specific knowledge. When an innovation initiative means continuing with the same competencies that an organization has been successfully applying, it remains in the flow of the organization's current competencies. This is an approach that can be viewed as playing it safe, but which, in fact, might be much less so when the postponement of necessary and inevitable changes raises the risk of falling behind. Conversely, if the competencies are new and aren't mastered by an organization, an innovation initiative that requires them is a stretch for the organization. There are risks in its execution, but which may be compensated by the possibility of reducing the long-term risk of falling behind competitors. Let us note that the intensity of novelty and the extent of the learning may differ from one organizational department to another. For example, if an organization decides to shift its activities to a new market that has a need for its competencies, despite the research and development department considering it as a perfect fit, the marketing and sales departments may consider it as being a stretch because there is learning involved in their being able to respond to the new market's characteristics. This learning perspective translates into 'in-flow innovation' or 'stretch innovation', as illustrated on left and the right sides of the democratized-innovation framework diagram in Fig. 1.1 (see Chapter 1).

Innovation is holistic in that its value isn't achieved until the novelty benefits someone, which usually means an external customer, but which can also frequently be another fellow worker or group of workers, or even the inventor himself or herself. Furthermore, because introducing a novelty to its target market or user-base usually involves learning as well, we also retained the notion of customers needing to learn about the novelty, to which Cooper (1999) referred in a straightforward manner as being "new to market". When an innovation is new to the market, its users may need to be educated about its advantages and taught how to use it. Sometimes the advantages are clear and quickly adopted such as portable digital music players that overcame Compact-Disks players which themselves had previously quickly supplanted analog vinyl-record players. On the contrary, some novelties need to be explained through extensive advertising, such as on-the-go pen-shaped stain removers. Hence, organizations also need to be preoccupied by their customers' learning because it could slow down the adoption of their novelties. Therefore, the operational learning and market education are two challenges in which an organization will need to become actively involved, often at great expense. Learning of these types may become hurdles that are likely to slow down product development and market adoption, both of which could put the success of innovation endeavors at risk.

These three learning-centric types of innovations should be kept in mind when establishing democratized innovation. We will disregard the types related to an innovation's degree of newness because it may be new on one market but commonplace on another, which could be confusing in an organization serving both markets. Furthermore, in our opinion, the innovation types that involve predicting the disruptive effects of an innovation on the market are based on speculation, making them too uncertain to be safely used in practice. Indeed, there is considerable uncertainty about a novelty's adoption by the market and unpredictability in the competitors' reactions to it; market contingencies are highly speculative and unreliable. Entrepreneurs typically over-estimate the rate of market adoption and under-estimate the effects of the competitors' defensive tactics, such as pre-announcements of their own versions of the novelty or extending the useful life of their solutions through defensive innovations that improve their performance slightly. Novelties may fail because the market traction for them was over-estimated. Causes are wide-ranging, such as imperfect information, lack of trust towards a new market player, insufficient brand strength, lack of – or spotty – reputation, regulations, technological lock-out or simply people's natural resistance to change.

Thus, our learning-centric innovation typology balances exploration and exploitation to enable democratized innovation. Exploration involves learning new competencies, for stretch innovation, while the continued use and improvement of current knowledge exercises exploitation which relates to in-flow innovation.

How can organizations benefit from expertise in innovation?

Previously, we highlighted the ambiguity surrounding the concept of innovation for practitioners, which begs the question: what can a capability in innovation concretely bring to an organization? To answer this question, we need to distinguish between organizations that are established in their fields or markets and those that are new to them, such as start-ups and established organizations entering markets that are new to them. Davidson and Ivanova (2011) calls the former 'incumbents' and the latter 'challengers'; we will use this terminology as well. The incumbents mostly focus on the exploitation of their capabilities usually on a specific market that they know well. Conversely, challengers apply most of their efforts on exploration and on finding a demand for their novelties. An organization may fit both these categories at the same time if it has an incumbent role on one market and a challenger role on another market. The incumbents' managers will mostly be concerned about cultivating their workers' innovativeness despite their organizations' focus on exploitation. Organizational silos may develop which can stifle collaboration and original creative thinking. Ensuring that such organizations maintain their sustainability in shifting market conditions is also a prime consideration.

The challengers' managers must quickly find a demand that will fuel their developing organization's – or business unit's – growth. They must be ready to quickly pivot to adjust their offers to the specificities of the demand on the markets on which they are trying to establish themselves. Faced with a disruptive event, an incumbent may either update its competencies to follow the shift or move to a new market where there is still a demand for its original competencies, which ironically would put it in a challenger role. Geoffrey Moore (2002) recommended that start-ups focus on a single niche market at a time. Once they established a dominant position on it, they should proceed to grow by moving successfully from one niche market to another. This is growth by conquering successive niche markets one after the other. Thus, the exploration-exploitation scenarios may be hybrid and depend on specific circumstances. One could say that it is a good practice for an incumbent to act more like a challenger, and for challengers to strive to take on the role of incumbent without losing their agility. In any case, there are significant uncertainties that shed doubt on the organization's successes irrespective of its role. Developing capabilities in innovation – or what one could call innovativeness – provides the means to address these uncertainties by dynamically balancing the organizations exploration and exploitation activities. In other words, it must be ambidextrous. Competency in the principles of innovation enhances the organization's capability to deal with these uncertainties. The innovation specialist will need to be the manager of this ambidexterity to ensure that it is creative and value producing.

Let us review some finer details. The incumbents must proactively manage their competencies and their capabilities to avoid being taken off guard. This objective usually involves ongoing worker training. In addition, they must capture the benefits of their progression along the learning curve through worker improvements and encourage their workers to develop original novelties. We recommended that the coupling between the organization's capabilities and market opportunities be kept loose to facilitate eventual moves to alternative markets if need be; selling on any particular market should be viewed as a temporary opportunity. Hence, innovation, with capability management and learning, must take place in the marketing departments as well.

It is important for start-ups to quickly pivot in response to the feedback that they receive on their offers (Ries 2011). They must integrate a capability to do so in their development plans until their assumptions have been validated; their evolving ideas eventually need to meet the reality of the market in what we could call their first successful touch-down onto it. Carrying out this short-cycled pivoting means that there is fast-paced learning about the field and about the market taking place. Early customer consultations establish a co-creation dynamic that can make this process less error prone by reducing the guesswork. Established organizations working with start-ups can share the risk and help foster a nimbler work culture through osmosis. A start-up is mostly about an idea, but it should also be about adjusting the idea with innovation capabilities. It needs to master the linkages between a nascent capability and the value that can be unlocked by meeting a market need. Integrating innovation expertise among its ranks will allow it to prepare for – and to navigate through – these adjustments. Pivoting involves adapting the idea or moving to another market or market segment to uncover the coveted value. Moreover, in keeping with the principle enunciated by Moore (2002), a successful start-up seeking to expand should move from one niche market to the next; it must maintain its pivoting capability to continue growing. This means that it needs to hone its learning-based innovation capabilities.

In both incumbent and challenger organizations, the people championing innovation will need to ensure that the organizational capabilities support the organization's quest for growth-sustaining or growth-enabling value. This astute management of ambidexterity, organizational capabilities and pivoting are the clear benefits that innovation can bring to both types of organizations. With democratized innovation that engages everyone in innovation, the innovation specialists will need to add the roles of innovation trainer, coach and facilitator; they will need to oversee the patterns of collaboration taking place in the organization to help them develop if need be. Effective people and management skills will be required to accomplish innovation through the collective imagination of a group of people.

Summation

In this chapter, we strived to clarify the ambiguity surrounding the concept of innovation. We proposed a concise definition that emphasizes two fundamental concepts, namely novelty and value-creation. A democratized innovation framework involves additional notions of collaboration amongst empowered workers conducting innovation. The exploration of the concept of innovation was further refined through an exclusion method by reviewing typical misconceptions about innovation and by identifying the typologies of innovation that are often used. We suggested that market disruptions are too unpredictable for innovators to use in practice. Hence, we devised a typology that emphasizes the extent to which an innovation is in the flow of what an organization already knows how to do or a stretch of its competencies, that is to say a typology that is based on the degree of learning involved in innovation projects. We included the new-to-market type (Cooper 1999) because it involved educating the user-base, that is to say learning targeted to an external group. Thus, learning is at the center of innovation and particularly of the democratized-innovation framework that involves workers who don't have formal education in innovation to engage in it. The knowledge-related components that come into play in the progression from organizational learning to value creation were reviewed. We concluded by clarifying the tangible benefits of innovation.

Chapter 5
Value-creating Knowledge

As we have previously mentioned, innovation is about creating value from something new. An organization may derive this value in two ways. One popular view is that organizations need to "hunt" for value by reacting to market changes and by astutely managing market dynamics. Another view is that value should be "cultivated" from within an organization by developing its capabilities. The approach that we advocate for democratized innovation leans mostly towards the latter view, although the former cannot be ignored. Therefore, we position the Framework as a resource-based view of innovation in organizations. While still keeping a watchful eye on market dynamics, it is a view according to which innovation should be stimulated to a greater extent from within the organization. Let us also keep in mind that marketing and sales functions should be included in a resource-based approach since they may develop innovative marketing and sales techniques.

There is an extensive body of research in the field of innovation and a considerable number of case studies and publications in this domain of knowledge. A primer in innovation could easily become voluminous. Therefore, in this chapter, we present a selected set of learning points on innovation for regular workers learning about democratized innovation that relate to common preoccupations that they may have and with which they will intuitively relate. These pieces of knowledge are not intended by any means to be part of a comprehensive review of the fundamentals of innovation. The points that are reviewed are rather designed to be segues into the subject of innovation that allow trainers to get the conversation about innovation easily started with the workers; the points are illustrative of the type of material that could get the democratized innovators quickly interested and motivated to learn more. The workers learning about innovation will naturally reorientate the discussions on innovation in directions that are the most pertinent to them; this cannot be planned in advance. We review some of the basic principles that come into play that should relate to the realities of their workplaces. The knowledge points are designed for learners who don't have prior formal training in innovation, but who are seeking to actively participate in a democratized-innovation work environment.

Inventing original novelties that could become innovations involves diverging from deep-seated design patterns to create new ones; this is a mental process that isn't necessarily easy to carry out. Once the new patterns found, real users will determine if the proposed design patterns provide the much-coveted value that defines innovation. Success will be tied to the achievement of this value, which is determined by how well the stakeholders' needs and expectations are met. Satisfaction may result from any number of criteria such as soundness, practicality, affordability, viability, accessibility to name just a few. Market stakeholders generally seek stability; they strive to converge on a single design pattern because it brings

https://doi.org/10.1515/9783110683837-008

simplification and efficiency. This propensity prompts them to agree – whether in a way that is explicit, tacit or imposed – on a design pattern that then becomes the new standard until it becomes obsolete, or until it is updated to continue meeting evolving requirements. This endless cyclical process of divergence, convergence, cooptation and standardization around design patterns illustrates the cycles of re-generative obsolescence and renewal that are typical of innovation.

The subject matter in this chapter is classified in four categories, namely: (i) opportunity and pivoting, (ii) design and engineering, (iii) workers and organization, and (iv) launch and diffusion.

Opportunity and pivoting: How does innovation relate to change?

Changing the status quo is one of the basic premises of innovation; innovators are agents of change. There is necessarily a transition from an initial state to an end state. However, the speed of the change may vary. The change may be implemented abruptly with a predefined switch-over date and time. This approach usually in-volves risks, which can be mitigated with a fair amount of preparation, staging, re-hearsals and simulations, stand-by assistance and possibly the option to switch back in case issues arise during the transition process. Alternatively, change may be gradually applied; the components of the current situation and the new one may co-exist for a transitional period, which reduces the risk, but increases the organiza-tion's operational complexity. During this period, the members of the affected user-base may learn about the novelty and get accustomed to it. They are expected to migrate any collateral material that they may have used or created under the envi-ronment that is being retired. The risks of work disruptions are reduced or at least mitigated. However, this approach may have the undesirable side-effect of catering to those who procrastinate or even openly resist change by providing them with a way to postpone their migration until the very end of the transitional period. Their actions allow them to purposely place themselves in an abrupt switch-over situa-tion despite the organization's preparation and accommodation for a smooth transi-tion. In the worst-case scenario, if they are in great numbers, they may jeopardize the switchover process and cause the de-facto rejection of the novelty. Procrastina-tion when facing a requirement to change is a common human reaction because change requires time and effort. The affected people may not have asked for it nor have seen it coming; they may not understand the need for the change. Hence, change needs to be explained and even socialized. It may impact people's habits and diminish their productivity, causing frustration; innovators need to take these considerations into account. Users need to learn new skills which may bring to light gaps in their knowledge. They may secretly entertain doubts about their ability to carry on their activities with the novelty in place. For all these reasons, change needs to be carefully managed; and therefore, the careful management of change facilitates the creation of the value that defines innovation. The scenario involving the co-existence of the new and the old may also mean duplication which is usually perceived as being wasteful and quickly eliminated. The old and the new may co-exist for extended periods of time and in ways that are both pertinent and justified when they have clearly distinctive user groups or purposes. In this case, bridging or interfacing solutions, such as converters, allow access to both solutions with more-or-less transparent exchanges of information between them. However, their effectiveness may be variable; the interconnectivity may range from being fully transparent to issue-prone especially when interconnectivity (or the lack thereof) is exploited by two rival organizations or design teams as a way to exclude one another from their respective user bases. On the positive side, bridging solutions may have the effect of connecting two user bases that were otherwise separated by different technologies; as a result, they become unified.

Change may precipitate the retirement of current technologies or solutions. It involves the adoption of something new that is deemed to be better in one way or another, immediately or in a foreseeable future; it represents an evolution or a revolution depending on how radical the change may be. The change may be arbitrary, which could raise concerns about its justification in the eyes of the affected users, or, at the very opposite, it may be motivated by a collective benefit that takes precedence over any other individual interests. The resistance to change, or inertia, is a strong force that may stifle innovation; it may result from fears of change or from self-serving interests that support the status quo; the expression "why change what isn't broken?" is often heard. In extreme cases, it could take a major event, possibly a dramatic one like an accident, a disaster or even a catastrophe to break through the inertia that may otherwise have prevented long-overdue change. Crises may break through such inertia and resistances because they change the priorities, force rationalizations, or alter the value systems. Change that occurs too quickly may be disruptive by ushering in transformations that may have dramatic and even devastating effects on workers, populations, industrial sectors and economies in a phenomenon that Schumpeter (1942) called 'creative destruction'.

Accommodating the simultaneous use of a novelty and an old solution allows for the continued use of the old solution's collateral material, which avoids a loss for its users. But in doing so it may stifle the development of new collateral material that better highlights the novelty's features and advantages. Alternatively, the absence of a migration path means a clean break with the past, but also the loss of any material that was enjoyed with the old solution. But in some cases, it may be beneficial because it forces the development of material that truly showcases the novelty's superior features, which ultimately helps to promote its adoption which means a greater rate of progress. There is however a loss of value in discarding the old material that the users will need to write off as sunk costs. Therefore, the absence of a bridging solution may represent a deliberate strategy to force the users to break away from the past in favor of a novelty. Such a radical decision is often stipulated by governmental decree or an organizational directive, or simply by other stakeholders, such as suppliers refusing to continue supporting the older version.

For the suppliers, a more accommodating and gradual migration approach increases the chances that the users will remain loyal to one's organization's solution whereas an abrupt switchover that causes disruption could prompt the users to consider moving to another supplier's solution. Thus, change represents a risk for suppliers imposing it since it gives their customers an opportunity to re-assess their options.

Adapting to change can be a matter of survival. Change in a shifting environment becomes mandatory to remain current with the times. Failure to adopt the change taking place carries the looming threat of obsolescence, loss of competitiveness and declining market share, all of which may jeopardize an organization's position and possibly even its very survival.

In practice, change may translate to many specific activities, such as version upgrading, code refactoring, technological generational leaps, new styles, new series, new paradigms, new fashions, etc. that is to say the many ways in which a novelty may supplant a current solution whether it had reached the natural end of its lifespan or if, on the contrary, its premature retirement was artificially precipitated and even calculated through planned obsolescence.

Democratized innovators must evaluate how the change that their novelties imply would be implemented and whether establishing a bridge with the past is desirable. Also, it is a good practice when navigating through change to prompt feedback from real-life users to understand what they want as early as possible. Issues will inevitably occur as a result of use cases or situations that were not anticipated and from design or production errors. Because of this process, it is always advisable to deploy early versions of a novelty to a small user base, preferably even one that has been carefully selected for its members' experience, motivation, resilience and patience given that they will be confronted with these development pains.

Design and engineering: How do standards influence innovation?

Standards are important in innovation because they represent a convergence on a particular design and a rejection of alternatives. They are the artifacts of agreements whether implicit or explicit. Once established and adopted by novelty producers, they enable market-mediated collaboration which involves their independently designing products that comply with the adopted standard. The concept of a standard could be expanded to include the locking effect that deeply ingrained practices or procedures often have. In its simplest form, the dominance of a design in a product or service category represents a virtual standard to which the other players on the corresponding market must comply to continue carrying out their business on this market. Utterback and Abernathy (1975) defined a three-phased process that characterizes how an agreement on a particular design establishes itself as a reference defining a new product category. Many early players experiment with different features in the "fluid phase". Early adopters respond or not to their solutions; the process is fast paced with many of the tentative solutions failing quickly. Eventually, the adopters show a preference for a particular design. As a result, a "dominant design" emerges which is a pivotal event in a transition to the second phase, known as the "transitional phase", as Utterback (1996) observed. The product category users' expectations are set from that point on; this shift favors a small set of winning firms with the other ones dropping out. Finally, in the "specialization phase", the market is well delineated with a small number of dominant firms serving the market. Interestingly, in this phase, a significant share of the technological inventiveness comes from an ecosystem of third-party suppliers that innovate by providing components to the principal firms that, in turn, often focus on the novelty's core components that have the highest added value; they subcontract the rest. This three-phased cycle may repeat itself as a new technological paradigm supplants another.

The democratized innovators should be cognizant of a novelty's progression in its product category. The initial novelties will likely be tentative. Finding the right solution may involve considering what has already being designed to avoid needless repetitions of options that were previously rejected. Experimentation will continue in the product category with a range of features and configurations trying to find the winning formula that defines the product category. At this highly exploratory stage, the innovators need to focus their minds on divergent thinking; they widen the number of options to try out. They iterate through several cycles of trial and error. After a design has gained traction, the ambiguity and the uncertainty will be partially resolved which reduces the risks, but also the opportunities. The designers' efforts shift to improvements that build on the dominant design, identifying process innovations that improve cost-efficiencies (Utterback 1996) and finding specialized market segments.

An interoperability standard is a technological convention that allows organizations to develop complementary solutions that seamlessly work together. In addition, it allows the end users to interchangeably make use of any of the components abiding by the standard or to assemble them as fully compatible integrated assemblages. Third-party component suppliers or producers of products that require interoperability are the first to adopt a standard. Coopting for a common standard means that the organizations adopting it implicitly cooperate with one another in developing a market comprising a range of compatible components without needing to explicitly coordinate their actions later on. Once the standard is set, all the firms need to do to participate in the market is to follow the standard. This implicit cooperation is said to be market-mediated because it occurs through the dynamics of the market with the players keeping their independence. There are duties and responsibilities imposed on those who coopt for a shared standard. It is defined and governed by a standard development organization (SDO) formed by representatives of several of these independent market players or by governmental authorities; the standard is managed in the sense that it is periodically reviewed and updated. A standard may be open and freely available or available for a fee with a binding commitment to scrupulously follow the standard. The open-standard adopters may also be required to share any improvements freely with others. Alternatively, standards can be proprietary and closed. Closed standards are often used by dominant firms to keep competitors out of their markets; however, case experience suggests that this is generally a losing strategy (Farrell and Saloner 1985). It restricts the possibilities for interorganizational partnerships that can create holistic value and implicit cooperation between competitors (Brandenburger and Nalebuff 1996). By comparison, the proponents of a closed standard will need to create a critical mass of adopters on their own. Closed standards are generally believed to allow for better quality control, but this advantage can be offset by an open standard with strong compliance rules.

An uncoordinated market with many competing standards may entice some users to hold off adopting any products out of concern that the market may consolidate causing the product that they chose to be discontinued which would mean losing their investment. Several standards in the same product category may co-exist, but often they are not interchangeable nor interoperable; their sponsors may engage in a confrontation for dominance of the market with a winner-takes-all outcome (Corbel 2009).

Since standards exist in many industrial sectors and for many types of products and services, the democratized innovators need to understand how to use them. They need to be aware of the opportunities for cooptation and of the risks that standard rivalries that may come about represent. For example, defining a standard and then making it freely available to whoever may want to use it, is a daring yet powerful strategy. The astute innovator will need to be cognizant of the opportunity offered by adopting an open standard developed by third parties. They should be wary of product categories for which two or more standards already compete.

There are other types of standards of interest for democratized innovators. Measurement standards may come into play in innovation because they can influence the modularity and sizes of solutions that involve component assemblies. For example, in the construction industry there are components and construction materials that come in standard sizes, which are usually cut in rounded measurement units. This type of standardization facilitates the design process, but at the same time it restricts the variety of options. Quality standards also provide reassurance for the end user looking to purchase with more confidence items that are hard to evaluate for a layperson. They guarantee a level of quality while relieving the purchasers from having to assess the quality by themselves which they may not be qualified to do. Some of the reservations that buyers could have had before purchasing an item may be removed especially if the quality standard is enforced by a government agency.

Democratized innovators need to keep measurement and quality standards in mind when designing their novelties. They should value the simplification that they bring, while dealing with the constraints that they involve. They were often developed to coordinate markets that had chaotic diversity. A totally uncoordinated market could hamper innovation because the diversity of solutions produces complexity and fragments the market; it can make the customers think twice and shy away from committing to any of the options offered.

Regulations are a form of standardization as well; they may be perceived by some as being roadblocks to innovation. At first glance, their stipulations may appear to be constraining, but there are also interesting benefits. Regulations force out outdated generations of technology clearing the ground for novelties by making the changes compulsory. In doing so, they help usher in innovations that may otherwise have been slow to gain market traction. This is particularly useful to break the resistance to change with which innovators are constantly confronted. Ashford, Heaton and Priest (1979) claim that regulations stimulate inventiveness by challenging solution developers to come up with new ways to comply with them, whereas without these regulations, they may have comfortably continued with the status quo. They create challenges for engineers to solve that stimulate their creativity. Flushing out outdated technologies may also simplify the environment in which a novelty needs to integrate by reducing the need for interoperability with older technologies. In other words, regulations can do away with these obsolete technologies on which some users cling for too long, often beyond their useful life. Democratized innovators should carefully review new regulations to find the impulse for innovation. They represent hidden opportunities because the forced compliance will likely translate into renewed market demand. Therefore, there are several reasons to view regulations as useful catalysts of progress. They can also facilitate the coordination between innovators without their needing to interact or to coordinate themselves.

Workers and organization: How can more original ideas be generated?

Ideation involves developing new concepts that break with commonplace patterns. This is much harder to do than one may think. The familiar designs and solutions condition our thinking and constrain our ability to come up with new ones. To stimulate one's creativity, these patterns need to be broken down to entertain what Kop and Carroll (2011) call "non-linear thinking". In addition, the human mind has limitations in its information processing capabilities – that Simon (1979, 1991) calls "bounded rationality" – that bring creators to settle on satisfactory solutions which are not necessarily optimal ones. Miller and Ireland (2005) and Hodgkinson et al. (2009) describe a mental process called "holistic intuition" that draws extensively on a form of expertise derived from past experience often intuitively at a subconscious level. Faced with ambiguity, the mind has the uncanny ability to fill in the gaps. Thus, ambiguous input can stimulate creativity by forcing the mind to try to make sense of it by creatively filling in the missing information.

Davidson (2015) classifies creativity techniques into three categories, namely: individual creativity, group creativity and eco-system creativity. Let us review some of these techniques. Representing the problem differently may stimulate creativity. For example, mind mapping a problem space as a diagram of concepts radiating out of a base concept draws out its conceptual structure. Creativity with this technique usually involves changing the structure of something in a novel manner; the graphical representation that highlights this structure helps to identify the appropriate change to make. The very statement of the problem may hinder one's ability to think out of the box. Brainwriting helps break down these known patterns by substituting a key concept in the statement by another – often at random – to find a solution to the modified problem statement. Once a solution is found, the designer attempts to transfer it back to the original problem which often reveals an original idea.

Pattern-breaking exercises can also be carried out in groups. Participants are challenged to relate a concept selected at random to the problem at hand. In doing so, they are forced to apply another frame of reference onto their problem which, like brainwriting, prompts their imagination and stimulates creative discussions. Convergent thinking may interfere with divergent thinking. To prevent this, brainstorming (Osborn 1988) separates ideation from evaluation. The intent is to avoid any participants refraining from expressing their ideas in fear of immediate judgement; all the ideas freely brought forward are evaluated in a second stage.

The Delphi technique stimulates additive ideation. The participants exchange written statements of their ideas or responses to a survey question, and they add any additional thoughts that they may have on each of them. In order to do so, they all exchange the documents in sequence until all ideas have been reviewed and extended by all participants. The ideas with the extended points are then reviewed and discussed in a follow-on plenary session. Role-playing techniques force each of the participants to present, to defend or to critique an idea from a particular standpoint (de Bono 1994). The participants are periodically required to switch roles as the process unfolds. This process ensures that the ideas are investigated from several angles.

Creativity may also come from external sources. A forward-thinking organization will strive to obtain feedback and ideas from as many sources as possible. Customers using its products or services day in day out may have invaluable observations on issues that they experienced and wishes, both of which could easily be turned into new feature ideas. There are usually too many of them, which must then be prioritized according to predefined criteria. Collecting ideas from one's employees is also a rich source of inspiration since they may provide feedback from work practices, issues that slow them down, or simply observations of unexpected and puzzling phenomena. The idea box may contain the seeds for the next brilliant ideas.

Hackathons build on the stimulating effect that a group event provides. In addition, there is instant diversity with on-the-spot ad-hoc team formation. The exercise involves a competition usually with prizes to gamify the event. One or more challenges are presented on which each team works during a set time period extending from an extended day to a weekend. The final solutions are presented to a panel of judges who evaluate them and assign the prizes before the crowd of participants in a festive atmosphere. Subsequently, the best ideas are further analyzed, and development projects launched.

With the advent of the Internet and the Web 2.0/3.0, group consultations can take place at a grander scale amongst a collectivity of people who may not even be part of the sponsoring organization. With crowdsourcing, creativity becomes an open and inclusive activity. Since the Internet is, by definition, open-ended, the number of people consulted can quickly become staggering. Computer software is usually required to help keep the process manageable. Participants may be challenged to find ideas to resolve posted problems or to evaluate and to vote on a set of ideas that are proposed to them. The gamification of the process with prizes or the association with a social cause dear to the participants will make it more popular. Social media in general provides candid unsolicited feedback, which even if it may be critical is still invaluable.

The democratized innovators should become familiar with several of these techniques to stimulate their imagination in different ways. Trying several techniques ensures that a problem gets investigated from different angles and with different mindsets.

Coming up with a single idea or a single design is never enough; it suggests that the ideation or design process wasn't pursued far enough. Most problems can be resolved in any number of ways. Considering multiple ideas generates debates, brings out differing views and focuses the discussions on the comparison of the respective attributes of each idea or design. Throughout the process it often happens that participants realize that they were working on the wrong problem. Being able to assess the respective merits or drawbacks of each solution means establishing evaluation criteria and setting priorities. Features from different solutions may be merged; compromises may be made. Through this process, original solutions are found.

Diversity and decentralization of the decision-making power can also stimulate creativity. Indeed, the rigidity of organizational practices may unwittingly lead to the establishment of a belief system that may limit and even stifle the workers' abilities to generate ideas that don't fit into its precepts. Furthermore, centralized decision-making power increases the distance between the decision-makers and the particular operational circumstances. This makes it harder to adapt the practices in order to find solutions that fit the context in an optimal manner; one could say that one size fits all never fits anyone well. In this age of ubiquitous instant communications through multiple channels and technologies, and cloud-based information systems that diffuse information throughout an organization almost instantly, distributing the decision-making power is easier to achieve while ensuring the necessary safeguards against misguided decisions. Distributed organizations are nimbler and more imaginative than centralized and uniform ones. Barnes, Gartland and Stack (2004) advocate a participative model that encourages ideas and decisions made on the organization's front lines.

Friendly competition stimulates creativity. Challenging two or more internal teams to simultaneously develop competing solutions brings them to outperform with a better solution usually being found. Moreover, opening internal challenges to external contributors (which could even be as audacious as inviting external suppliers) ensures that the internal standards match those that prevails in the external market. This reduces the risk of complacency.

Most inventions are inspired by external sources (i.e., academic institutions, research organizations or others) rather than being created from scratch; Cohen and Levinthal (1990) defined the concept of "absorptive capacity" that allows an organization to recognize the value of developments in a given field and to develop the capabilities to assimilate them in order to derive a benefit from them. It is a form of associative learning thanks to which the new elements of knowledge are related to an organization's context. Given the fact that many lines of business are increasingly becoming knowledge-based, it includes knowing where to find information for a particular field; patent databases may provide useful starting points or one's own backlog of ideas that were never carried out because previously the conditions weren't right. New knowledge should be quickly put into practice. As a result, the innovators are quickly confronted with the practicalities of applying a new body of knowledge to their unique situation. Domain knowledge is usually codified and readily transferrable, but the related know-how is often highly contextual and tacit; it may be hard to transfer to others. A learner who doesn't have practical experience may find it difficult to understand it. Indeed, without practical experience it is hard to even entertain useful discussions about the subjects at hand because one needs the shared experience to communicate effectively, let alone to understand the shared meaning. There is no better way to acquire it than getting down to it and learning by doing or at least learning by trying. For the democratized innovators, this means that if one intends to champion a new competency in the organization, one should launch a pilot project as early as possible which should involve starting with a simple and achievable goal; it focuses the learning by confronting the domain knowledge to practical considerations. The learning will be richer.

Humbleness opens the mind to creative thinking. Democratized innovators should ask themselves: "how could our successful product be one-upped by an imaginary (or not-so-imaginary) competitor?" Being proactive in this exercise and humble in recognizing that one's novelty's leadership position may not last forever are key attributes of the democratized innovators' spirit. One should never be fully satisfied with what one has accomplished, and proactively engage in brainstorming sessions to find ways to beat one's own novelty. If it is hard to do, then it may be necessary to bring in external consultants or end-users to avoid complacency.

As we have seen in Part 1, the Framework is, by definition, distributed and diversified with the team members being engaged by applying a principle of spreading activation. Participants join and leave as the project needs arise, evolve or are met. As much as possible, the decision power is left to the people who have the appropriate specialized expertise to debate it constructively in a negotiated innovation dynamic amongst the stakeholders. Making groups vote on matters provides further reassurance for management because a formal record is taken of each vote which entices people to be mindful of the way that they vote. Thus, de-facto, the Framework integrates the seeds for creativity that should be cultivated throughout the organization.

Launch and diffusion: How can a novelty be successfully introduced?

The introduction of a novelty may synchronize with the previous solution's end of life. Often, it couldn't keep up with the growing demands made on it. This is a straightforward situation that involves little resistance to its introduction. However, most cases aren't as straightforward; it may incur considerable resistance from its intended user base.

A novelty that is first in its category represents a particular challenge. Indeed, when entering a brand-new market, the first challenges to face involve confirming that there is truly a demand for the novelty and educating the would-be adopters. In fact, even on a new market that doesn't have any direct competitors per se, the users' needs may already be filled by a substitute solution or technique that may not formally be in the same product or service category as one's novelty. It may even be a manual method. Hence, an unmet need is often a fallacy or, at best, a misnomer since the need likely already exists even if it is addressed differently. One should then determine how laborious, pricey or, more generally, resource-consuming this existing solution may be, and whether it could qualify as a pain point. However, on most markets, there are already competitors, which confirms that there is a demand to meet. If there is a single firm – the pioneer – the first thing to do is to examine its pricing strategy if that information is available. The pioneer may be profiting from its monopolistic position on the market with high umbrella pricing, that is to say pricing that becomes a reference point for would-be competitors to assess the profitability of their potentially entering the nascent market. As a rule, a high umbrella price point attracts competitors. It also allows a competitor to enter at a lower price point while still being profitable. Analyzing the pioneering firm's offer, its history on the market and its capabilities should shed light on the maturity of the market. It will reveal the attractiveness of the opportunity for another player to enter the market and the extent of the challenges that may lay ahead. Competitors leaving the market would obviously be a warning signs of low-profitability issues; one should try to understand what motivated them to do so. Is the product or service being talked about in the social media? Are there reviews and possibly comparisons, such as benchmarking data from a neutral third-party organization? How would one's novelty be different and hopefully more compelling than the pioneer's or the substitutes? Is there a subset of the total population that may be more receptive to a novelty from a lesser-known brand? These might include users who are more adventurous or tech-savvy. Some may like to impress their following with a novelty never seen before, while yet others have the means to switch and to forego the residual value of the solutions that they currently use.

Introducing a novelty to a standard-based market involves particular challenges. One needs to assess the degree of homogeneity of the users' profiles and preferences. A market that is very homogeneous will be highly prone to being locked by one player with a suitable solution and a well-known brand. On the contrary, if the user profiles and preferences are very heterogeneous, the network effects induced by a leading standard taper off quickly; this is a phenomenon known as "infra-marginal network effects" (Liebowitz and Margolis 1994). A heterogeneous market cannot be entirely locked by a single standard which allows multiple standards to coexist, each with a segment of the market characterized by a set of specific user preferences. In other words, challengers should go after heterogeneous markets, while dominant players could use their size and might to control homogeneous ones, as long as another dominant player hasn't already locked them. Size will have little impact on a heterogeneous market, but it matters when economies of scale can be leveraged. For the democratized innovators, this means that if they are part of a challenger organization, they should look for the diversity of user needs. However, this also means that, as they grow in size, they will not be able to dominate the market either; it could remain vulnerable to new competitors. However, early successes in such a market allows a small player to establish itself and to grow; it could then tackle another market that is more homogeneous to leverage its newly acquired size and to achieve sustainability. The consulting market is a quintessential example of a heterogeneous market.

Maybe the userbase isn't external, but rather an internal group of co-workers; maybe this novelty would only be used by its inventor. In this case, the benefits should be identified and quantified, if the idea is at the proposal stage, the development costs should be assessed; they should include the opportunity cost resulting from the organization not having some of its employees working in their regular occupations while they develop the novelty. The expected return on investment should be estimated. Interfacing issues with existing practices, technologies and tools should also be reviewed. The skills and training that would be required to develop it and later to operate it should be examined. In addition, one shouldn't forget about the cost of maintaining the novelty. When comparing several competing novelties that involve radically different capital and operating costs, it may be advantageous to consider the total cost of ownership to determine which one is truly the most advantageous.

Assuming that the novelty is well advanced, and that the developer isn't the principal beneficiary, a lead user should be identified. The earlier this user is involved, the earlier the feedback will be available. A lead user who joins at the inception of the innovation project is, in fact, a co-creator. The lead users may be motivated to participate by being the first to get access to the novelty from which they may derive a competitive advantage. They may simply be seeking the prestige of being on the cutting edge or recognized as being the novelty's champion or sponsor in their organizations. Co-creators may be entitled to a compensation. Whatever the motivation may be, having the help of a lead user ends up being invaluable in most cases, especially, if it avoids needing to pivot the project later which can be time consuming. Furthermore, in some cases, the lead user's organization may even sponsor the project with an early purchase. Alternatively, sponsoring market studies or organizing customer surveys or focus groups could help gain useful user or market insights.

Engaging in consulting activities is a fertile ground for learning and exploration of what the target users need. An interesting option is to provide, first on a consulting basis, the service that the novelty would later automate. When the novelty is at the pre-commercial stage, one could use it oneself to aid in providing the service. It goes without saying that the creators of the novelty would be patient lead users, albeit not fully objective since they would be evaluating their own novelty. Eventually, once the novelty becomes available, it could be commercialized, while phasing out the consulting business or transferring it to a value-added reseller (VAR) or to another consulting firm.

It is highly recommended to discuss the risks involved with using an early version of a novelty with the lead users and to clarify the objectives sought in doing so for both parties. These objectives could clash if the lead user expects features that are too specific for a generic product. In which case, having a VAR partner to propose could avoid disagreements and save the partnership in a mutually beneficial manner.

Having to choose between several options is always a puzzle for consumers unsure about which one to select. Typically, in absence of knowledge and information, new would-be adopters will look for explicit or implicit guidance in their purchasing decisions from those who have already committed to one of the options. The preferred standard may not necessarily be the most technologically advanced, the best designed or the best from the viewpoint of any other criteria. It is usually the one that manages to garner the most adopters, signalling a form of collective wisdom. In order to create some leverage from market adoption, one should focus on selling to customers (or signing up users) who could influence others to do the same either explicitly by their public statements or implicitly by the reference that their simple use of the novelty represents. To make them effective influencers – whether or not they explicitly refer to themselves as such – they need to have a high-profile status in their industry either for their technical expertise or simply from their general notoriety.

Introducing one's novelty on a niche market is usually an effective strategy to shield oneself from powerful competitors. When this market is too small to be of interest to them, the niche market wouldn't be on their radar screens so to speak. The niche may simply be defined as a particular segment of a larger market, in which case one's novelty should be specialized to respond particularly well to its users' needs, preferences, constraints and expectations preferably better than the larger competitors' solutions. One could also focus on a regional market that has a particularity that shields it from competitors, such as an uncommon language or complex social structures. The competitive forces may be less intense on a regional market or a foreign country, allowing one's organization to grow more easily. One should take care to keep the orders under the threshold of interest for established players. Also, keeping the novelty's pricing under the allowable threshold for sole-sourced orders can be invaluable in the early stages to avoid a formal tendering process being required by some purchasers. The aim could also be to just make the first order happen and initiate a cash flow whatever the profit margin may be; if the customers or users like the novelty, then they will be likely to order more of it later on. If they are delighted, they may even tell their acquaintances (Beckwith 2014) implicitly helping in the effort to market the novelty. The delight factor may be directly associated with the novelty or with other related value-generating activities, such as customer service or training. Reducing the risks involved in adopting a novelty that doesn't have a brand name by offering a free trial period, full money-back policy or extended warrantees can go a long way to diminishing any hesitations that the users may have.

If one has other successful products, the novelty could be introduced with a cross-marketing technique, such as providing a free sample with the other product, combined packaging, or simply discount coupons. In doing so, one strives to introduce the novelty to one's existing user base, bridging both markets. Greater quantities offered at the same price as the competitors' offer could prove to be enticing for some customers, but one should beware of the fact that when faced with the difficulty to evaluate a solution, they may consciously or sub-consciously use the price as a proxy for quality. In other words, they intuitively expect that a higher-price should be applied on an item of higher quality; lesser quality is usually less expensive to produce and thus cheaper – a word that commonly denotes lack of quality.

An important thing to keep in mind is that, although one may have managed to remain stealthy during one's development phase, once the novelty is introduced to the market, it will certainly come to the competitors' attention. They are likely to react with price cuts or pre-announcements of their own upcoming versions of the novelty even if they haven't developed them yet. Their brand strength and reputation could bring customers to wait for their brand-name versions while ignoring the challenger's novelty despite it being already available. This delay would derail the novelty's launch and deprive the new market entrant from much needed revenue, potentially even jeopardizing its survival. It is always safe to assume that one's entry on the market will be harder than anticipated and that adoption will take longer than planned. If the novelty is intended for internal use, one shouldn't underestimate the resistance to change that one may face.

If the market still comprises many users who haven't committed to any solutions, it is preferable to go after them in priority of course. However, when market saturation makes it necessary to draw the competitors' users away which entails switching costs, offering to cover these costs removes a barrier albeit at a high cost for their sponsor. Switching to another more attractive market, such as one that is still in its early-development stage should be considered to find sales growth. One should keep in mind that markets are fleeting.

Summation

The innovation subject matter presented in this chapter relates to the typical preoccupations and scope that democratized innovators in training are likely to entertain. Identifying which specific body of innovation domain knowledge may be appropriate for a particular group of regular workers depends on each organization. The training in innovation is highly context-dependent because the perspective needs to be anchored in practice which is obviously contextual. Thus, we presented topics intended to be illustrative of the type of material that is typically of interest to regular workers. The trainer could make use of them to get the discussions started; the study points could then be adapted to whatever sparks the learners' interest. Additional study points could be developed by the trainer or by external training partners to expand on innovation topics particularly relevant to one's organization. As shown in the points presented in this chapter, the perspective must be predominantly practical. Using 'how' questions in the statements of the study points helps frame them in a way that corresponds to the democratized innovators' needs rather than being presentations of theoretical points. First and foremost, it is of utmost importance to develop the learners' curiosity and interest for the subject to motivate them to research, to experiment and to practice even more by themselves or in groups; as Sir Kenneth Robinson is reported to have said: "Curiosity is the engine of achievement". Therefore, the primary goal is to develop their curiosity and interest; the knowledge and practice will then come naturally soon after.

Chapter 6
Innovation Modelling

The ambiguity that typically characterizes innovation projects creates risk. The organization's capabilities that aren't properly managed may suddenly become misaligned with the skills that are required to carry out innovation projects. An organization's production doesn't occur in a void; it integrates into a complex sequence of value streams. There are many possible strategic orientations that may be selected for an innovation project. A comprehensive innovation strategy will guide the decision-making in keeping with the orientation that is selected both at the planning stage and as the project is being carried out. In this chapter, we investigate these challenges. We present two conceptual models that may be applied when innovating, one that relates to risk management and the other to innovation strategizing. In addition, we define on what the management of an organization's knowledge assets should focus, and the concepts of value chains and value streams in innovation are reviewed. The points presented highlight the multidimensional aspects of the innovators' reflections.

How can the risks that innovation involves be managed?

Risk relates to an expected outcome that doesn't occur or to an undesirable result that causes a loss. Innovation always involves risks because it is a venture into the unknown. The chances of success of innovation initiatives are often hard to predict. Innovators must understand and assess the risks associated with their projects to manage them appropriately. Risk may have a delaying effect by causing entrepreneurs to procrastinate. Projects that are risky or perceived as being risky may be less attractive for investors who may hesitate to commit their funding, which may delay the launch or which may cause them to demand financial terms that compensate for the risk. Excessive optimism may lead to risks being misunderstood and underestimated which may jeopardize the innovation projects' ultimate success when they are much more advanced and after extensive costs have been engaged. For example, it is common that feasibility studies are mistakenly carried out as an innovation project's first phase of development, when their purpose is really to clear the unknowns that make the innovation project difficult to plan and to estimate; its practicality must be confirmed. A feasibility study should comprise activities that clarify the project's areas of ambiguity that create risks and provide plans to manage them; the outcome should support the project-planning phase. In addition, it is important to keep in mind that the experimentation that is part of the feasibility studies may not directly be reusable in the later stages of the project. One should resist the temptation to alter or even to distort the purpose of a feasibility

https://doi.org/10.1515/9783110683837-009

study simply to reuse components for their later use in the eventual development stage.

The risk exposure could also be quantified as: the probability of a loss multiplied by the size of the loss. This simple equation draws out five risk management strategies to which we will refer with the acronym ATRAM; one may:

- Assume the risk, which means taking on the risk and establishing a form of self-insurance. In practice, this means setting aside or pre-arranging the funding that may be required to remedy its eventual consequences.
- Transfer the risk, in full or in part, by seeking insurance coverage which, in fact, is a form of mutualization of the risk in exchange of a fixed premium, partnering in a joint-venture or outsourcing parts of a project that the organization doesn't have the capabilities to carry out by itself to a partner that does.
- Reduce the risk, by reducing the scale of a project; for example, this situation would apply when there is a high level of contextual uncertainty or ambiguity that cannot be resolved; in the risk exposure equation, this relates to reducing the size of the potential loss.
- Avoid the risk, which means that the risk is eliminated by not engaging in – or by withdrawing from – the risk-bearing activity; in other words, the size of the loss is reduced to zero. However, this also means that one chooses to pass on any gains that the project could have generated. The risk associated with the status quo should also be assessed.
- Mitigate the risk, which means that measures are taken to reduce the probability of a risk's negative consequences occurring, such as conducting preventative maintenance on machinery to reduce the risks of it breaking down in the field at an unexpected and possibly inopportune time, including experts on a project who ideally have worked on similar projects, having knowledgeable technicians on stand-by at critical times ready to intervene in case of problems, or buying technologies rather than developing them in-house.

One may combine several of these strategies, such as, for example, combining both the reduce and mitigate strategies by creating a working prototype for a smaller set of users with a Commercial-off-the-shelf (COTS) tool that is fully supported by a third-party organization. It facilitates the development even if the tool's features don't fit the purpose as well as customized development would. The smaller user-base reduces the outcry in case of problems.

The risk factors identified for an innovation project may change as it progresses; monitoring them actively makes it possible to adjust the risk strategy if need be. It goes without saying that risk management strategizing requires the strategy to be put in place before the loss or the undesirable outcome occurs. Let us also note that different stakeholders may have different tolerances to risks and that agreement on the risk management strategy may involve negotiations amongst them which should be part of what we called negotiated innovation.

Barry Boehm (2000) introduced a spiral model designed especially for software development projects, which highlights an evolutionary process featuring a widening project scope. Risk analyses are carried out at each cycle. He related the model to the game of stud poker for which a set of cards are handed out some face up some face down. This illustrates the risks related to the ambiguity and the uncertainty surrounding the value of one's hand compared to the other players' hands; additional clues are provided to the players as the game progresses and as the cards are revealed. Like Design Thinking, the spiral model guides the users through the possible steps that they can carry out or reiterate or, on the contrary, over which they may skip or leap forward, rather than following a fixed sequence through a set of rigidly predefined steps.

We designed a new model that we called the 'iVortoid framework which stands for 'Innovation Vortex-like framework. The iVortoid reflects the fact that it comprises a depth dimension contrary to a spiral which is on a single plane. At each cycle, a risk is identified, and a risk management strategy is selected; various activities are then carried out to investigate and to manage the risk. This model is a map not an itinerary; the steps that don't apply to a given situation can be skipped over. These cycles could focus on one of the following investigations that illustrate some typical risks associated with innovation projects:

- the insufficient knowledge of the users' needs or requirements, or the misunderstanding or misinterpretation of the problem to address (a Design-Thinking Empathise-domain study could be conducted, and the user acceptance criteria defined);
- the availability and readiness of the capabilities that are needed to carry out the project (which could involve their development, their procurement or arranging for training initiatives);
- the identification of a project portfolio which balances opportunities and risks, when managing several projects concurrently (the mix of projects with different risk levels balances the overall portfolio risk);
- the appropriateness of the solution architecture (which may need to be revisited if the initial prototype, working prototype and finished novelty are implemented with different underlying technologies; prototyping and scaling may point to different tools and techniques with different inherent risks);
- the planning of the resources and the estimation of the project costs (including development, commercialization or deployment, and the total cost of ownership; the extent to which these costs could increase should be considered; stocking or hedging strategies could be considered);
- the availability of quality assurance techniques and tests to prevent defects in the novelty (testing against the project requirements and the service-level agreements, for example);

- the existence of regulations (depending on the industry, independent verification and validation may be required; one should consider whether these regulations could change in the foreseeable future);
- unforeseen changes in market or user-related circumstances (external or internal; i.e., decreasing demand or new competition);
- unexpected requirement changes which usually means increasing scope (identifying and managing the so-called "requirements creep" which is often addressed by identifying items that are out of the original scope of work and renegotiating the terms of the project with additional costs, as 'extras', associated with the new work items);
- unplanned organizational changes (i.e., mergers and acquisitions, partner disengagement, disablement of key participants or bankruptcies, etc.);
- uncertainties about the practicality of the assembly of a novelty in the field which is often addressed by staging it to uncover any delivery and integration issues before it is deployed;
- unanticipated circumstances when deploying or commercializing the novelty (such as the resistance to change or the competitors' reactions to one's novelty's market introduction);
- the challenges of maintaining the novelty's condition and readiness and respecting the terms of its warranty after its delivery to the customers;
- the challenges of operating the novelty and its integration in a value chain of wider scope, which are sometimes addressed with design-build-operate-transfer agreements (DBOT) that involve the designing organization operating the novelty for a prescribed period of time to iron out the integration issues before transferring its ownership to the customer;
- sustainability and lifecycle of the novelty including the on-going pertinence of the novelty in its conditions of use and with respect to competing solutions (including the availability of key components such as underlying technologies, materials and business models, as well as the resources required to operate it).

Figure 6.1 shows the iVortoid framework in which the risk management strategies allow for the gradual reduction of the ambiguity by moving down the iVortoid towards a state of clarity at its center; considering the three-dimensional (3D) perspective, one could also say that the goal is to move through the iVortoid towards its exit at the center. The model's typical risk-bearing issues should be adjusted to an organization's line of business, its practices and processes, as well as to its particular context and circumstances. It needs to be regularly revisited to assess the impact of any changes that occur and to monitor the continued suitability of the risk management strategy as the innovation project progresses and as the ambiguity surrounding the project gradually clears. This is a four-phased cyclical model that runs clockwise. In a first phase (see Fig. 6.1 upper right), the unknowns that cause a risk exposure are identified; these may involve some of the typical ones

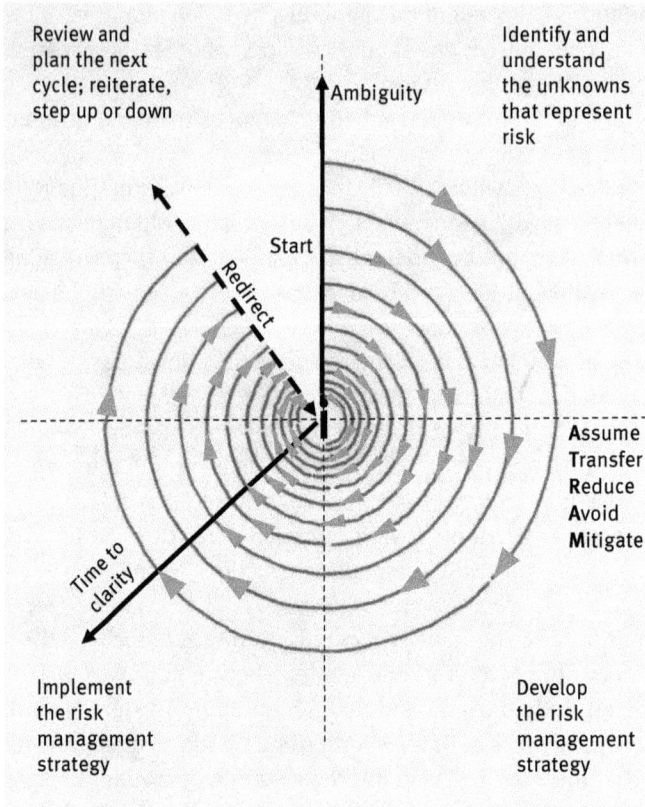

Fig. 6.1: The iVortoid framework used to develop a risk management strategy.

that we previously listed. They are investigated to gain an understanding of them; the innovators may choose to focus on one of the unknowns at a time in each iteration. The model user should start somewhere in the middle of the iVortoid because the investigations may reveal later conditions that increase the project's ambiguity beyond what was originally thought at the start. The second phase (see Fig. 6.1 lower right) involves the development of a risk management strategy using the ATRAM options. The connection between the risk and the risk management strategy should be documented and the steps that the strategy requires should be planned. In the third phase (see Fig. 6.1 lower left), the activities that the strategy involves are carried out and the results collected. Finally, in a fourth phase (see Fig. 6.1. upper left), the results from the iteration that completed are analyzed. If the strategy that was applied allowed to clarify an unknown, the process continues at a lower (i.e., deeper) level in the iVortoid. If on the contrary, the iteration revealed issues that increase the ambiguity, then the next iteration would need to proceed at a higher level in the iVortoid. We call these incremental jumps 'redirections' of the path through the iVortoid. One can jump up or down by any number of levels, if need be, which can also be viewed as moving forward and backward in the model given the three-dimensional perspective. At this point in the process, the innovator may plan a new iteration taking into account the new information collected in the performance of the iteration that just completed, or he or she may select another risk-bearing unknown previously set aside to investigate. The depth in the iVortoid which is visible from the 3D perspective is also measured with the 45-degree depth axis representing the time separating the current understanding of the project to its clarity (see Fig. 6.1 lower left). The model iterates as often as necessary with the ultimate goal of reaching this point in the center of the iVortoid. The inward-oriented coils of the iVortoid illustrate the reduction of the ambiguity at each cycle. The process continues inwards towards the state of clarity or at least significantly diminished ambiguity which allows for the project to be planned and executed with more confidence. The time-to-clarity variable is the time that separates the project's present ambiguous situation in the iVortoid to the state of clarity. It may increase or decrease as the iterations are carried out in the iVortoid clearing unknowns which reduces ambiguity or on the contrary uncovering new unknowns which need to be investigated making the objective of reaching the state of clarity more elusive and remote.

Contrary to Boehm's spiral model, the vertical axis does not represent the increasing project cost; it measures the overall ambiguity in the innovation project. The expenses applied to risk management activities will ultimately pay off; no matter what is done, they will always be a small fraction of the costs that could otherwise have been needed to address the issues when the full development of the project is underway, to say nothing about the lost project time and delays. Thus, gauging the project's ambiguity matters more than the project cost at this stage; cost isn't a prime consideration, within reason of course. The iVortoid framework integrates an iterative process in case new project information comes into play that reintroduces ambiguity. As a result, a risk management procedure previously carried out may need to be repeated or it may have revealed new ambiguities about which one may not have been aware. To illustrate this graphically in the model, there is a gap next to the vertical axis after each cycle's review-and-planning stage (see Fig. 6.1 at the top center) that allows paths to be reiterated which means that the overall level of project ambiguity is readjusted; stepping back higher in the iVortoid means that the iteration hasn't reduced the ambiguity. Jumping up or down one or more cycles (i.e. farther away from clarity or closer to it) reflects the situation in which more ambiguity has been uncovered or, on the contrary, situations in which ambiguity has been cleared or appropriately understood.

Another way of looking at the model, is that the coils of the vortex-like shape illustrate the layers of disambiguation that that are attempted at each iteration and the progression towards the state of clarity (or of well-managed risks) at the center as the risk analysis proceeds. Once the ambiguity has significantly diminished thanks to the various risk management measures, the project is in known territory so to speak. At that point, it could be managed like any other regular project with standard project management techniques.

How should organizations manage their innovation capabilities?

We believe that the management of knowledge assets is a central consideration in the management of innovation. Knowledge assets are what brings an innovation initiative to fruition. This line of investigation addresses the question: "are we (or how could we be) capable of carrying out an innovation initiative?" Contrary to value chains and value streams that model the value-creating business functions and activities, this dimension relates to organizational learning and organizational readiness.

In Chapter 4, we proposed an innovation typology based on learning. Competencies involve knowledge and know-how. They are enabled by a chain of knowledge-development processes that extend from the genesis of theoretical principles (i.e., fundamental knowledge) usually in research settings to the value-generating competencies that organizations apply. As illustrated on Fig. 6.2, scientific discoveries and theoretical principles produced by fundamental science and research eventually feed applied science which in turn puts them to practical use by producing inventions and technologies which represent knowledge. These inventions and technologies may be adopted by organizations through knowledge transfers. They further experiment with them and learn about them producing related know-how that can be explicitly codified such as:
- techniques that operationalize a skill,
- methods on the application of algorithms, tools, models or frameworks to achieve a given result,
- customary or habitual organizational practices (i.e., directives and guidelines), and
- processes that comprise sequences of activities or tasks leading to value-producing results.

Other areas of know-how relate to the development of practical points of experience that remain tacit in that they cannot be easily codified. They are usually implicitly transferred amongst workers through mentoring, simulations and coaching. The final step involves the incorporation of the know-how in the organization's production processes. These components are operationalized to form what is needed for an organization to claim that it has a competency in a domain and in a given context (i.e., an industry, line of business or region).

The steps that lead to the creation of competencies from the knowledge and know-how require a significant amount of training; greater depth in the genesis of

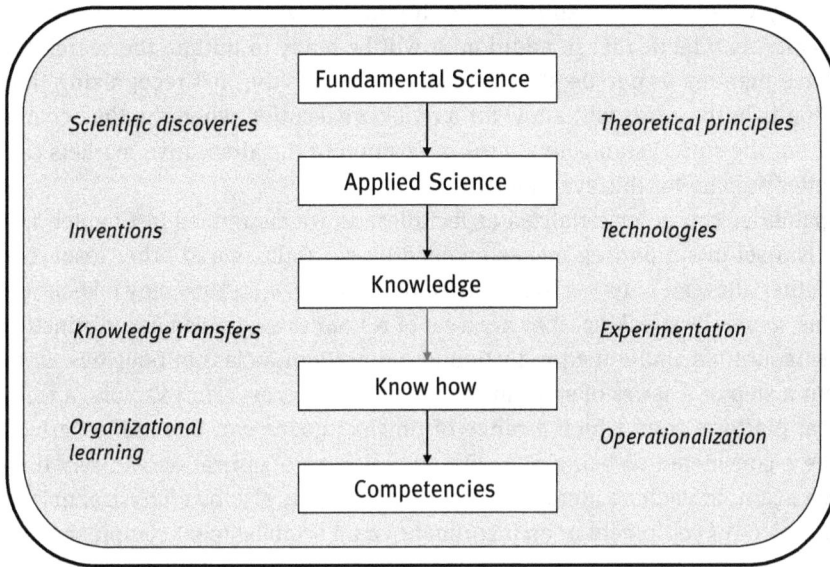

Fig. 6.2: Knowledge-to-competencies development chain.

competencies may be developed by establishing ties with research organizations that generate the fundamental knowledge or with internship or fellowship programs providing temporary employment to students or to recent graduates who are or were involved in fundamental or applied research. Core competencies are those that are tied to an organization's distinctiveness and competitiveness. Competencies enable capabilities by drawing on one or more areas of expertise to fulfill a specific goal as illustrated in Fig. 4.1 in Chapter 4.

We believe that it is more important for organizations to map, track, manage and update their capabilities rather than their focusing on their product lines and production processes to improve their overall resiliency and sustainability in ever-changing business circumstances. Start-ups need to do this at an even faster pace by pivoting a few times before their seed funding runs out. Products and processes need to be frequently modified to catch up with the continuous shifts in market demand, which forces an organization to be reactive. When an organization is overwhelmed by these frequent tactical changes, the management of capabilities enables a high-level view of the organization's readiness. The state of readiness or capability preparedness, as it is called, may be strategically planned much longer in advance than the tactical adjustments to products and processes that are attempted in response to market shifts. Hence, managing capabilities proactively allows an organization to be better prepared for any eventuality. Indeed, market demand can shift quickly, while capabilities require time to be updated or to be developed from scratch. An organization that manages its capabilities has a better chance of being ready when a market shift occurs. It could be viewed as managing more strategically than tactically. In addition, it will be ready to initiate the search for alternative markets to pursue should it become necessary; just recognizing that the option is in the cards will allow for a quicker execution when the time comes to carry out the shift. Establishing a token position in the alternative markets can even better prepare for this eventuality.

Capabilities can be materialized as facilities. As we mentioned in Chapter 4, a facility is a set of supporting means enabled by capabilities and other resources that together allow an outcome to be carried out (see Fig. 4.1). They may take different forms; generally speaking, they are a set of resources assembled as a distinctive establishment to facilitate the production of a novelty or a class of novelties, or to carry out a step or a series of steps in the innovation process. For example, a technological platform from which a range of finished goods can be readily derived could be a considered as being a facility on which an organization can rely time and time again. In its more literal meaning, a facility may also be a physical object, such as a piece of equipment or an instrument, or an establishment comprising one or more buildings, including staff and equipment – such as a research lab – that provides the innovators all the access, administrative support and equipment to conduct their investigations in specific domains. When the operating costs are very high, the facilities can be shared with other organizations. Facilities need to be operated, managed and periodically updated, which requires time and resources. Thus, the pertinence of establishing them should be carefully weighed against other options, such as renting, leasing or sharing them. Other organizations may deliberately do the opposite by outsourcing business functions (with the related capabilities and facilities) that don't leverage their core competencies. This means doing away with a facility or transferring it to a partnering organization. The original facility-operation capability is replaced by a capability to manage more cost-effective long-term partnerships or subcontractors who may be using the transferred facility or similar ones more knowledgeably and efficiently. Facilities have a pre-determined life span; they are not necessarily established forever. They may serve a purpose until their serviceability elapses, at which point, they need to be upgraded to continue meeting their intended purpose or replaced. An organization may also decide to phase out, spin off or close down the facilities that no longer align with its strategy. Facilities need to be documented with explicit descriptions of the competencies, the capabilities and the resources required to operate them and to use them.

Organizations need to manage their competencies, capabilities and facilities diligently. This means establishing and updating an inventory of their knowledge assets with comprehensive descriptions, maintenance plans and training. Of course, the guiding principle is how they all contribute to creating value for the stakeholders, which is, as the reader may recall, the last component illustrated on Fig. 4.1.

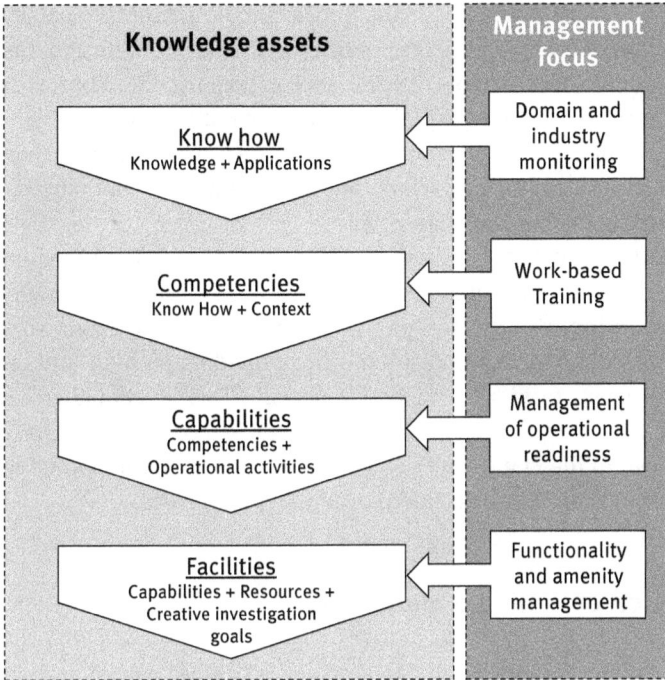

Fig. 6.3: Knowledge assets and their related management.

Let us recapitulate how all these knowledge assets should be managed. Figure 6.3 illustrates on the left-hand side the progression from know-how to facilities with each level building on the previous one. On the right-hand side, the management focus for each type of knowledge asset is shown. Know-how is developed when a body of knowledge is applied for a given purpose. Its management involves monitoring updates of practices in the corresponding domain or industry, which could mean in practice participating in various professional activities or gatherings, such as conventions, conferences, workshops, get-togethers organized by trade associations which make it possible to informally exchange with one's peers in one's industry; organizations may also consider partnerships with research organizations even to the extent of sponsoring them in exchange for a first right of refusal on the IP produced. Competencies may need to be periodically updated through training that should ideally be work-based to maintain the closest connection with the particularities of one's workplace. Capabilities draw on competencies and tie in the organization's operational activities. Their management involves reassessing and managing their readiness with any corrective measures being applied if they are found to be deficient in one way or another. Finally at the lower level in Fig. 6.3, the facilities make use of capabilities and resources to accomplish creative exploratory goals. As knowledge assets, their functionality and their amenity need to be periodically reassessed and updated. Xavier Baron (2016) emphasized the importance that the concept of amenity plays in determining how well the facility's users carry out their tasks. Indeed, beyond the purely functional considerations, a facility's components should provide convenience and safety in the performance of the activities that it supports, and possibly comfort and enjoyment as well depending on its purpose. Hence, it is a qualitative consideration that relates to human factors, but that can have a very tangible effect on the effectiveness of the innovation process.

Adopting democratized innovation involves developing a capability based on the Framework's principles in one's organization. To support its regular workers turned into democratized innovators, an organization may choose to establish a training and coaching facility like an innovation office providing support and refresher training on one aspect or another of the Framework. This functional group may also oversee how well the collaborative exchanges take place and proactively stimulate them as needed. In the Framework's structure, the democratized-innovation capability could also be a managed by a dedicated community of practice.

How can the creation of value be managed?

Michael Porter (1985) defined a value chain as the strategic business functions that come into play to deliver valuable products or services to a given market; these functions may be primary, that is to say that they are directly involved in the production of the goods or services that an organization produces or provides. They may also support the primary functions. Later, Womack and Jones (1997) added the notion of value stream that they defined as being an end-to-end set of activities that produces the value that a customer expects.

The full extent of an innovation initiative from ideation to launch may be carried out entirely within an organization. The value may be passed on to its customers in exchange of a financial compensation, or it may be captured internally when the beneficiaries are amongst the organization's workers. However, in another scenario, the novelty's inception and the creation of value may be separated in space and time. The process may span across several organizations that either explicitly collaborate or implicitly interact with one another through the mediation of the market. For example, customers may assemble a computer system with compatible components made by different suppliers. This forms a value chain that may extend over a durable form of vertical integration or that simply reflects an impromptu sale transaction. For instance, an industrial-machinery maker may sell its latest novelty to a manufacturing firm that would then use it to automate a key process, making it more efficient. The efficiency gains allow the manufacturer to sell its products at a more competitive price which increases the value offered to its customers. The value chain may extend beyond that point if the customers have customers of their own to whom they provide more value as well.

In some cases, the value flows in a single direction, while in others it may si-multaneously flow in both directions. For example, von Hippel (2005) described the co-creation that on occasion occurs between lead users and manufacturers. On the one hand, the lead users benefit from gaining early access to a novelty which may be worth their having to deal with the inevitable glitches that they will encounter with its early or pre-commercial versions. In addition, thanks to the manufacturer providing them with pre-commercial versions to try out, they can spear-head the development of a value-creation initiative in their own field or line of business. This may bring value to them in terms of performance, prestige, competitiveness, ad-vanced learning or getting ahead in the race to innovate in their own line of busi-ness. On the other hand, the services that a lead customer provides back to the manufacturer also have a considerable value. The manufacturer can observe how they use pre-commercial versions of the novelty and collect feedback on its early use; this early testing may confirm the novelty's viability and reveal any flaws that it may have with a patient user without its reputation being negatively impacted. This collaboration accelerates innovation and reduces the risks of design misfits; it establishes a de-facto co-creation field laboratory. The lead users provide invalu-able insights into a target market's needs and expectations. They test early proto-types in real-life conditions in a fault-tolerant environment usually with a quick turn-around time; this level of dedication cannot be hired nor bought.

Therefore, value may flow in several directions and through several stakehold-ers. Innovation initiatives may involve several of these outward-extending or criss-crossing value streams; often the outcome from one value stream feeds into another value stream within the organization or outside of it. What characterizes each stream is the value towards which it builds, and the intermediate value components that are created along the way. Value streams highlight the linkages between the capabilities (that involve competencies and operational activities) and, if applica-ble, the facilities that come into play to create value. They can be assembled and configured to respond to specific demand scenarios that span the whole novelty-invention-to-value-creation scope. A given capability could enable several value streams. Complex streams may be created by aggregating more basic ones; these complex streams may involve several capabilities. Innovation involves setting up new value streams or enhancing existing ones. The achievement of the value by the customers as they use one's novelty should be carefully managed. To this aim, an organization should dedicate resources to support the innovation that takes place in the customers' organizations by setting up a customer innovation support capa-bility. The reader may have guessed that, in the Framework, this responsibility rests with a dedicated community of practice.

It is worthwhile to map them out. An innovation initiative's value stream in-cludes the sources of innovation and an outcome in the form of a novelty used by someone; value is created between these two points by applying the organization's capabilities and facilities or by developing new ones. Figure 6.4 illustrates the different sources from which value streams could be initiated.

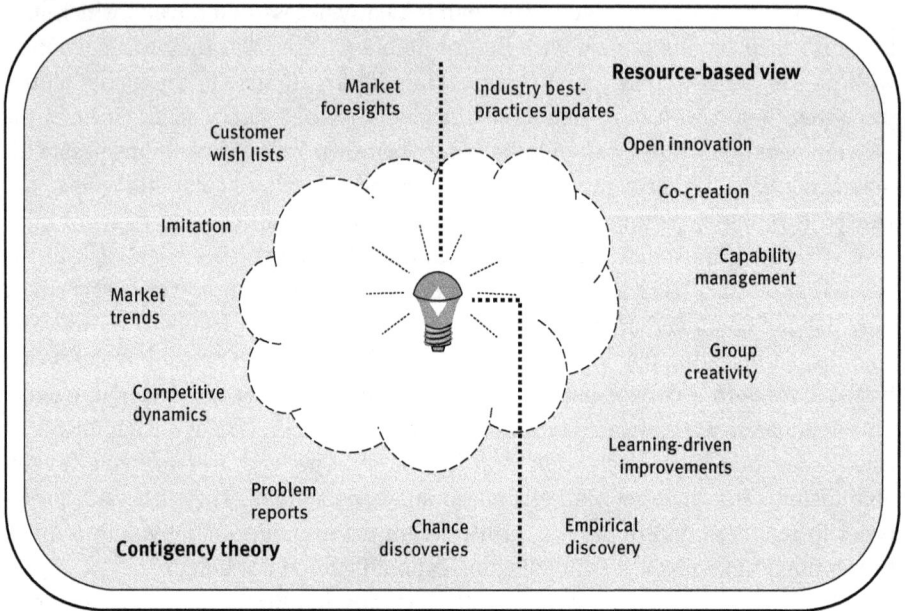

Fig. 6.4: Sources from which value streams may be initiated.

Like value chains, value streams may be primary in the sense of being part of production or supporting activities, such as research and development or development and operations (DevOps). The former creates value that is directly delivered to an organization's customers, while the latter develops the business solutions used by the production value streams. This dichotomy distinguishes between the value produced by the research and development function traditionally associated with the invention of the novelty from that generated by the organization's production and operations functions. This distinction corresponds to production-innovation capabilities compared to innovation capability management.

The concept of "mission threads" is used by the military when it applies or manages its capabilities as a system of systems (SoS) (Owens 1996). There are three types of mission threads, namely operational, development or sustainment mission threads. They need to satisfy several types of quality attributes. Interestingly, the quality attributes for the sustainment mission threads includes a review of the instrumentation that supports training. Thus, this is yet another case that places training at the center of the management of the capabilities that an organization needs to innovate. In keeping with the resource-based view of the innovative organization that is applied in our Framework, we focused our attention on the capability management aspect of value streams; in particular, the enablement and sustainment of competencies. In addition, this parallel supports our learning-centric innovation typology.

How can value-creating capabilities be innovated?

Expanding on this capability-enabled value stream model, we devised the concept of 'value-stream innovation'. In this view, rather than focusing on processes, this concept relates to the business architecture of value streams, which maps the capabilities that come into play to produce value. Hence, value-stream innovation is the innovation of these value-producing capabilities. Let us note that this concept differs from the concept of "innovation value streams" proposed by Hansen and Birkenshaw (2007) which is a three-step process, comprising idea generation, development and implementation. The difference is in the positioning of the word innovation; a little difference that changes the meaning altogether. Positioning the word innovation before the terms value stream implies a novelty development process. Value-stream innovation, that is to say with the word innovation positioned after the term value-stream, concerns the management of the organization's capabilities that may in turn be applied to produce innovative novelties. Value-stream innovation includes the development, improvement and sustainability of these capabilities. These activities should be carried out by the corresponding communities of practice. For example, in artificial intelligence (AI), the ability to process perceptual data usually requires a machine-learning capability, whereas automating the decision-making related to the interpretation of the perceptual data and especially explaining the system's decisions generally requires a capability in symbolic AI. These are two distinctive sets of skills. The establishment of these capabilities relates to innovation capability management. AI-system developers may draw on either or both these capabilities to assemble innovative AI applications that will eventually be delivered to customers through value streams that apply production-innovation capabilities. This example highlights the distinction that exists between the capabilities to innovate – to which we referred earlier as innovation capability management – and the object of the innovation – that we called production-innovation capabilities. Furthermore, in the previous AI example, feeding perceptual data into a decision-module associates two distinctive capabilities as part of a hybrid system. The two value streams merge into one. A composite novelty may comprise several value streams that merge to deliver value to a group of stakeholders.

To situate the approach in adjacent methodologies and practices, we note that, interestingly, the management of the value created by a novelty also relates to the field of benefit management. The key aspect of benefit management that carries over to innovation value management is the documentation of the benefit to realize. This documentation covers the identification, planning, measurement, tracking and assessment of the benefits that a project or program should produce. Similarly, before engaging in an innovation project, the stakeholders should have identified and agreed on what the expected benefits or value may be. A benefit generally has a narrower scope than a value; it is often expressed as a gain or an improvement of a key performance parameter that provides a user or user-group with an advantage in performing a task. By comparison, a value is a more diffuse concept: it is the effect provided by a novelty that renders something more valuable or desirable. Despite these differences in scope, the practice of documenting the expected benefit (or value) that is central in benefit management is one that the democratized innovators should diligently adopt. They will find it convenient to regularly refer to these descriptions as an innovation project advances to guide their decision making or to validate them later on. It helps to ensure that the innovation initiative remains true to its intended purpose. It may also come in handy in case one needs to reconfirm the project's purpose to senior management if any doubts about it are raised. In addition, it is interesting to note that several benefit management methodologies highlight a point that relates to training. Indeed, rather than simply being trained on a novelty, benefit management methodology stipulates that the users of the novelty should be "educated" on how to exploit it to carry out their work better. The difference is in the realization that training is enabling while education is transformational. Training and education are once again central considerations in innovation.

How can an innovation strategy be defined?

An innovation endeavor should start with the definition of its innovation strategy; it will guide the innovators in making a set of strategic decisions. Each endeavor has its own strategy although it is likely that several endeavors may apply similar ones. To do so, we adapted the innovation-strategizing model defined by Davidson and Ivanova (2011) and which was later expanded as the "iNuggets" innovation strategy framework by Davidson, Malard and Ivanova (2012). A variation was devised to analyze innovation strategies in organizations. It involves four main groupings of considerations, that we call strategic viewpoints. They come into play in defining a comprehensive innovation strategy; They are identified as: (i) Opportunity and Pivoting, (ii) Design and Engineering, (iii) Workers and Organization, and (iv) Launch and Diffusion. These viewpoints form four quadrants as illustrated in Fig. 6.5.

The hemicycle on the left-hand side of Fig. 6.5 represents the viewpoints that relate to market contingencies and the management of demand that are external to an organization, while the hemicycle on the right-hand side of Fig. 6.5 relates to organizational resource management or in this case, the management of capabilities (that are mostly internal, but which may also extend beyond the organizational boundaries for co-creation and partnerships). Each hemicycle comprises two quadrants reflecting different aspects of it. There is a process to define a strategy for a

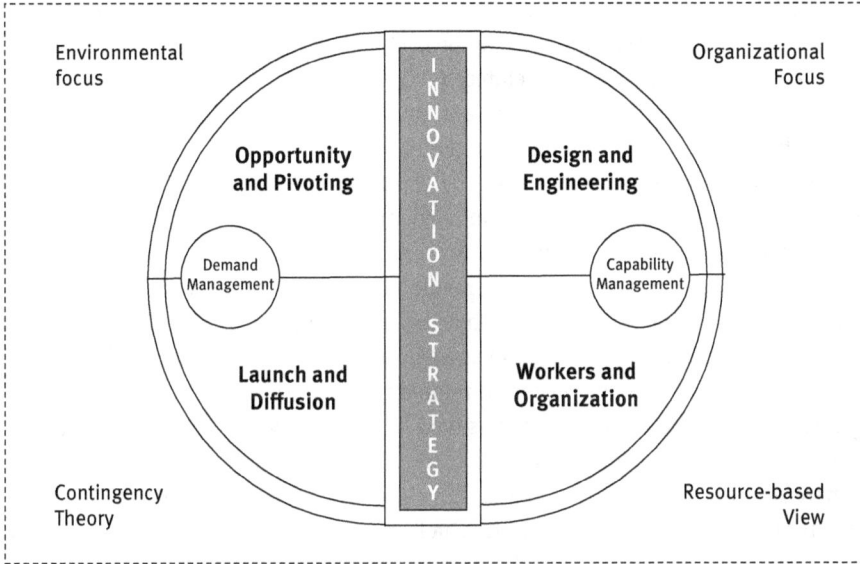

Fig. 6.5: The iNuggets innovation strategy framework.

specific innovation endeavor that overlays this viewpoint classification. Before describing the process, let us first note that the quadrants in the model reflect functional groupings of considerations rather than formal steps in a rigorous sequential process. In other words, switching from one quadrant to another implies moving from one viewpoint to another which is like looking at the endeavor through a different lens (e.g., from design-and-engineering to workers-and-organizational considerations, or from launch-and-diffusion to opportunity-and-pivoting ones). The lens analogy is illustrated by the arcs of the two opposing hemicycles and the two quadrants that each one comprises in the diagram in Fig. 6.5. The points collected in the model represent the endeavor's innovation strategy. These points may be related to the innovation best practices pertaining to the quadrant under review. For example, when in the opportunity-and-pivoting quadrant, the user could pick the strategy of targeting a small and specific market segment and then relate it to the well-known best practice for start-ups to enter a less competitive niche market, especially one that allows to circumvent dominant players. Typically, the innovation strategist incrementally assembles the points and relates them to recognized best practices in each quadrant then moves to another one to do the same. Generally, the process edges clockwise from the opportunity-and-pivoting quadrant through to the launch-and-diffusion one (see Fig. 6.5). It can loop back or jump forward allowing to reiterate any of the previously visited quadrants or to skip ahead to the next quadrants. The strategic decisions that are progressively made as the strategy is defined may impact some of the ones already made or constrain the remaining options (Davidson 1985). In this way, the process flexibly edges towards the end goal of developing a comprehensive strategy that covers most if not all of these viewpoints. The strategy may be updated as the innovation endeavor progresses, and until the ambiguities related to it are clarified. Updates may also be carried out as new information is gleaned, and as new strategic decisions are made and added to the strategy; this 're-actualizes' the innovation strategy. Also, an innovation endeavor that doesn't produce the expected value should pivot and cycle again (and possibly even several times) which means revisiting some of the four quadrants if not all of them while updating the strategy for a new direction hoping this time to find the value that the users need and, as a result, commercial viability. Cycling through several cycles of the model reflects the hit-and-miss nature of exploration. A trace of the process applied in developing the strategy keeps a record of the decisions that were made and the events that occurred related to the innovation strategy. A successful pattern of strategic points could be saved and formalized as an internal customized strategy that then becomes part of the knowledge assets.

Therefore, this is a flexible process that shifts the focus of the innovation strategizing from one viewpoint to another, which may require the participation or consultation of people who have specialized expertise in one area or the other. Decisions made in one quadrant may have impacts on those made in other quadrants. The decision-makers in each quadrant should remain abreast of any new information that may have an impact on their prior decisions and on their strategies. For example, pivoting may involve switching to another market with minimal technical changes but with significant impacts on the organization's marketing capabilities. Conversely, changes resulting from marketing decisions that are at first glance mundane such as deciding to make a basic version of one's online services freely available as a loss-leader, may have significant technological impacts because of the increased traffic that open access to it would involve. This innovation strategy framework is an effective way to focus the team discussions when democratized innovators get together to strategize; it entices them to consider a range of perspectives.

The value created thanks to the strategies defined through this cyclical process is highly temporal and contextual, which means that it doesn't last forever since the context is subject to change; the value may erode over time with life-cycle developments, or it could be challenged by disruptive events bringing about its sudden dissolution. Thus, it is essential to periodically revisit the innovation strategy for all of one's innovation endeavors and novelties including those that are currently successful and those that didn't make it to market. The former case focuses on sustaining the value that has been achieved, while the latter one monitors whether new windows of opportunity for previously failed, suspended or abandoned novelties may have suddenly opened. In fast-moving industrial sectors, this activity may require constant monitoring and situation reassessments resulting from fast changes occurring on the market, such as changes in demand, trends and competition. In practice, this means that the innovation strategist should run through the quadrants with updated information and knowledge to identify any value-affecting changes; he or she should update the strategy accordingly. For example, a new scientific discovery may provide a hint that new technologies may appear on the market within a few years which are likely to eventually compete with one's established products and services. A novelty that a competitor introduced on one's market may have a more immediate effect by rendering obsolete one's current offering, or by diminishing or even eradicating its value. In strategist roles, the democratized innovators may then decide to engage in defensive innovation or make a pre-announcement to get one's user base to wait rather than switching to the challenger's novelty (which incidentally are both best practices of innovation). A market change, such as previously independent competitors partnering or coopting for a competing technology or standard is another event that can quickly affect one's organization. Ironically, an organization's novelties may also cannibalize its own existing commodity production lines; this is something to realize even if this negative effect may be beneficial in the long term which justifies allowing them to carry on. More importantly, by realizing that medium-to-long term changes are coming, the organization may engage in the task of updating its capabilities or investigate new markets for them, which makes the process more resource-related.

As an example, let us consider the case of a fictitious start-up that started with the idea of selling high-end art online with a Dutch auction system; the key differentiators are: 1) that the sellers don't need to reveal their reservation price, and 2) that buyers tend to bid at the high end of their budget brackets producing better proceeds. Let us imagine that the start-up founder came up with the idea when visiting a Dutch auction house specialized in selling large batches of flowers for the wholesale market and on the following day, visiting a fine-arts museum in Amsterdam. She put two and two together in a spark of creative imagination. Thus, to translate this start-up's approach in the opportunity-and-pivoting quadrant into strategic management terms, she related the art market to the best practice of selecting a market with heterogeneous preferences which is advantageous for a start-up and unlikely to be dominated by a strong competitor, and the strategy of selling to high-end art collectors to the best practice of 'selling to a high-end market' or in other words, going for where the money is.

The community of practice mandated with the management of the democratized-innovation capability should support the regular workers in their strategizing, not to carry it out for them, but to train them and to advise them on how to do it themselves.

Summation

In the Framework, innovation needs to become a shared responsibility, a community value and a collective reflex in which all workers are engaged and that one exercises on a daily basis. The regular workers need knowledge in innovation to do so. Collectively they build the organization's innovation capability. It doesn't need to be perfect and complete to get things started. It is important to foster a critical mindset about all considerations related to innovation, whether these relate to one's innovation endeavors or to the very frameworks and tools that are used, because criticism, dissatisfaction about the status quo, curiosity and the perpetual quest for new knowledge and learning are generally the starting points of innovation. One shouldn't hesitate to adapt one's models, frameworks and tools to one's particular needs. Questions such as the following ones should come naturally to everyone's mind: Why am I doing this? How can I make this better? Is there a better way of doing this? Has anyone resolved this before? Let's get other people's views and ideas on this matter.

Let us also conclude by recapitulating the tangible benefits that innovation brings to organizations. The managers of established organizations should be concerned about their organizations' sustainability in changing market conditions, while start-up owners are, of course, mostly focused on finding a market that can fuel their nascent organization's growth; they may need to pivot several times before being successful. In both cases there are ambiguities and uncertainties that make proper planning of innovation initiatives difficult to carry out. A better approach is to develop the capability to address these unknowns. For the established organizations, the key is to astutely manage the risks of innovation, their competencies, capabilities, and value streams, as well as managing the continued pertinence of their innovation strategies. Learning is at the center of innovation since new or updated capabilities imply new knowledge and skills to acquire. The innovation manager is mostly a capability manager with an organizational training mandate; strategizing and managing risk are also part of the job. The coupling between capabilities and market demand should be purposefully kept loose to facilitate eventual moves to new markets where demand for one's organization's capabilities can once again be found. Alternatively, the organization should proactively adapt its capabilities to shifting conditions. Selling on a market should simply be viewed as a temporary touch down onto it.

For the start-up and challenger group, the key will be to quickly pivot to adjust the sketchy original idea and development plan to the realities of market demand. The short-cycled pivoting that start-ups need to carry out means that there is fast-paced learning about the market that takes place through a trial-and-error process. A start-up needs to develop its ability to quickly adapt to this pivoting which means that it needs to understand, to redefine and to master the linkage between capabilities and value in record time. This pivoting capability, as we call it, should be planned with an innovation specialist before the project is even initiated; as a result, pivoting, when it occurs, will be greatly facilitated. Pivoting may involve adapting the engineering – involving technical knowledge – or moving to another market or market segment with its distinctiveness to find the coveted value – which means that they will need to acquire knowledge about the new market and to develop new marketing competencies and capabilities. In the latter case, one may wonder whether it is a contingency perspective or a resource-based one. In fact, the management of the market-pivoting capability is a resource-based one despite the marketing objective sought that relates to the contingency approach. In other words, it is an example of mixed modes of innovation with both an innovation capability and an operational innovation purpose. Looking at the situation from a different viewpoint can bring insights. Beyond the start-up's eventual first success, it might want to grow by moving from one niche market to another as recommended by Geoffrey Moore (2002) which again requires fast capability adjustments and learning. The start-up's innovation specialist holds mostly the roles of pivoting manager and strategy advisor.

Hence, the astute management of innovation capabilities benefits both established organizations as well as start-ups including the other types of challengers. Overall, the in-house innovation specialist will need to advise the democratized innovators on capability management, innovation project risk management and innovation strategizing that are carried out in the Framework's cornerstones. In addition, he or she will need to take on the roles of trainer, coach, and workshop facilitator. The person in this role must always keep in mind that democratized innovation means that they should simply advise and guide the regular workers who carry out the innovation. Therefore, this is a multi-dimensional role that requires effective people-skills since innovation will need to be accomplished through many minds working together.

Part 3: **The Training**

The conversion of the Framework into an organization's particular manifestation of democratized innovation relies to a great extent on the regular workers' individual and team initiatives. They need to adapt it to their needs. For this purpose, they must first master the principles and practices of the Framework that we proposed and of the domain of innovation. The training approach draws them into the subject matter as active participants; this sets the stage for them to make the knowledge theirs. The trainer is a guide and a facilitator in the process. We analyze the training situation systematically and describe an innovative approach to the training of aspiring democratized innovators. Then, we review a comprehensive set of practical considerations that come into play when conducting democratized-innovation workshops. Finally, we investigate advanced topics such as addressing the learners' resistance to change and the use of exploratory and creative dialectics for the purposes of instruction. The trainer needs to develop a high-level of proficiency with these dialectics to guide the learners in a way that is effective from an instructional point of view and that naturally entices the learners to strive to reproduce the skill in their own creative deliberations.

https://doi.org/10.1515/9783110683837-010

Chapter 7
Training Challenges and Approach

Previously, we emphasized that, to be more successful, organizations need to draw on the innovativeness of their regular workers to a greater extent than they currently do. This means that their workers need to be actively engaged in innovation and empowered to undertake activities pertaining to innovation. Also, we stressed that the existing organizational structure remains in place unaffected. The interconnections between the regular workers form a virtual knowledge network that makes the decision-making related to innovation more knowledgeable. There are well-defined interfaces with management to ensure proper oversight of the activities taking place within the Framework. Thus, the workers' empowerment occurs throughout the Framework's four cornerstones.

First, this empowerment needs to be granted by senior management, and the expectations related to it must be clearly communicated to the workers. Second, the workers must be encouraged to exercise this new power that has been bestowed upon them. Counterintuitively, this may not naturally come to all, since with empowerment comes engagement, commitment and accountability. With democratized innovation, workers are granted more control over the innovation that applies to their work, and a say on the orientations of innovation in their organizations, but this comes with additional responsibilities to which some of them may not be accustomed. Getting them to spontaneously display initiative, creativity and a flair for uncovering value, all of which could be compounded as being part of innovativeness, may represent an uneasy challenge as well. The training in democratized innovation involves more than the acquisition of new knowledge. The workers need to be taught to think and to act as democratized innovators. There are significant behavioral changes to instill through the training process; some of these may be tacit and therefore challenging to teach.

How can workers be trained to use deliberations to stimulate creativity?

Previously, we argued that the workers derive the legitimacy to participate in democratized innovation from the enhancement of their knowledge in innovation, which in turn produces the empowerment that is sought (Davidson 2019a). They will develop self-confidence in voicing their opinions about innovation and in exercising their imagination in bringing forward initiatives that relate to improvements or to novelties with clear value propositions. The training must be offered to all the workers to make democratized innovation a ubiquitous skill in organizations; there are both hard and soft skills to acquire. Being empowered to innovate doesn't mean that

https://doi.org/10.1515/9783110683837-011

any half-baked idea that someone may have dreamed up on a whim will be adopted without extensive scrutiny. Quite on the contrary, in the Framework, there is hard work taking place jointly with other innovators in the knowledge network to clarify an idea, to develop it further and to bring it to the next level, which may even mean redesigning it entirely. There are more stakeholders to convince than ever before, more opinions to consider, and more concerns to address. Getting an idea adopted involves resolving diverging viewpoints which requires extensive and intensive deliberations. Acute negotiation skills come into play to find the appropriate compromises that optimizing value usually involves. In democratized innovation, collaborative imagination must pass the test of collective wisdom. Ideas mature in a collaborative environment supported by the knowledge network. Hardly have ideas been conceptualized that they are evaluated collectively by being again challenged or supported by the wide range of expertise available in the knowledge network; incongruities are quickly detected well before extensive costs are engaged. Quick pivoting occurs naturally when one has access to a wide range of perspectives. Thus, given the omnipresence of this spirit of collaboration at all steps of the process, the workers must develop the ability to devise and to articulate appropriate arguments for their proposed novelties; those reviewing them must also articulate their points of view constructively. The proposers must be able to make convincing cases while remaining open to the option of making the appropriate redesigns and compromises that result from the feedback. The exercise is like testing the potential of one's ideas against the experience of others; the feedback should be perceived as being invaluable because it prevents costly mistakes and accelerates the innovation cycle. It may be hard at times, possibly even frustrating, but certainly gratifying in the end knowing that one's novelty has been supported, reviewed and endorsed by one's knowledge network, which is a state that we proposed to qualify as one's innovation having been "negotiated" from the early inception to its final acceptance. It is the ultimate state of acceptance after having worked its way through the collaborative process. If an idea didn't survive the collective scrutiny; it should be taken as being a learning experience that can be used in developing the next one. Ideas not retained at one point in time may be reused later for another purpose. Significant and valuable ideas develop through a continuum of creativity with interconnected sparks of imagination in a virtual collective mind. The knowledge network is a source of inspiration for the organization, a sounding board and a virtual testbench; it is all of that and more right at the democratized innovators' disposal.

For democratized innovation to be successfully introduced to an organization, that is to say that its 'manifestation' is allowed to flourish, an executive-level champion must promote it, possibly with the help of an external consultant and facilitator. Thus, the impulse is unlikely to have originated from the ranks of the regular workers. As a result, the regular workers, who are used to the current way of doing things in the organization, may need to be sold on the idea and on the advantages of making this change; it may be viewed with suspicion. Unsurprisingly (and even typically), some may resist the notion of any change claiming that the current modus operandi works "just fine". This feeling may come from both the individual contributors and the line managers. However, to reduce these concerns, it should be underscored that one isn't replacing the existing organizational structures and processes, but rather that one is adding more expertise to activities that require creativity. A virtual knowledge network with related processes brings out the regular workers' creativity into the open; it could be viewed as being a reliable background capability. Therefore, establishing the manifestation of the Framework shouldn't be called an organizational change, but rather an organizational addition or enablement. It isn't change per se; it is rather bringing out something that is already present, yet somewhat dormant, in one's organization. The training must aid in the achievement of this revelation.

It is a given that the workers have prior professional or trade education and experience; one must relate the new knowledge to their backgrounds. In addition, they will be expected to act as implicit partners in this organizational enhancement by adapting the manifestation of democratized innovation to their organization's particular case. The training must be carried out while the organization continues operating as usual, which can be challenging. How does one bring the workers to embrace this enablement and to readily engage in the related training? In this chapter, we will explore the approaches and techniques to motivate them to willingly and enthusiastically learn the skills required to make democratized innovation a practical reality in their organizations. Thus, let us review the challenges involved in training regular workers in democratized innovation.

How can the challenges of training on the Framework be addressed?

To state the overall goal that is sought from the start, the intent of the training program is to quickly bring the workers at a point where they are familiar enough with the Framework to be able to start exercising it in their day-to-day activities. Little time should be spent on theorizing about it; the training needs to be very quickly grounded in action by prompting the learners to relate the workshop's material to their regular work. As we hinted earlier, the implementation of democratized innovation is the manifestation of a natural inclination that the workers have that is waiting to be unleashed. The precise expression of it requires some adaptation that will be defined through the attendees' input both as learners in the workshops and as practitioners of the Framework on their place of work. Therefore, as much as possible, worker training and Framework implementation should occur concurrently. The practice of the Framework will justify the effort involved in learning about it in the eyes of the workers; it will feed their motivation to learn. Framework simulations in the classroom should also be part of the exposure to the Framework as soon as possible. One shouldn't aim for perfection which would cause unnecessary delays before practicing the Framework. Any mistakes made in trying out the Framework in real-life, albeit executed at a measured pace, supports a learning-by-doing technique (Dewey 1938; DuFour et al. 2016) that has proven to be effective with adult learners. Any issues encountered in the initial runs through the Framework once reported and analyzed in class provide effective learning opportunities. Practically speaking, the training program will require the acquisition of both knowledge on the working principles of the Framework and in the field of innovation, which incidentally were respectively the subjects of the two first parts of this book. Let us review the principles underpinning this training program.

The recommended training approach involves extensive learner participation. They must be brought to rediscover the principles at play by themselves through discussions and in a workshop setting with the inconspicuous guidance of the trainer who acts more as a facilitator in this case. The learners being trained must get the feeling that they had the concepts in their minds all along as if this knowledge just needed to be uncovered and revealed. As a result of this process, they will make the knowledge learned theirs which goes a long way towards their wanting to use it in their work.

The learners must experience in the workshops the very same dynamics of creative collaboration that they will be required to carry out later for their innovation endeavors. In other words, the classroom learning dynamics epitomize the subject matter to be learned. Through mimicry (perhaps subconsciously), they must learn the behaviors leading to collaborative conceptualization, exploration and validation. From the outset, it should be explained that collaboration doesn't mean always agreeing with one another or bowing to a vocal participant: this would be an expression of the groupthink phenomenon that must absolutely be avoided. Of course, conversely, creative collaboration doesn't mean social loafing either. Everybody needs to participate or, for quieter personalities, to be skillfully prompted to do so in a way that entices them to bring forward their thoughts. Overall, these collaborative dynamics mean finding the flow state described by Sawyer (2007) and further investigated by Bashwiner et al. (2016, 2020) with the jazz-band improvisation analogy that we previously examined. They must not be passive recipients of the subject matter, but rather active members in the forging of their shared understanding of it with some limited guidance from the trainer that hopefully can be reduced as they progress. Ideally, they should eventually be able to carry out these discussions without any facilitator being required. Creative collaboration must become a common practice even a natural reflex. Through their active participation, they will be creating their own instance of the workshop on democratized innovation, that is to say a workshop that is perfectly adapted to their unique needs.

The democratized-innovation training program is a frame of reference intended to guide the trainer in "shepherding" the learners through the course material. In order to achieve this, it is designed to be flexible. The trainer must start by mastering the principles of work-based training for adult learners; the workshop's sequence of study points investigated will naturally follow as the workshop unfolds. Let us review these fundamental training principles; we used a categorization of viewpoints derived from a work-based training analysis model that was also previously applied in Davidson (2013) which includes the following aspects: the organization, the training context (that we derived from the original model terminology that made use of the word "environment"), the learners, the subject matter and the training agents (which refers to the resources at large involved in the training).

The organization

An organization may be prompted to adopt the Framework to boost its innovativeness. There may be underlying motivations, such as better dealing with increased market fragmentation and complexity, lessening the impacts of disruptions on an organization's traditional markets, that is to say by improving its sustainability, or pivoting with more ease, to mention a few. There may be industry-specific considerations, such as industries that are more risk averse than others or market disruptions taking place, such as merging markets (Davidson and Ivanova 2011). The organization's particular situation may come into play as well, such as its seeking diversification or its reacting to a shrinking market share. There might be contextual stresses of which the trainer should be aware to gauge the challenge and to prepare appropriately. Senior management may want to explain the rationale for adopting democratized innovation to its workers before they engage in the training to better frame the context for them and to secure their cooperation.

The trainer should also understand the existing organizational structure. It should be clearly explained from the outset to all the stakeholders that the Framework simply adds a knowledge network to the existing organizational structure. It isn't intended to replace or to compete with the existing organizational structure by any means. The Framework shouldn't be perceived as a threat to the status quo, but rather as a revelation of an already existing pool of creativity that may not always have had the opportunity to flourish because of operational priorities and constraints.

The training context

There may be practical considerations that affect the learners' receptivity to the training. The challenges of adult learning will be amplified by two additional organizational factors. First, its introduction will likely have been promulgated by senior management, possibly even with the personal intervention of a particular senior manager – acting as the champion – promoting its adoption. Therefore, it is unlikely to be fully voluntary; initiatives coming from the perceived authorities in an organization may naturally be viewed with a certain degree of grudging reluctance especially if it pushes people outside of their comfort zones. As a result, the workers' motivation to participate will need to be cultivated. Second, the workers will need to continue their day-to-day activities while undergoing the training. Time on their busy schedules will certainly need to be officially freed for the training workshops, but the trainer still needs to be cognizant that the workers will be timesharing with other activities, and that getting them to participate, to persevere and to focus their full attention on the training will be an on-going challenge. The trainer will need to be watchful that their other work activities don't take priority over the training.

Traditional classroom lecture-based methods should be avoided. Indeed, it is not effective to make adult learners in a work-based setting sit through lectures passively absorbing training material. Knowledge points must be grounded in practice and in action. Experiencing the skills is even more effective because the knowledge develops quicker in their minds. Challenges, friendly competition and gamification bring the learners to take on an active role in class and to associate various emotions with the training process which, if they are positively channelled, are conducive to better learning.

The Learners

As mentioned in our introductory comments, an organization's workers are adults who, as learners, have particular characteristics. The training program is designed to cater to their distinctive training needs. They are independent thinkers who will be driven by self-induced motivation; any attempt to impose training that they don't deem useful will be rejected outright. They will constantly validate and reassess the pertinence of the training, which may easily lead to disenchantment and even to disengagement if the trainer fails to properly anchor the new knowledge in justifications to which their can relate. It is even better to prompt them to muse on how the material could be applied to their work. One can expect that the learners will focus on the specific aspects of the subject matter that are the most interesting to them both collectively and individually. This is a form of mental filter that makes their minds try to relate the new knowledge to what they already know. In addition, they naturally focus on the study points that fall within the scope of their personal interests and professional goals. As a result, two learners participating in the same workshop may end up with slightly different takeaways if their goals and interests happen to be different. Such variations are perfectly fine since the objective of the training sessions is to bring the workers to develop their own mental models and practices derived from the Framework that work specifically for each one of them.

This is a personal appropriation of the workshop's knowledge that should be encouraged. The training program simply represents a guideline.

To frame the training approach in theory, training adults is a distinctive subfield of education science known as "andragogy", which roughly relates to the field of adult learning and education (ALE). Adult workers have busy lives as every one of us knows of course. Everyday, they need to deal with their work responsibilities, pressures to produce and to provide, and people who depend on them or on whom they rely. They generally multi-task, switching from one task to another sometimes even from one role to another throughout a typical workday. They are often subjected to time constraints which can induce stress. These considerations are part of the typical professional lives experienced by most workers. Their professional backgrounds, that is to say the combination of their education and their experiences, may also influence the way in which they approach study points and think about them. They may have deeply engrained views and biases with which the trainer may need to contend. They have competencies and habits that may have served them well throughout their professional lives that they will exhibit in the workshop discussions. They will often try to relate the new study points with their current knowledge seeking connections which is a reflex that should be encouraged since these conceptual connections will help anchor the new knowledge in their minds. In fact, their failure to openly relate the new knowledge to their current one, may be a hint of an even greater and possibly looming challenge for the trainer to address: resistance to change. It is a common reaction amongst adult learners that may be expressed by their detrimental behaviors during the workshops either covertly by their lack of participation at the workshops and their failing to apply the learned skills in their daily activities, or sometimes even overtly by disrupting the discussions with confrontational remarks. Given the workshop's focus on participation and knowledge rediscovery, these behaviors will indubitably undermine the workshop's effectiveness. They must be addressed as soon as they become apparent. The behaviors suggest that they are unwilling to adapt to the proposed change, which could be the result of the rationale of the change not having been appropriately explained to them or that they don't accept it, let alone approve of it.

To sum up, they are accomplished professionals; they are anything but neophytes in their respective fields. As a result, they may have a certain degree of skepticism towards any training initiative that is offered to them. To be successful, the trainer will need to be sensitive to each learner's particular needs and distinctive expectations. The training must be presented as complementing their expertise in their respective fields.

The subject matter

In Chapter 4, we described the ambiguity surrounding the concept of innovation; this ambiguity will need to be addressed otherwise some learners may claim that they are already actively innovating, and that the training in innovation isn't necessary. Indeed, sometimes it takes a fair amount of knowledge to be cognizant of the limitations of one's knowledge on a particular subject. They need to realize that innovation is a domain of expertise in its own right with a genuine body of knowledge associated with it.

The training needs to focus as much as possible on practicing innovation to experience the principles at play. Formal instruction on theory should be kept to a strict minimum; problem-solving with case examples and simulations should be preferred.

The learners will expect the benefits of the workshops to be quickly apparent. The trainer needs to pay close attention to this by asking for feedback on how the learners may have applied the previous session's subject matter and discuss any difficulties that they may have encountered; typically, time for this type of feedback should be scheduled before moving to new training points.

Because of their diversified backgrounds, the learners will often reword the workshop subject matter in ways that are more telling for them. This is something to encourage because it is indicative that they are trying to make sense of the new knowledge. It shows that they are trying to make the training points theirs. The trainer will also need to develop active listening skills to rephrase learning points using the learners preferred terminology as expressed in their questions and comments.

The most challenging skill to instill in the learners is the ability to explore new ideas collaboratively or colloquially putting all the participants heads together. This will be accomplished through creative collaborative discussions. First, this involves being open to new ideas and being willing to investigate them with the other participants even if their ideas compete with one's own. The learners need to develop their curiosity and their probing skills; some self-doubt and humbleness help too. This is a skill that is hard to explain; it is tacit. It should rather be observed and experienced through mentoring and coaching. Since the workshops involve discovering the principle of democratized innovation, the very dynamics of this learning process must illustrate how collaborative discussions may be constructively conducted. This is a form of bootstrapping, in the sense that the trainer uses the techniques to be acquired as the training technique for the workshop. Starting in a mentoring mode (i.e., showing the behavior), the trainer engages an exploratory discussion with open questions with the intent to subconsciously inspire the workshops participants to respond and to reproduce the behavior. Little by little, as the participants start using open questions and arguments themselves, the trainer will be able to shift to a simple coaching mode that simply requires overseeing how the discussions unfold to ensure that they doesn't stray away from the subject matter.

In addition, the learners need to acquire an interest in learning, because innovation is to a great extent about learning about novelties that involve new domain knowledge. They should be brought to embrace what is new, unfamiliar and ambiguous rather than seeing it as something that is unsettling. They need to be comfortable in going beyond what they know or what is commonly known; the unknown should become attractive. They need to develop life-long learning skills that should be motivated by a continuous quest for value through knowledge.

The training agents

The training approach that we advocate emphasizes the rediscovery of the subject-matter to better anchor the training material in the learners' minds. Therefore, the learners are active partners in managing how their own training unfolds; the trainer is simply a coach and a facilitator in this process. The trainer must engage the learners to pull them into active participation. Simulations will make it experiential; gamification will stimulate motivation by establishing a more light-hearted spirit that may make them less aware that there are learning. The workshop's participant-centric model will instill a sense of control over the learning process that should appease the learners who display skepticism and reluctance from the start; it is hard to criticize when one is in the proverbial driver's seat. However, the trainer will need to subtly orient or reorientate the discussions to ensure that the workshop's subject matter is appropriately covered.

We mentioned previously that each adult learner may absorb the subject matter in slightly different ways because of varying interests. As a result, they will also expect to manage their own learning process by themselves which will make them want to visualize the coverage of their developing knowledge and to be aware of any gaps. Therefore, the training material must be organized in short modules from which they can pick and choose. Since most of the workshops involve group activities, there needs to be agreement on the subjects to investigate which will allow them to exercise the negotiation skills early on. This is again another example of bootstrapping at play in the workshop training process.

It is to be expected that some may engage in the subject matter more assiduously than others. They can each learn at their own pace about different study points at varying depths. This is characteristic of learning in adults; the trainer shouldn't attempt to force any uniformity in the learning experience across the members of a given group or from one training group to another. People will naturally focus on what is most important to them. More importantly, if they find value in particular study points, they will apply them in their daily activities. To a large extent, training adults is a best-effort endeavor.

How can an approach for training in democratized innovation be defined?

The traditional training technique involves well-structured lectures fully prepared beforehand and delivered in a classroom setting; in this model the learners are formally taught a body of knowledge. Their learning reflects the degree to which they are attentive and motivated by the subject matter. Validation of the effectiveness of the learning process involves testing the students to confirm how well they assimilated the body of knowledge at least to the extent of being able to regurgitate the memorized subject matter at an exam. However, there is typically little if any validation of their ability to practice what they learned. In addition, in this educational model, learning is a singular event which doesn't take into account the reality that people forget the knowledge that they don't regularly exercise. This technique, that is known as "behavioral", fails when the knowledge is tacit, that is to say when it isn't explicitly codified let alone codifiable. With this approach, knowledge is something that needs to be communicated to – and absorbed by – learners who attend the lectures rather passively other than for the occasional allowances for question periods that are designed to clarify what they may not have properly understood. Some courses conducted with this method include field exercises or lab work to provide some element of practice and self-directed discovery, albeit limited.

When it is important to ensure that the learned skills are actually practiced once that the training is completed, learning techniques that engage the learners and that involve experiencing the skills in the workshop setting are more effective than the behavioral approach. These techniques place the learners in situations in which they need to solve problems that are typical of the activities that they will be carrying out in their workplaces, usually with incrementally increasing complexity. Lave and Wenger (1996) described the concept of "situated learning" in which the learners acquire professional skills that relate to their seeking membership in a working community that we interpret as meaning their knowledge network. The learner-centered problem-solving approach to teaching was also advocated by Dewey (1938) for its dynamic exploration of the knowledge through questions that the learners are challenged to investigate on their own or in small groups; he claimed that it allowed the learners to develop a deeper understanding of the knowledge. This approach features learning the skills in a context that is either literally one's workplace, a context that simulates it or more conceptually with the use of the same tools that the workers would be using later. Knowledge is co-constructed usually through mentoring and coaching. Learning is a highly social activity.

Forgetting is an important function of the mind which underlines the reality that learning isn't a one-time event; conscious effort must be applied to maintain one's acquired knowledge. Forgetting is how the mind naturally manages to remain current in a shifting context. Memories – including knowledge and skills – that are seldom accessed and rarely used end up being forgotten; however, let us note that the memories don't completely disappear. They may be recalled at a later time with less effort than that applied for their initial learning; re-learning is a reactivation of one's recollections of the knowledge that faded in one's mind. Forgetting allows the mind to focus on what is important at any particular time in a continuously evolving environment. However, this also means that one needs to maintain one's proficiency at previously learned skills through periodical refresher training beyond the completion of the initial training sessions. Even while the workshop curriculum unfolds, repetitions are always useful. Training in democratized innovation doesn't escape this reality; it needs to be actively exercised or old habits of individual thinking and unilateral decision-making will quickly settle in again.

Repetitions can help better anchor the knowledge in the learners' minds. Furthermore, when the learners start noticing the repetitions, it means that they have assimilated the subject matter. On occasion, we applied this principle in the contents of this book as the attentive reader may have noticed. However, too much repetition may come across as rambling; it is a matter of striking a happy balance.

How does the training concept cater to individual learning preferences?

Everyone has his or her preferred learning technique. Some people may favor visual cues, while others may better respond to auditory techniques. The iconography used to illustrate the significant parts of the Framework, such as the cornerstones in its four-quadrant representation, relates to visual learning. The trainer may choose to add auditory mnemotechnics to the workshop, such as catchy acronyms; for example, the iVortoid' model's ATRAM acronym helps the learner recall the five risk management strategies. Yet other learners may respond better to a kinetic technique, that is to say learning through gestures and movements, even as limited as writing down notes or drawing out diagrams derived from the subject matter being learned. These preferences relate to the sensorimotor processing of the information presented in the classroom. Given the existence of these preferences amongst learners, it is always a good idea to combine several of these techniques in the classroom to cater to all these individual preferences.

Yet another mode of learning, known as "reflective learning", engages the learners at a higher level of cognition. Some learners need a period of time to absorb the subject matter on their own and to think through its implications and other ancillary considerations before engaging in its application or before taking part in group activities in which they need to show that they understood it. By selecting the study topics for the following workshop at the end of each session, the learners with this type of preference may carry out readings ahead of the workshops or simply organize their thoughts ahead of time. However, as we described previously, adult learners also need to understand how the knowledge may be useful to them which is something that they may not always be able to figure out by themselves. This means that when a reflective period is provided, the trainer needs to quickly proceed with the practical applications of the knowledge and to engage in the group discussions.

This focus on practicing knowledge relates to Aristotle's (2012) belief that theory cannot be well understood until the learner has had the opportunity to apply it and to John Dewey's "experiential learning" (1938) which involves a person learning from experiences and learning by reflecting on what one is doing or has done. In other words, it involves having the opportunity to directly experience the skills on the job or in a simulated environment and then using metacognition – that is to say the thinking about one's thinking – to gain insight into the experience to convert it into working knowledge. In practice, this means experiencing the skill possibly through a trial-and-error process, then stepping back and reflecting on one's attempts while using one's cognitive abilities to make better sense of the experience (whether successful or not) and of the knowledge at play. Learning is thus enriched through a cognitive feedback loop. Other similar learning approaches have been devised, such as the "reflective practice" (Boud, Keogh and Walker 1985) which institutionalizes the reflective process to enable continuous learning. Interestingly once the learners have developed the habit of reflecting on their experiences, they may continue doing so without the teacher or facilitator being present. It highlights processes such as self-assessing one's performance, learning from one's mistakes when performing a task all the way up to learning from failed projects, that involve a larger scale and greater consequences. It is seeking valuable learnings by making sense of one's experiences. This approach to learning applies particularly well when the learners need to develop reasoning and problem-solving abilities, as well as the behavioral and mental abilities to apply a piece of knowledge in context. Another significant benefit is that it also feeds the participants' motivation to learn, which is a key consideration in adult learning as we have already mentioned.

How can one learn through a process of social interactions?

The training technique that we advocate is participatory, experiential, discursive, and reflective. The knowledge must be rediscovered through a process of social interactions. The Cambridge online dictionary defined constructivism as "a theory . . . [according to which] learning is an active process . . . [allowing] people [to] gain knowledge and understanding through the combination of experiences and ideas". The keyword in this definition is "combination". Let us turn this time to the online Merriam-Webster dictionary that interestingly states that a combination can be "two or more people working as a team". Thus, these definitions suggest that a constructive mingling of experiences and ideas towards the advancement of

knowledge and understanding can best be performed in the context of group interactions; add a common purpose to the mix and we have a team as once again the
Merriam-Webster dictionary suggests. Therefore, the fundamental premise of the
approach that we advocate is that individual learning (because each learner's purpose may be slightly different) is still more effective when it takes place at least partially in a social context emphasizing interactions with others. Deeper understandings
are developed by testing one another's developing conceptualizations, theories and
ideas. At the center of this approach is the ability to communicate one's thoughts and
to process, associate and transform them through discourse. Adding individual personalities, motivations and passions to the mix, we obtain lively and stimulating
debates in which the participants search deeper and deeper for the shared understanding through the testing of their ideas amongst the group. Thus, participants
must be able to debate in a constructive manner that is to say in a way that advances
the development of a shared understanding towards the discovery or rediscovery of
knowledge. Ambiguity must be transformed into clarity of understanding through
the virtual commingling of several minds.

Let us consider how this commingling of minds may be realized; it should be
externalized and formalized to a point of being predictable, systematic and reproduceable. Socratic dialectic learning involves a group of people debating a subject
in a search for truth (which corresponds to the learning points in the case of the
training workshops). This process of interactive exchange of ideas or "discursive
reasoning" unfolds as a dialogue of arguments and counterarguments takes place.
These arguments take the form of logical propositions and counterpropositions. A
fundamental principle of this approach is that the proponents of a proposition must
consent to change their views if their propositions are proven to be unfounded;
ideas are nothing more than thoughts needing to be tested. We relate this truth-
seeking process to the evidence-based exploration and rationale-building taking
place in the democratized innovators' quest for the solution which value best satisfies its stakeholders, that is to say the negotiated innovation. A sequence of open
questions allows to clarify a vague or ambiguous initial belief (i.e., the original
idea) through its logical consequences and through conceptual transformations as
the exchange proceeds. In the Framework, the propositions don't need to be as rigorously grounded in logic as formal Socratic dialectic would require, but the participants' interventions still need to be factual and to reflect coherent (to avoid saying
rational) thinking. Ideas are refined and validated through respectful deliberations;
all must hold a deep reverence for the truth which can be equated to finding what
is best for the affected stakeholders in a given context. Plato (Plato and Bloom 1991)
adopts a similar evolutionary perspective by suggesting that, through dialectics,
one incrementally develops one's conceptualization and understanding of a given
reality until enlightenment is reached in a process that he qualifies as being slow
and difficult. He claims that one works from one idea to another idea in a process
that culminates in the emergence of an idea with supreme qualities. Giving up an

idea that doesn't survive the test may be painful, but if it leads to better shared understanding, as such, it still has a positive effect which should be celebrated.

The notions of shared understanding and illumination reached through discourse leads us to the notion of social constructivism (Vygotsky 1978) in which experience in learning is blended with social interactions. It is based on the view that learning is a process that takes place through interactions with others. It highlights group discussions intended to make sense of a subject matter through deliberations conducted with others to reach a state of understanding on which all participants agree. Similarly, Van Eemersen and Grootendost (1984) describe the shared construction of knowledge through the resolution of opposing views in their research on argumentative discussions. Along analogous lines of reasoning, McKinley (2015) highlights the importance of critical thinking in a collaborative learning environment for training in English-as-a-foreign-language writing. In addition, he observes that the students' abilities and successes in the training may be influenced by their social norms and by each student-author's identity construction with respect to their desire to be included in a community. A key component of their framework relates to critical argumentation. We relate McKinsey's social norms and what he calls accumulated schemata to the conditioning effect of the learners' professional backgrounds, and his concept of identity-construction to the learners' natural propensity to seek recognition in the manifestation of the Framework. This yearning for recognition is a powerful motivator to entice workers to set aside their own activities at least for a little while to help out their colleagues who reach out to them. The knowledge that is produced through the passions of argumentation will be better appropriated by the group. Thus, participation, joint exploration, challenging one another through questions shedding light on areas of ambiguity, seeking evidence, coherent arguments and rational justifications, experiencing the skills through trial and error, simulations and on-the-job practice, discourse, critical thinking, deliberations and negotiations, all these techniques come into play in the training in democratized innovation and the application of it in practice. The bootstrapping principle applies again with the skills that are exercised during the workshop learning process applying as well in the negotiated-innovation process that takes place in the Framework.

Summation

In this chapter, we reviewed the challenges involved in the training of adult workers using a structured analysis of the work-based training situation. Adult learners have special needs that must be addressed for the training to be effective. Failure to do so with traditional classroom teacher-centric training techniques will result in disappointing results. The trainer should leverage the characteristics of the training situation rather than treating them as pitfalls. The idiosyncrasies of adult learners must be leveraged to ensure that more effective learning takes place.

The workshops must emphasize learner participation in rediscovering the subject matter to ensure that the learners appropriate it. In addition, we advocated the importance for the learners to experience the Framework through action-oriented training techniques. The learners must rediscover the knowledge through their group deliberations, which makes them exercise a skill that is fundamental for the Framework's negotiated innovation. It is a bootstrapping learning technique. Most importantly, one should get started with one's manifestation of the Framework as soon as possible in the training process. A manifestation suggests engagement, action and practice. The learnings are already present in the learners' minds; they simply need to be revealed through the dynamics of creative group deliberations.

Chapter 8
Workshop Techniques

As we have seen, the trainers should act more as facilitators of the learners' redis-covery of the workshop's subject matter than as instructors per se. They must thor-oughly master the study points to be able to adapt them on the fly to the shifting orientations of the group discussions. There is hardly any plan per se that needs to be set ahead of each session since the workshops follow the learners' interests, but attention should still be applied to ensure that overall a proper curriculum in inno-vation is covered. The path through the study points may be circuitous, possibly even meandering at times. The trainers must be flexible, and they must be good lis-teners to go with the flow, but with the skill to subtly nudge the discussions back to the workshop's subject matter when the learners stray too much off track. The train-ers must master the art of training in a context of constant improvisation; they must expect the unexpected. No two workshops will be the same; however, common pat-terns in the way that they unfold will emerge. The workshops must be dynamic, engaging, friendly and, as much as possible captivating because learner motivation is something to cultivate for the workshops to be successful. The workshops are "performances" carried out by both the participants and the trainer featuring ex-pressions of creativity in training in a live and improvised setting which isn't unlike performance art. Similarly, the process is improvised and exploratory. The trainer inconspicuously edges them through the rediscovery of various knowledge points. The participants are left free to find their own way to the points of knowledge even if the path to it may be anything but linear at times. Misconceptions that the partic-ipants eventually develop throughout their deliberations become powerful opportu-nities for re-examinations leading to deeper understanding. The rectification of their mistaken beliefs through more fully articulated explanations will allow them to better anchor the new knowledge in their minds. It goes without saying that it is a process that requires time and patience on the trainer's part; the workshops are completed when the learners are considered to be proficient in democratized inno-vation. The progress in the workshop is measured by assessing the overall perfor-mance exhibited by the learners; it isn't simply based on their advancement in the training program as is usually the case with traditional training. It is tested in terms of their proficiency in their application of the Framework.

The workshops must illustrate through its dynamics how collaborative explora-tion should later be conducted in the Framework. In the performance of these work-shops, the learners will experience how to cultivate the creative flow state that is so important in the Framework without their needing to be aware of it. This is a form of subliminal learning. Despite this training being implicit, the learners should still be able to recall or to mimic the skill when needed. Their minds will have been con-ditioned to approach ambiguity through a discursive technique. The reflex becomes

https://doi.org/10.1515/9783110683837-012

indissociable from the person's being. The ability to deliberate collaboratively towards a creative, exploratory or problem-solving goal is the most important skill for the learners to acquire. The trainer needs to be cognizant of each participant's progress in this regard astutely prompting those exhibiting a propensity to hold back, drawing them in the active deliberations.

The training should be conducted in a way that inspires the learners to embrace their own manifestation of the Framework and to make it work for them. We used the notion of inspiring in this statement because the motivation to adopt this new knowledge must come from them. The trainer simply provides benevolent guidance throughout the process.

How should the training sessions be positioned?

The training should be framed as being workshops rather than formal instruction per se. It should be conveyed to the workers attending it that they aren't students in the literal sense of the word, but rather active partners in implementing the organization's particular manifestation of democratized innovation. They need to figure out how it should be integrated into the organization's work processes. Therefore, the learners are expected to be far more than students; they will be instrumental in making the organization's manifestation of the Framework a working reality at their workplace. They will enable it first, virtually in their minds and then, second, in practice by applying it to their day-to-day activities. Time in the workshop should be regularly set aside to discuss how they may have applied the workshop's learnings. As a few members report their practical experiences, others will be enticed to do the same.

Previously, we argued that the learners needed to become familiar with the notions related to innovation. However, innovativeness may be viewed by some as a personal quality rather than a hard skill; they may claim that they are already innovative. Add the common resistance to change to this situation, and the trainer may face a flat refusal to participate in the workshops. There are useful tactics to manage this situation: one of them is to explain that they will be selecting the study points which allows them to elevate the workshop at any level that they choose. Another tactic is to make them realize the ambiguity surrounding the concept of innovation. This can easily be illustrated by the divergent interpretations of it that are likely to exist amongst the workshop attendees. Usually, each person has his or her own definition of what innovation may be. The trainer should ask them to write down their interpretations individually as short statements that are then collected, read aloud, and discussed as a group. The definitions will likely differ considerably. The need to find a common understanding of it will, as a result, become obvious to all.

The workshops are participatory and experiential with short theoretical learning capsules as it unfolds when misconceptions become evident or to reframe the points brought up by the participants and to relate them to known theoretical principles. Throughout this unconventional approach to training, genuine learning will take place hopefully without the learners being overly aware of it. The workshops must be engaging possibly even entertaining; ideally, the learners must look forward to them.

How should discussion groups be configured to maximize collaboration?

The workshop teams should be assembled to maximise the possible team combinations; the trainer must check that the compositions of the teams change regularly to expose the learners to as much team diversity as possible and to allow them to experience all the cornerstones and roles in the Framework. A random selection procedure or a round-robin approach with one member systematically switching teams at each session, could be applied to make these changes easy and mechanical. This avoids the need for people to select their teammates, which could easily become time-consuming and awkward if some people feel left out. Learners coming from the same work groups in the organization should as much as possible join different teams to avoid introducing in the workshop any pre-existing interpersonal behaviors, either good or bad. If the workshop group is noticeably homogeneous, the trainer may consider purposely inviting other members with different backgrounds to artificially introduce the diversity that is lacking in the group. Diversity helps people think outside of their usual thought patterns.

Based on their research in the field of neuroscience with experimentation related to the improvisations made in jazz, Bashwiner et al. (2016, 2020) suggested that people are most creative when they manage to loosen the strong pre-existing associations in their minds. They must temporarily silence the inner critic that the researchers relate to the mind's "executive attention network". They should activate with more intensity what Kaufman (2013) calls the "imagination network" that relates to thinking about the future which, more precisely, means envisioning different possible scenarios and developing a mental representation of something that one has never encountered before. In addition, interestingly, one's imagination network also comes into play when trying to figure out what someone else is thinking. It is common knowledge that when experiencing creative block, a stimulating conversation with other creative people may get one's creativity going again. Hence, there is extensive anecdotal evidence that suggests that creative thinking may be stimulated by creative discussions. Creative thoughts also activate the mind's "salient network" which acts like a switch that perceives and integrates sensory stimuli and that processes cognitive information. It promotes different lines of thought.

Collaborative group creativity involves first provoking creative thoughts aiming at forming inceptive or embryonic mental constructs, and second, engaging in creative discussions to articulate them to the others to solicit their creative input. It is truly co-creation. This two-step process forces the originator of an idea to better define, to structure and sometimes to clarify his or her thoughts that naturally may still be vague. This exchange with other creative conversationalists leads to a state of shared understanding through which an exercise of joint exploration may engage into what is, conceptually, the unknown. In the state of flow, the leadership of the developing line of reasoning moves from one participant to the next as if the minds were working as one.

For this flow state – which is indicative of peek performance – to occur, each participant must be in tune with the other team members to mentally follow one another's contributions to the shared line of reasoning. Different perspectives concurrently weave together, diverging and converging in sequence to finally merge into one singular creation. This process draws heavily on the participants' mental capacity and produces exhilarating excitement, but also significant effort that may even be physically draining. This cross-member mental conjunction relates to the theory of mind concept used in psychology (Harris 1991). This is the ability to intuitively perceive and to implicitly understand other people's beliefs, expectations, desires and mental states or to make inferences about their thoughts and their perspectives based on observations. This mental connection allows the participants to anticipate what they are about to say next or to do, and to discern their general intentions. When such a virtual connection is established, it is frequent for people in an animated discussion to somewhat impatiently jump ahead of what a fellow conversationalist is about to say once they inferred a point, or on the contrary to express their perplexity when the direction of the line of reasoning isn't made clear quickly enough. Other mannerisms typical of people in a state of creative flow may be observed, such as people completing one another's sentences, squinting their eyes as if to better see something that is out of focus, placing their fingers against their foreheads or pinching their chins in a pondering pose, scratching their heads in puzzlement, pacing back and forth in the room and other gestures and facial expressions indicative of their being at the same time perplexed and mesmerized by what they are jointly trying to fathom.

In the negotiated-innovation process, which is a step closer to decision-making, the principles of the theory of mind again come into play at an even greater extent because one needs to uncover what the other party may not be explicitly saying or may even be purposefully holding off revealing. As we have seen in Chapter 2, one must probe beyond the problematic demands to bring to light the underlying motivations which could be satisfied in alternative ways that hopefully are more acceptable to all parties involved. Thus, the participants must be able to induce this sharing of minds. Through deliberations, proposals are transformed. We use the word 'transformed' because collaborative creativity involves the interplay of two or more concepts. Usually, arguments seek to transform an idea put forward in a given manner. The proponent of a new argument could be challenged to explain how it impacts the original idea being deliberated.

Because creative collaboration teams may involve decision-making in a climate of trust and in a tone of confidence, the total number of participants in such discussions must be small and remain an odd number to avoid any ties occurring when the time comes to vote; ties could lead to stalemates that prevent any further action, and, sadly, preclude any value from being generated for anyone.

There needs to be frank discussions, while avoiding a cacophony and ensuring that all the participating stakeholders (or their representatives) have a fair opportunity to express their points of view. It is common that groups that are too large to support efficient discussions split into smaller groups. In addition, the sub-groups should still comprise odd numbers of members and enable the two-thirds supermajority decision-making that is part of the notion of negotiated innovation described in Chapter 2. Therefore, this suggests that there should be a minimum of three people in any team; we will consider the maximum number of team members in the next section.

How should the workshops be configured to maximize collaboration?

The learners are expected to actively engage in collaborative discussions which means that the number of people who can be accommodated in the workshops is necessarily limited. Krems, Dunbar and Neuberg (2016) conducted a study on the optimal size of conversation groups. They found that these conversation groups naturally comprise no more than four people. This observation is based on the limitations of the human mind's ability to "mentalize" the minds of the other people with whom one converses. In addition, the risk of overloading the people's information-processing capabilities and the practical constraints of being able to hear what other people in a small group are saying, may also play a role in limiting the size of a conversation group. They observed that beyond four people, groups tend to split in smaller conversation groups which produces separate conversations. Furthermore, when the conversationalists talk about an absent party whose mind also implicitly needs to be modelled, the number of conversationalists is further reduced by one. In other words, this absent person about whom the people are talking creates the same mental drain on the conversationalists as if he or she were physically present.

In the democratized-innovation workshops, the size of a deliberation team is restricted by the limitations of the participant's mental-modelling abilities. Discussions aiming at rediscovering collaboratively the workshop's subject matter represent a considerable cognitive demand on their minds as they strive to model the other participants' developing lines of reasoning. Indeed, the type of collaborative creativity that we seek to develop in the workshop setting involves finding a flow state, which means that all participants interactively construct a shared virtual creation that exists only in their minds while they interact. The mental effort required to carry this out is significant.

Furthermore, in the Framework's exploratory discussions that exercise a user-centric Design Thinking approach, the novelty's end-user (or a typical one) represents an absent person whose mind needs to be modelled as well in the discussions. In the workshop's training context, the Framework's learning points that the participants are challenged to rediscover on their own represents a virtual entity to take into account as well that is equivalent to an absent person in the conversational group study. Thus, the optimal number of participants in such discussions is again three. However, the total number of participants in the workshop can exceed three in the following manner.

A workshop group should include no more than nine people who can break up into three teams of three for learner-driven knowledge rediscovery discussions. When the three teams have concluded their independent deliberations, each of these teams must designate a person to represent each of them in the subsequent plenary discussions that involve the trainer. The representatives will deliberate in the name of their team in the plenary session. This maintains the optimal number of four when one includes the trainer in the count. Indeed, the trainer counts as a fourth person in the optimal conversation group size. The remaining two members of each team may still support their representative as the plenary session unfolds by feeding their thoughts or ideas to him or her as written notes on sheets torn off small notepads or on small whiteboards that should be available to them; they may also confer at impromptu recesses. Alternatively, if the team members are equipped with laptop computers and smart phones, the team members could send their thoughts to their representatives as chat or text messages. For that purpose, they should move their tables closer to the plenary discussion table; moving the tables around is easier if they are mounted on casters. The round shape of the tables supports the perception of equal status amongst those sitting around them which supports in the workshop setting an important principle of democratized innovation. Figures 8.1 and 8.2 illustrates how the group splits in three teams to deliberate independently as the trainer looks on, and later they all reconvene in the plenary session.

For the Framework classroom simulation exercises, as illustrated in Fig. 8.3, the nine-person group should be organized in the following way: first, five workshop members will represent a community of practice (see Fig. 8.3 lower left). This group may be larger than the prescribed four people for group creativity conversations, because they usually discuss facts and not beliefs or intentions about the work carried out by their colleagues in other cornerstones of the Framework. This is supported again by Krems, Dunbar and Neuberg (2016) who suggest that the discussion of facts involves a lesser cognitive load on the participants' minds. When the community of practice needs to investigate in more depth specific subjects that involve collaborative discussions (such as, for example, the updating of one of the

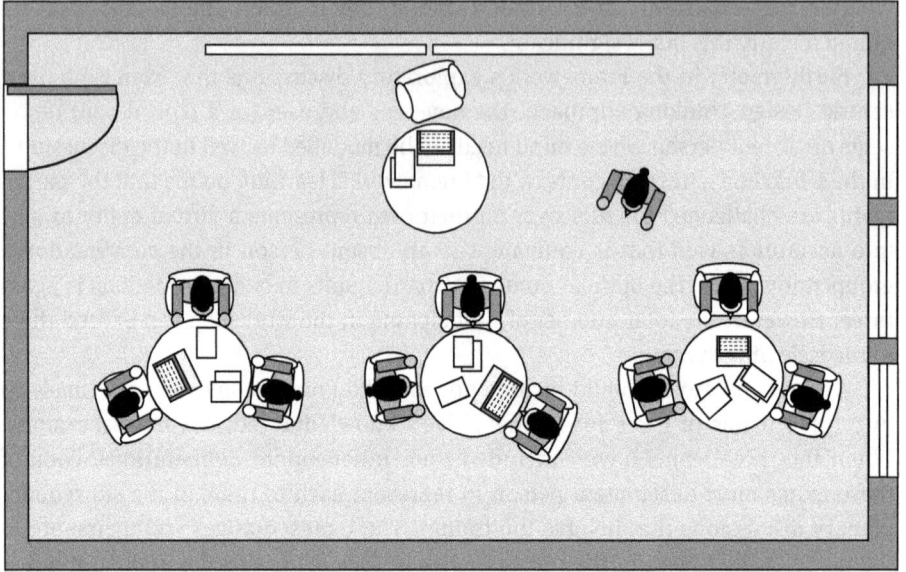

Fig. 8.1: The learners deliberate in three teams.

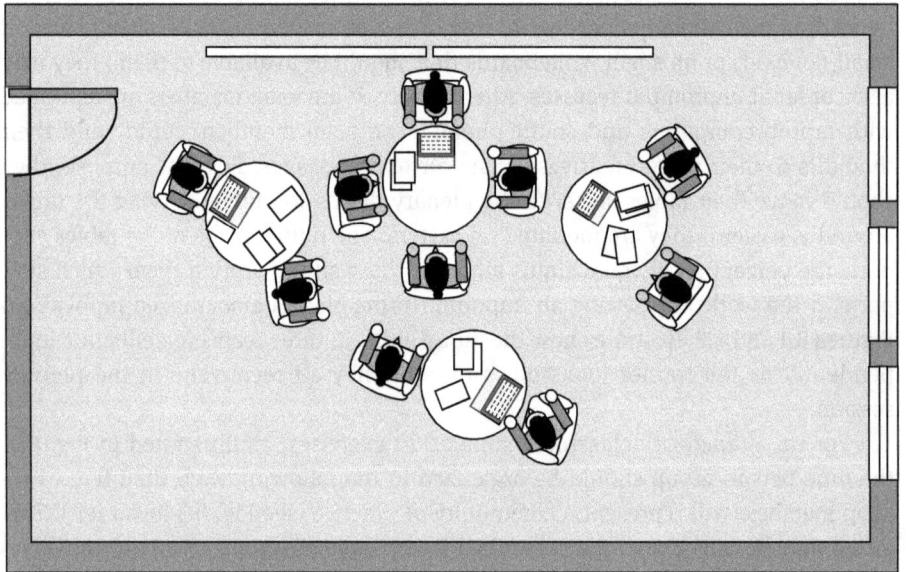

Fig. 8.2: Three team representatives deliberate with the trainer.

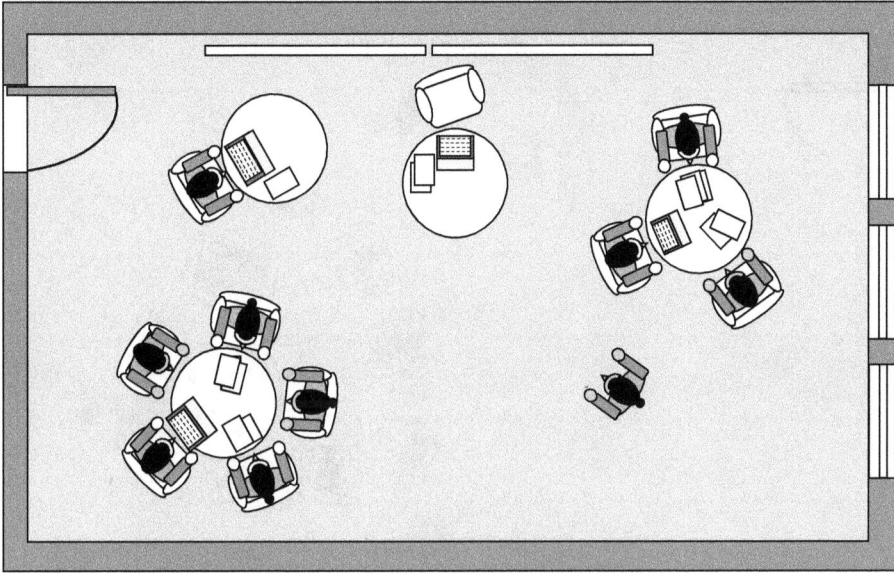

Fig. 8.3: Simulation of learners working in three of the four cornerstones.

organization's capabilities), they must designate sub-committees of three people that may be composed of any combination of the available community members plus external expert-consultants, if need be, who wouldn't vote. An innovation project core team (see Fig. 8.3 upper right) should involve three people because collaborative discussions about conceptual and exploratory beliefs is a significant part of their activities; in real-life situations there would be many more absentee members. These types of discussions cause a significant cognitive load, as we have seen. The last remaining person out of the total nine people will double as a production worker proposing a field improvement for the community of practice to approve, or he or she will test a novelty developed by the innovation project team at the community of practice's request (see Fig. 8.3 upper left). This person will also serve as an invited domain expert for the innovation project team. The trainer looks on ready to provide clues to the learners who require help (see Fig. 8.3 lower right).

While still in the simulation exercises, all the nine workshop members assemble to engage in the group-wide consultations aiming at finding the orientations of innovation in the organization. They may either work all together in a crowdsourcing activity or gather in teams of three to clarify their proposals which is again a conceptual activity. They all physically congregate together to impress that this is a group-wide activity while the trainer looks on, as illustrated on Fig. 8.4. The lower-left location in the room corresponds to the position of the orientation cornerstone in the Framework diagram (see Fig. 1.1 in Chapter 1). In this scenario, the trainer will take on the role of a member

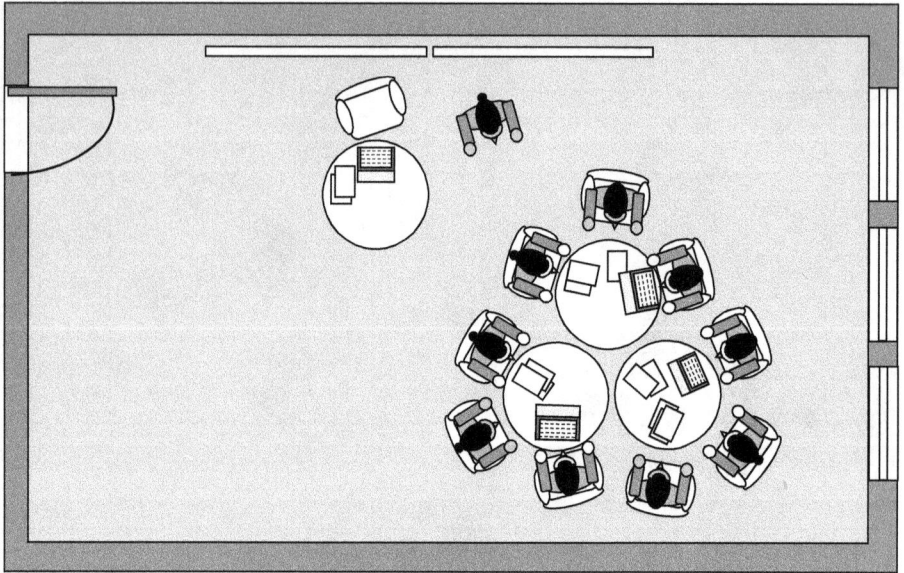

Fig. 8.4: Simulation of the group-wide consultations on innovation orientation.

of the stretch-innovation oversight committee required to review and to approve the various recommendations stemming from the Framework in action.

Attendance at the workshops should be mandatory since assiduous participation is indicative of one's seriousness in contributing to the Framework being implemented. However, if a trainer expects or finds absenteeism to be a problem, the groups could include a few more participants (but no more than three) who could play the roles of observers as the three independent discussion groups of three learners deliberate and as additional improvers from the imaginary Production function. Another approach is to arrange for several groups being trained contemporaneously but not literally concurrently, allowing participants to be drawn from another group to replace missing participants on the fly so to speak.

Two workshop groups of nine people could merge into one for more extensive Framework-simulation exercises. For example, this allows several concurrent innovation project teams to be enacted. The three-member core teams that represent the optimal number for the flow state to occur should be maintained; this limited team size simply needs to be replicated to include all the learners. If an innovation project is complex and requires more workers, it should be split up in smaller sub-teams of three members. More elaborate scenarios could be devised with more consultants assisting each innovation team as their concepts evolve. A second community of practice could be established as well providing sufficient people to simulate more elaborate scenarios. Most importantly, the team compositions need to change to ensure that all the members experience all the roles in all four of the Framework's cornerstones.

How should the Framework simulations be conducted in the workshops?

Simulations apply the principle of 'scaffolding' in education (Yin et al. 2009). Scaffolding provides safeguard measures that reduce the complexity of the situations or an environment in which the learners can safely exercise their developing skills without concerns about the consequences of making mistakes. The level of complexity of the simulations can be gradually increased as the learners improve on their skills, before shifting to real-life work situations with coaching. Having an allowance for safely making mistakes in the simulations reduces the stress and anxiety for the learners; they are placed in a more relaxed and receptive state of mind which is more conducing to learning. To start, the simulations should relate to fictitious cases that have been especially designed to simplify the considerations at play. This initial simplified simulation could be followed by more realistic ones that reproduce more closely situations that they encounter on their real workplaces. They may be asked to suggest cases that they experienced as ideas from which new simulations could be derived. Both fictitious and real-life simulations can be repeated with variations that add various complexities to ensure that the learners remain appropriately challenged. This transfer from a fictitious case to a realistic one illustrates one of the key principles of scaffolding, which is the gradual removal of the instructional support as the learners' gain familiarity with the knowledge and confidence in their skills.

When role-playing in simulation exercises, the trainer may decide either to let the learners pick their preferred role – which usually plays into one of their natural strengths or, on the contrary, to entice the learners to take on roles that are out of their comfort zones to expand their abilities. For example, some people may be more comfortable in an evaluation role while others prefer to work on new ideas. The first time on a simulation, the trainer may choose to let the learners play roles that align with their natural abilities to develop a feeling of self-efficacy (Bandura 1993) which contributes to developing their confidence and motivation, but later they should apply a round-robin switching procedure to ensure that everyone experiences all the roles. Generally, the simulations will gamify the training.

How do mentoring and coaching apply to knowledge rediscovery training?

Mentoring and coaching are commonly used work-based training techniques. They are a must for learning tacit knowledge that isn't explicitly codified nor even codifiable. Mentoring involves the learner observing how an experienced worker carries out a task. Preferably, the mentor should express aloud the reasoning process that takes place when carrying out a task to maximize the learning. The learner should also be allowed to ask questions as the task is performed or after it is completed if the mentor cannot take his or her attention away from the task. In particular, the mentor should explain how to evaluate how well a task is carried out and how to assess the quality of its outcome. Coaching often follows a period of mentoring. This time, the learner attempts to carry out the task while the experienced worker looks on providing advice and critiques as he or she proceeds.

In the training program, workers who are experienced in the Framework shouldn't participate in the workshops before the new learners have experienced the knowledge rediscovery training technique; this would defeat the purpose since they would simply tell the learners what the knowledge points are. The knowledge rediscovery needs to be appropriately challenging to push the learners out of their comfort zones while not being so hard that they would want to capitulate.

How does one teach people to deliberate constructively?

The participants must learn how to constructively carry out critical thinking as a group without anyone feeling put on the spot. Whether the subject of the deliberations are points in the training curriculum to rediscover, or, later in the workplace, ideas to develop when working on innovation endeavors, the fundamental skill to acquire is the ability to respectfully carry out collaborative investigation of a subject that is highly ambiguous. In addition, a tangible time-limited goal is needed to keep the learners focused. This is a skill that cannot be passively learned; it must be experienced for it to be fully mastered.

Another principle guiding creative deliberations is that the participants must exercise kindness and curiosity in allowing the people who are naturally less expressive to contribute their thoughts and ideas as well. They may need to be regularly prompted to do so. A consideration to keep in mind is that one's fellow participants may in fact hold the key to solving a problem on which one is stumbling. Thus, it is as important to create the conditions that allow creative ideas to rise out of these deliberations as it is to try to convince the other participants of the merits of one's own ideas. A fair amount of humility in this regard is beneficial to ensure a positive outcome to the deliberations. The outcomes of collaborative deliberations should be celebrated to reinforce this belief, irrespective of whose idea was retained.

In Chapter 2, we described a set of thinkLets for creative deliberations that add to the consensus thinkLets that have been developed over the years by several researchers and that are readily available online. The democratized-innovation learners need to become familiar with them. Beyond these techniques, the trainers must develop a mastery of what we called 'exploratory and creative dialectics' that are designed to reorganize and to reframe the points raised by the learners in the workshop setting to relate them to the workshop's subject matter in the process of knowledge rediscovery and revelation by the learners. One could view exploratory and creative dialectics as advanced deliberation skills that are used for the purpose of knowledge-rediscovery-based instruction. We will investigate the principles of this type of dialectics in more details in Chapter 9.

How should gamification be used as a motivational technique?

Let us start by paraphrasing Paul Valery's 1941 statement that "a serious . . . [person] has few ideas while a . . . [person] with ideas is never serious" (Dicocitations 2021). This highlights how some good-hearted playfulness may effectively stimulate ideation and learning by establishing favorable conditions for reaching the coveted state of creative flow. Neuroscientists might explain this phenomenon as reducing the activation of the executive attention network responsible for thoughtful problem resolution grounded in acquired knowledge and experience in favor of less structured imaginative out-of-the-box thinking based on intuition. The overall workshop dynamics could also be viewed as the gamification of the learning process. The workshops need to be engaging and entertaining; who said that learning needs to be tedious and boring?

However, the specialists' reservations about using gamification in instruction (Dahlstrøm 2017; Lewis, Swartz and Lyons 2016) should also be considered to avoid its pitfalls. Indeed, the critics warn that rewards represent an extrinsic motivator for the learners that may have the undesirable side-effect of reducing their intrinsic motivation. In other words, the learners may become addicted to the rewards and could lose their natural motivation when they are no longer offered which would be the case at their workplaces. Indeed, to ensure the success of their manifestation of democratized innovation, it is important that the learners maintain a persistent motivation to continue applying the knowledge learned in the workshops to their regular activities beyond the completion of the workshop. Therefore, one should take heed of this warning when considering using the pleasantness that games provide to entice the learners to look forward to the workshops. No explicit rewards should be offered to them, except a diffuse and ephemeral feeling of satisfaction that they may experience when winning at a game. Self-efficacy at democratized innovation should remain the only intrinsic reward.

How should one convert knowledge points into competencies?

A competency involves multifaceted knowledge; theoretical knowledge alone isn't sufficient for a worker to be fully operational in a work setting. French researcher, Le Boterf (2002) identified several types of knowledge that come into play in work-based training. For a worker to claim to be competent in a given domain, he or she needs to master the following types of knowledge. Let us illustrate each type of knowledge with some examples from the domain of democratized innovation.

- *Theoretical knowledge* are the principles and concepts of a given domain. In the Frameworks, it includes considerations such as, for example, the understanding of the Framework's cornerstones, the principles of innovation, such as our learning-based innovation typology, and, for the training of trainers, the challenges of adult education or how the theory of mind explains the limitations on the number of people who can take part in conversations.
- *Situational knowledge* of how one should apply and adapt the general principles to specific situations: it relates to the definition of the organization's particular manifestation of the Framework, which could mean adapting it to its industry's usages or the organization's culture and practices. It also comes into play when adapting the innovation knowledge to an organization's particular situation. For example, depending on whether the organization is an incumbent in its field or a challenger, some innovation strategies may apply, others not.
- *Procedural knowledge* are pre-defined methods, procedures and sequences of actions that should rigorously be followed to achieve something: it comprises considerations, such as the step-by-step method that we recommended to establish the Framework in an organization. We also recommended starting or ending the workshops by asking the learners to choose the topic for the next workshop out of a suggested list of three or four in different categories.
- *Operational know-how* relates to the use of tools and techniques; for example, in the domain of innovation, it includes our iVortoid framework that brings the learner to reflect on the risks involved in early ambiguous projects and on ways to reduce them through risk management strategies. Often these tools and techniques reduce the cognitive workload of the workers who use them; in addition, they allow workers to make use of these tools without their needing to fully understand the underlying technical intricacies that came into play in their development.
- *Experiential and empirical knowledge* of heuristics or tricks of the trade that facilitate a process: it covers for example, how to manage the propensity for risk taking that groups may unwittingly have; many of this chapter's practical

recommendations about the management of the workshops clearly fall into this category as well.

- *Relational knowledge* that encompasses how a worker should interact with other workers and stakeholders: it comes into play in managing the interactions between people. For example, workers should readily make themselves available for colleagues who reach out to them for help. We also described how workers negotiating their innovations should try to find out the other party's underlying interests to find mutually satisfactory ways to satisfy the points in contention.
- *Cognitive knowledge* that covers the ability to process the information relating to a task and to reason about it: for example, our Framework's critical thinking, negotiated innovation and creative dialectics fit precisely into this category. Being able to work one's way from an initial state of ambiguity to the clarity of shared understanding while maximizing a novelty's value by deliberating rationally about the stakeholders' requirements illustrate task-related cognition at play.

The trainer must take care to engage the learners in all these knowledge categories to ensure that the learning in the workshop is well balanced. Failure to do so could result in incomplete learning that could limit their abilities as democratized innovators. In order to do so, the trainer must keep track of the knowledge categories to which the visited learning points belong. A typical mistake is to overdo the theory which relates to the classical lecture-style mode of instruction against which we have already argued. Each trainer may choose his or her own technique to register the study points. A simple table on a spreadsheet comprising these knowledge types for the trainer to check off will show how balanced the coverage of the knowledge may be at the blink of an eye. Overdoing one category signals that one needs to apply more effort on the other ones. Maintaining a global vision of the knowledge being uncovered in the midst of meandering discussions allows the trainer to skillfully intervene to ensure that the learning is comprehensive. Hints, open questions and knowledge capsules come in handy to do so.

How should the workshop topics be managed?

The training workshop should be organized as a selection of self-contained modules to fit into the typical workshop session's timeframe which can range from two to three hours to avoid learner restlessness. The reader may have noticed that most of the section headings in this book are expressed as 'how' questions. As open questions, they will naturally launch the discussions on the given topic, at first amongst the three separate teams of three learners, and afterwards in the plenary session with the three team representatives arguing in favor of their respective group's findings with the trainer. This scheme of phrasing headings as questions was established on purpose. Indeed, in doing so, the book's table of contents provides the trainer with a convenient and structured list of thought-provoking study points. One should keep in mind that the book is structured according to the trilogy of understanding, knowledge and wisdom both across and within the parts of this book. The points in sections that relate to understanding are mostly explanatory in nature; knowledge sections represent in-depth explorations of the subject, while wisdom covers advanced topics. Another way of seeing them is that they situate, deepen and elevate the perspective on a subject. Part 3 contains subject matter concerning the training on the Framework, which is also structured in this manner.

One can expect that the members of the team-discussion tables flag the trainer to ask for clarifications on the question provided as a challenge; they may be unsure about either the terminology used or about its scope. The trainer should move from table to table ready to provide the required clarification preventing them from going too far in a direction that would be completely foreign to the topic, but still taking care to let the teams spontaneously explore the topic as they please; one should keep in mind that misconceptions may later become useful learning opportunities. Observing the team members' body language may also provide clues about how well they engage in the discussions. Perplexed expressions at one table could prompt the trainer to engage the team members to get them over what may be a minor hurdle. If there are perplexed expressions at all the tables, then it is worth resetting the exercise by pausing all the group discussions to find out what they may not have understood.

The first time that learners experience rediscovery-based learning it may naturally be somewhat disconcerting to them; the tables are turned in a way that is presumably unfamiliar to them since it breaks away from the traditional teacher-centric instructional approach that they all experienced throughout their prior education. Uninitiated learners may be unsure about what to do. Coaching may be required with a few recommendations; mentoring may be more effective by showing them the dynamics of exploratory and creative dialectics in action. For example, the trainer could illustrate investigative deliberations by asking questions to understand how to navigate through public transportation systems in the learners' hometowns. A traveller who is new to a town may ask open questions to understand how the public transportation fare payment system works. Beyond establishing shared understanding, the trainer must show them how this investigation could lead them to find innovative payment techniques. Tourism street smarts are convenient examples of which to make use because everyone has wondered about them at one point or another when travelling abroad.

In Chapter 7, we pointed out that adult learners expect to manage their own training curriculum. Therefore, we recommend that the trainers present three or four topic options from which the learners may choose at the end of a session in preparation for the next one. The table of contents relates the topics to the three parts of the book and to the chapters which will easily allow the trainers to visualize their context. Trainer preparation for an upcoming session could simply involve reading the pages in the book that are related to the topic that the learners selected. Now, one should keep in mind that this text covers the knowledge points; the trainer must allow the learners to express their findings before the trainer starts relating them to the book's material. It is to be expected that the workshop will stray away from the points listed in this book since innovation is a wide topic. The conversation about innovation will never be fully finished, neither should it since it is future-oriented and a continuously developing domain of knowledge.

How should workshop notes be drafted?

As the deliberations proceed in the workshop's plenary sessions, the trainer should jot down the keywords that represent each of the points made on a whiteboard or flipcharts on an easel. The learners may use small portable whiteboards to jot down their ideas as they deliberate ahead of the plenary session. Towards the end of a workshop session, the trainer will use a second whiteboard (or flipcharts) to recapitulate and to reframe the points raised during the workshop session according to the Framework's concepts. Knowledge appropriation by the learners is important in adult learning and education; therefore, the trainer must take care to relate the learning points to those raised by the learners. The learner points that aren't used at that time should be kept for later use. Both the learners and the trainer should take digital pictures of the whiteboard, typically with their smartphones, to keep as workshop documentation for later reference. Some learners may prefer to write up their own notes. The workshop learners must keep their notes for themselves to ensure that other workshop groups experience the full benefits of the same knowledge rediscovery process.

How should the learners be evaluated?

As far as grading participants, the long and the short of it is that there isn't any need for grades. In practice, what really matters is what the workers learn and how keenly they apply what they learned; one could call these the takeaways. Their evaluation of the pertinence of the workshop is a more important consideration. They should be asked for feedback at the end of each session or at the beginning of the next, and globally at the end of the workshop. The trainer should strive to adjust to the learners' feedback or explain the rationale of the training method if the dissatisfaction results from uneasiness with it. Adult learners like to self-evaluate. The participants should self-assess their own progress on the basis of the extent to which they managed to apply the workshop learnings to their regular work. They should be encouraged to share their experiences with the group.

Jakobsen and Knetermann's (2017) "team-based learning" concept involves learners being required to go through learning material before each course. To ensure that people have indeed done so, they start the course with a short quiz. Those who don't succeed are then required to carry out additional study assignments. For the Framework training, we chose not to have this expectation. Their carrying on with their regular work usually precludes them from dedicating any time to read or to research any material beforehand. However, if some of them do, it certainly shouldn't be discouraged, but care should be taken that they don't spoil the knowledge rediscovery process. If it is a single individual, he or she could be asked to play the role of trainer's assistant by taking down the points raised in the discussions on a whiteboard during the plenary session.

If many learners read material ahead of the workshops, the trainer should organizing fast-track workshops that gather the keenest learners together to keep them appropriately challenged. The format of the course would then relate more closely to Jakobsen and Knetermann's (2017) team-based learning method, with the discussions in the workshops focusing on the application of the material absorbed by the learners prior to the session.

How should the learning points be illustrated with running examples?

As we mentioned in Chapter 7, adult learners expect the knowledge learned to quickly translate to practice. To that aim, the trainer may invite the learners to describe how the workshop material relates to their daily activities. Since all the learners are likely to have a diversified range of interests that may be difficult to reconcile, the trainer may prefer to use several general-purpose running examples to which the trainer may refer as the workshops unfold. Moreover, there may be times when an example outside of the learners' specific work contexts is preferable to avoid running too quickly into emotionally loaded opinions indicative of sectarian thinking in the organization that could detract from the study points. When the trainer perceives such a risk, it is better to fall back on an example from a neutral domain. We propose the following examples, namely: an improvement case, a design challenge, a case that involves touchy interpersonal ramifications, and a capability management case. None of these cases require prior domain expertise; indeed, the learners shouldn't have to invest any time and effort in acquiring new knowledge in a field that isn't theirs.

Improvement cases

We all naturally and intuitively look for ways to improve on activities that are frequently carried out. Efficiency may improve as the skills are mastered, or as the activities are carried out more mechanically. The learners will likely come up with numerous examples when prompted, but in case they draw a blank, the trainer could mention the following case that relates to a business practice. It involves a maneuver when driving a train pulling heavy railway cars about to reach the top of a hill. In this industry, a recognized practice is to ensure that the railway cars reconnect tightly together right before the train initiates its descent. Indeed, the connection between two adjacent railway cars is purposefully loose to prevent the full load of the train from concentrating on any single connector knuckle, when a train initiates its forward motion from a stationary position; the forces of inertia of the train's full load would easily break it. Because of this concern, each knuckles comprises a gap that allows each car's inertia to be overcome one at a time; any knuckle is subjected to no more than the load of one single car at a time. However, when rolling down a hill, the gap in the coupler knuckles close up under the effects of the accelerating cars propelled by the force of gravity induced by the downward slope of the hill. As a result, a sequence of sharp jolts occurs as each car goes over the ridge and the gap of its leading connector knuckle closes one after the other. To prevent this undesirable effect from happening, the train driver needs to slow down before reaching the crest of the hill to ensure that the cars' coupler knuckles gently reconnect with each other. Keeping them tightly in this proper forward position before engaging in the downward slope prevents any jolts from occurring. In addition, preventing the nasty jolts reduces metal fatigue and extends the life of the coupler knuckles; there is more to it than simply a smooth ride. The identity of the person who came up with this practice is lost to the ages, but it illustrates the value that a single person may bring to his or her organization by bringing forward an astute practice from which all can benefit.

After describing this example, the trainer should prompt the learners to find similar improvement cases. These may be as mundane as finding itinerary efficiencies when commuting to and from the office or riding the public transportation systems.

Design challenge case

For this case, the learners are challenged to design what the kitchen of the future could look like. The trainer should start by prompting the learners to express their pet peeves with their own kitchens; this will highlight that there is room for improvements. Open kitchen concepts have been in vogue for quite a while, but what could be the next big thing in kitchen design? Get them to consider radical functional trends, such as whether people will cook at all. Maybe time will come when it will be cheaper to buy fully prepared meals from a caterer rather than cooking them by one-self at home. How would they be delivered? Maybe by drone? How would the drones drop off their payloads without spilling anything? The learners should work in groups of three to come up with original designs. If they can't agree on any particular point, they should be encouraged to vote amongst themselves with the Framework's consensus-seeking principle in mind. The solutions that they propose could reveal their boldness as designers.

Interpersonal issues case

This case illustrates the challenges of managing stakeholder relationships when sitting on condominium (condo) boards. As many people may have experienced, it is a thankless and often trying job that requires strong negotiation skills. Condo owners are naturally very opinionated about their condo units because they are both financial assets and their homes. Hence, they tend to be both rational and emotional about them. People complain about the upkeep, while demanding that the condo fees be kept low. One could say that many co-owners want to have their cake and eat it too as the saying goes. Board members may pull their hair out trying to find happy compromises. In our experience, the most effective board members are those who put their minds together to understand and to solve the issues creatively; it is both a problem-solving and co-creation process. They may have little if any experience in construction and building maintenance. Yet, through exploratory discussions and open-minded deliberations, they can find the best ways to proceed. Since many people may have experienced condo boards firsthand, the learners are likely to immediately understand the case and to relate to it. Themes, such as rising insurance renewals costs in a context of a condo established in a building of historical significance (see if they find out about replacement vs. reproduction vs. reconstruction evaluations and historical preservation laws), a leaky roof, a classical fence dispute, complaints about noisy neighbors or an issue involving one of the board members (that is to say a situation with ethical issues to be managed), or, if the learners feel particularly brave, selecting paint color schemes or carpet patterns, are all guaranteed to produce lively deliberations.

Capability management case

This is a case that involves developing a new line of business. It comes in two flavors: one corresponding to an established organization and the other to a challenger (i.e., a start-up or an established company entering a new market). This example doesn't require any domain knowledge to figure out. It was used by

Davidson, Malard and Ivanova (2012) for a study in innovation that involved presenting a simple case to busy technology executives as a preamble for a survey questionnaire.

The case is a variation of the Dutch auction example presented in Chapter 6. It involves a fictitious Internet-services firm developing an online version of the Dutch auction system. The rationale for doing so is that Dutch auctions are more effective and profitable than traditional auctions. In a traditional auction, the parties interested by an item being offered start bidding at a low-end starting price and gradually step up their bids in a highly competitive context. Most bidders fold as the bidding goes higher than what they can afford to pay. The process continues with a diminishing number of bidders until only one single unchallenged bid wins the coveted item. By comparison, Dutch auctions start high; the auctioneer reduces the asking price – usually at an astoundingly fast pace – until a bidder commits to buy at a particular price which freezes the process abruptly and concludes the transaction. There are none of the theatrics and bidding wars that are part of the traditional auction's folklore. Dutch auctions tend to be dispassionate, which contrasts with the excitement of traditional auctions which are social gatherings and opportunities for people to show off their wealth, power and audacity often at their own financial peril. We stated previously that Dutch auctions tend to be more profitable because first, a greater number of transactions can be carried out over the same period of time, and second, more importantly, the process testing the bidders' self-control, people have a tendency to bid at the high end of their budgets.

In the incumbent variation of the case, a hypothetical existing online traditional auction firm wishes to experiment with the Dutch auction concept. It experiments with caution to avoid disturbing its existing revenue stream. Furthermore, the mechanical process may not sit well with some customers who are used to the spectacle of traditional auctions and who may get frustrated and possibly even bored. There are pros and cons of each of these types of auctions to consider.

For the challenger variation of the case, the new market entrant needs to quickly establish its Dutch auction model with a winning offer in a niche market. It cannot leverage a strong brand name. Also, it must not challenge established online auction firms head on. It must find a niche market to showcase its Dutch auctions. It will need to establish barriers to the entry of competitors, which could include the development of capabilities that are difficult to reproduce. It may need to pivot from one product category to another as it tries to find a profitable market. Also, if it is already a player on another market, it could leverage its know-how or the strength of its brand on its original market with a cross-marketing offer.

This case lends itself well to the investigation of a range of innovation strategies, market challenges and organizational issues. The learners could start by considering what competencies and capabilities are required to develop an online Dutch auction. The incumbent may consider how its existing capabilities would apply, while a start-up may need to move quickly to find a market that sticks. In both cases, adjustments of competencies and capabilities are likely to be required. Getting the learners to name their fictitious firms will gamify the case and entice them to make the case theirs by personalizing it.

Summation

In this chapter, we reviewed a series of practical considerations related to the organization of the training workshops, as well as workshop dynamics and techniques. The workshop's format is designed to cater to the needs of adult learners in a work-based setting. In a principle of bootstrapping, its participatory format featuring the learners' rediscovery of the knowledge points is an application of the collaborative deliberation skills that the democratized innovators will later need to apply in the performance of their work. Therefore, the workshop includes a body of knowledge to acquire but its dynamics also contribute to their subconsciously developing the behaviors and interpersonal skills that are part of democratized innovation.

Also, we examined the optimal workshop attendance which should aim at including three deliberation teams of three learners that is to say nine people in total. Clearly, training a large number of people will require a train-the-trainer approach, with potential new trainers being recruited within the organization. Although it is important to keep track of learner attendances, grading learners is excluded. What matters is to develop the learners' motivation for democratized innovation; whatever subject matter sticks in their minds should suffice to allow them to make their own manifestation of democratized innovation work for them.

Chapter 9
Training of the Trainers

In Chapter 7, the typical challenges that are encountered when training adult learners in a work-based setting were presented and analyzed. We described an approach that effectively addresses these challenges while supporting the training in democratized innovation. It highlights learner participation and the rediscovery of the workshop subject matter through social interactions and discourse. As a result, the learners become more engaged in their own learning. Then, in Chapter 8, we covered a range of practical considerations when conducting the training workshops. Most importantly, we prescribed the maximum number of people who can simultaneously participate in the workshop to allow for productive deliberations. Exploratory and creative deliberations are fundamental components of the adult training approach that we advocated. Negotiating one's innovation is a step in the process that ensures that the interests of all stakeholders are integrated in the outcome. As the Framework's manifestation is more and more exercised, deliberations increasingly take place in the organization. As we shall see in this chapter, exploratory and creative discourse also comes into play when addressing one of the most common challenges in adult education, that is to say the overcoming of their natural propensity to resist change. Therefore, proficiency at this type of discourse serves three purposes: innovating collaboratively, participative training and overcoming the workers' reservations about novelties that disturb their regular beliefs and habits.

As a side-effect of the workshops, the learners are expected to acquire a basic level of proficiency in the art of deliberation. They rediscover the workshop's subject matter supported by the inconspicuous guidance of the trainer. Later, they could apply the same skills on their own, when carrying out deliberations related to their innovation endeavors. Any ability at exploratory and creative discourse that rubs off from their participation in the workshops will serve the intended purpose without requiring more extensive and formal training in it. Simply the fact that they acquire the habit of talking constructively to one another and putting their minds together to solve problems represents in itself a remarkable success. However, as far as the trainers are concerned, they need to develop a mastery of exploratory and creative dialectics and proficiency in applying them to effectively drive the workshops.

How does the training technique affect the learners' resistance to change?

Resistance to change is a common reaction exhibited by adult learners. It must be addressed otherwise it will inhibit their learning. The knowledge that the learners currently possess may have served them well for a long time. As a result, it isn't surprising

https://doi.org/10.1515/9783110683837-013

that any suggestion to replace it by a new body of knowledge with which they aren't accustomed will be unsettling. They invested time and effort to develop their expertise; it is part of their inner being. Furthermore, they are likely to have enhanced their knowledge with experience by practicing it in real-life situations. This allowed them to develop valuable complementary knowledge such as know-how and heuristics. They may also have earned a recognition for their expertise. Indeed, resistance to change is often based on concerns about losing one's professional and social status acquired through the expertise that one has developed over the years, and, in a very practical way, fear of being unable to carry out one's work with the same efficiency and effectiveness as one exhibited before. Thus, the reluctance to put all of this at risk for something unfamiliar is understandable. Furthermore, they may be unwilling to learn new knowledge from the basics and to stumble through a process of trial and error; they may associate this ramp-up process as being functionally incapacitated.

Langer (2000) defines the concept of "mindful learning", that is to say the "act of drawing novel distinctions". This implies entertaining the possibility that knowledge points may not be absolutely certain. For example, a mindful-learning trainer might say that tires "can be used" on wheels, rather than a more affirmative statement such as "tires are designed to go on wheels", even if, in effect, they have been designed for that primary purpose. This opens up the mind to other uses of tires if not even substituting them by something else on vehicles. Along similar lines, Mezirow (2000) refers to "transformational learning" that mutates the frames of reference that people take for granted; new information should bring learners to adjust their beliefs. For example, this is an exercise that populations all over the world have been required to do with ever shifting pandemic confinement directives.

To extend Mezirow's thinking, if the learners acquiesce to the merits of the direction of the change, it becomes an evolutionary process. Therefore, one may wonder whether this evolutionary perspective could be induced at the same time that the knowledge is originally acquired? This approach would mean that people focus their learning on the path that brought them to the knowledge rather than the piece of knowledge itself taken in isolation. A path suggests something that can naturally be extended; implanting this consideration through knowledge rediscovery will mentally prepare the learner to expect new knowledge discoveries further along the same path. In other words, the recollections of how knowledge was elicited and the understanding that knowledge isn't immutable opens the minds from the start to later updates to it. This epistemological learning – that is to say learning that is based on a reflection on the limits and the validity of knowledge – is likely to reduce the resistance to change when change become necessary. Furthermore, if the original quest for knowledge was participatory and experiential – as is the case with the knowledge rediscovery training technique that we advocate – the path becomes a mental journey intertwined with personal memories of how it occurred. Add deliberations and negotiations to the mix and the learners will have become emotionally invested in the knowledge rediscovery process. As a result, the knowledge rediscovery path will have more significance than the goal of acquiring a piece of knowledge; in other words, the journey is more cognitively important than the destination. Furthermore, recognizing the path to knowledge will also facilitate recalling knowledge that may have faded over time. Treading along a path that has been visited before is always easier. This is the rationale underpinning learning through the knowledge rediscovery approach that we advocate. This is how we believe that learning should be carried out to cultivate life-long learning and openness to new ideas in the future. Unfortunately, most workers have learned their skills with what Langer (2000) called "mindless learning" based on the passive assimilation of knowledge presented as irrefutable certainties.

How should the trainer overcome the learners' resistance to change?

Learning in adults requires them to update a complex network of interdependent cognitive elements in their minds to which we will refer as their belief systems. These belief systems define how they view and understand their undertakings, their roles and their work environments. Their thinking and their actions at work are conditioned by these beliefs. As we suggested previously, Langer (2000) refers to the "power of uncertainty" in suggesting that new teaching material should be introduced in a conditional perspective (as opposed to statements of certainty) because it opens the learners' minds to consider different perspectives related to it later. Unfortunately, traditional teaching generally focuses on the learners mindlessly absorbing knowledge points in a way that fosters rigid mindsets. This rigidity diminishes the learners' ability to update their thinking later and to think out of the proverbial box. For example, one of the author's favorite pastimes is to wander through the isles of hardware stores with a divergent thinking process, that is to say by trying to find components that could be used or assembled to fix a household problem for which they weren't originally designed. Incidentally, let us note that it is common for marine engineers to scavenge parts from non-essential equipment throughout their ships to repair broken critical components when at sea far from any shipyard. Similarly, at the hardware store, it isn't because plastic tube connectors are placed in the display racks in the plumbing department that they can't be used to, say, prop up a piece of furniture for example. We share the view that all bodies of knowledge should be presented to the learners in a way that invites critical reflection about them later; this approach opens the learner's mind from the start. Doubt is a powerful force for the advancement of knowledge. Irrespective of the progress of knowledge in a domain, the value of knowledge depends on each learner's context and goals, which are also both potentially shifting considerations. The learner-driven knowledge rediscovery approach that we adopted for teaching democratized innovation creates this mindset from the outset because the learners contributed to rediscovering its principles; they found the path to the knowledge, therefore they will feel empowered to update this path, if need be, later on. Generally, they will be more likely to develop a habit of diverging from what may appear normal if they subconsciously harbor doubts about it.

Coming to grips with new perspectives that challenge knowledge that may have been acquired mindlessly, as Langer (2000) puts it, triggers resistance. Mindless learning precludes critical thinking related to the knowledge acquired through it; it assumes that the learners take the knowledge at face value with little allowance for skepticism. How can anyone raise doubts about a belief presented as being unquestionably true, possibly even as being foundational without stirring up objections? The stage is set for the unqualified rejection of the unsettling change. The rigidity in the original learnings plus their repeated validation over a significant period of time stifles the learner's ability to question the teachings. Thus, one needs to restore the learners' ability to engage in critical thinking in the areas that they consider as being unequivocal beliefs before the acquisition of new knowledge and new skills may even be contemplated. Mezirow (2000) calls these deep-seated beliefs "assumptions" which highlights the fact that these are knowledge points that one assumes to be true, but that may not necessarily be so as a matter of fact. Ambiguity may be considered as a more common state of humanity's quest for knowledge with certitude being a fleeting and relative state.

In other words, when people stop questioning the validity of their beliefs, their beliefs become assumptions that is to say facts that they view as being absolute truths. As a result, new learnings that undermine these beliefs are subconsciously rejected, because the assumptions are indubitable in their minds. This rigid mindset precludes questioning the knowledge; it stifles any opportunity for adaptations and advancements; teachings are elevated to the status of received wisdom. At an organizational level it adds up to organizational myopia (Henderson and Clark 1990) which may in the worst of cases end up undermining the organization's very sustainability, or, to paraphrase Leonard-Barton (1992), it produces core competencies that become core rigidities. This is often the result of what Langer (2000) calls mindless learning, that is to say learning that is very matter of fact without any provision for doubt. This state of mind usually fosters resistance to change. The reality is that very few things in science, technology and even life are invariably or unfailingly true, but rather are simply perceived as such in people's minds. There is a French saying according to which "the exception proves a rule". The latter part of the saying "in the cases that aren't excluded" is usually dropped in the colloquial use of the saying, but it makes an important point. Interestingly, it integrates a critical reflection about the universality of a fundamental principle based on the justification of an exception. If the exception is debunked, then the rule's universality is maintained, but if the exception is justified, then it suggests the existence of a new distinction. For this reason, while abstaining from falling into the deceptive argumentation of sophistry, we advocate viewing truth in a belief system as a simple probability dependent on what is currently known about a domain of knowledge at a given time rather than something that is invariably true. This truth should be viewed as being a convenient approximation of certainty; below that level, terms such as probable, plausible, possible, doubtful, unlikely, or any number of synonyms illustrate varying levels of confidence that one may associated with a belief. An assumption that is taken for granted by someone should rather be framed as a presumption, that is to say a belief based on probabilities of being true by taking into account what is know about it at a given point in time, which could in fact be limited. Moreover, the appropriateness of a belief reflects how well it is suited to a given context. It is a conditional attribute associated with its practical application. If the contextual conditions change, something that may have been tagged as having a high level of appropriateness, may no longer be viewed as such. Therefore, as we alluded previously, to open minds one needs to cultivate a healthy level of doubt which is developed through the practice of skepticism. This state of mind addresses both the rational and subjective aspects of beliefs. Questioning the learners' assumptions may be particularly challenging because, first, they work into a complex system of interdependent beliefs and, second, because they may be intimately intertwined with emotional considerations, such as the learner's self-concept (that is to say the beliefs that they hold about themselves) and their self-efficacy (that is to say their beliefs in their abilities to perform). Therefore, updating a specific belief system in a localized manner, that is to say without affecting other related ones may be challenging. In addition, the emotional considerations make learning a destabilizing and possibly even a trying exercise. People may perceive that their inner self is at risk of being deconstructed, while in fact the update at play may only be limited to focused considerations (e.g., one technique replacing another) allowing their overall experience in the field to carry over without profound upheaval.

Let us now consider a process designed to address the learners' resistance to change. To start, they need to come to the realization that the change is induced by a shifting context. It is needed to reach a positive outcome, that is to say the sustainability of the organization in an ever-changing and possibly threatening environment. In practice, this means that the impulse for making the adjustments is beneficial for the organization which means that it is likely to have a positive impact on the workers as well. When presenting the need for a change, it should be made clear that there isn't any nefarious intent, such as staff reductions for example. Even the perception that there may be a hidden agenda will intensify the resistance because it becomes a matter of work stability. Turmoil in the workplace will inevitably ensue. Senior management may want to confirm that it is committed to retraining its staff to alleviate this concern. Some beliefs need to be adjusted throughout an organization's workforce to ensure that it continues thriving. Individually, this means of course that each learner's belief systems must be harmonized to support the organization's adaptation to the shifting conditions.

The following process is designed to overcome the learners' resistance to change. It is inspired by Mezirow's (2000) "transformation theory". It fosters an acceptance of the change by the learners to overcome their resistance to it. The initial step in navigating through the change involves expanding the learners' awareness of the conditions and of the constraints that triggered the need for the change which in turn makes the acquisition of the new knowledge necessary to support it. A carrot-and-stick approach usually works. Emphasis could be placed on the risks involved if the organization were to disregard the change, such as losing its competitiveness, for example. Highlighting the career opportunities that the new context may create can stimulate some interest from the learners. In the second step, the learners are invited to engage in an exercise of critical reflection around the justifications and limitations of their current beliefs that are at issue based on the examination of objective evidence and similar case story telling. The shortcomings of the current beliefs should be framed in their context by relating them to the needs to fulfill the new conditions and constraints. This reduces the learners' propensity to express subjective or sectarian thinking, since the statements must be rationally supported by a need; "Why do we still need to do that?" could be a typical question to ask as a rebuttal. It should be clear that the circumstances point towards a line of action, rather than simple preferences. Grounding the discussions in this manner helps support the feasibility of the exercise because there is no reference to what may be right or wrong in absolute terms; the suitability of the beliefs is determined by the circumstances. Then, this step leads to a third step that focuses on an exercise of collective reflection involving the discovery of the new beliefs and their dialectic validation related to the current beliefs as a group. This means an interplay of arguments and counterarguments. Common areas should be identified and emphasized because they are reassuring for the learners, and the distinctions understood. In practice, this exercise aims at updating the network of justifications of the learners' current belief systems to integrate (one could even use the expression "to splice in") the new beliefs into it. Integrating rather than changing will help the learners make the new beliefs theirs. The process ends with a fourth step that features the experimentation of the beliefs supported by an understanding of – and appreciation for – the new context. This step entices the learners to try out the new or transformed beliefs if they haven't already done so as part of the awareness awakening step. This ensures that the new beliefs are exercised in practice, and that they start developing a sense of self-efficacy related to it. Feeling that one is quickly getting good at the new skill will go a long way towards it being accepted; mentoring and coaching should be provided. Sometimes a beginner may be stumped by the smallest of details that has little to do with the gist of the change. Simulations may help overcome the fears of making mistakes because it removes any real consequences. In addition, in some cases, once the initial trial has been carried out, these simulations could be continued individually, allowing the learner fearful of public image to stumble privately. However, feelings of frustration are more likely to develop when they are in isolation. The exercise should be monitored by the trainer prompting for feedback privately and offering help as required.

How can critical thinking overcome the learners' resistance to change?

Let us have a closer look at the behavioral response that occurs when people resist change. It reflects that a person is struggling to maintain, and possibly even to defend, the coherence of his or her belief system when being presented with new knowledge that challenges it. Mezirow (2000) refers to the "deconstruction" of prior blocking assumptions. We believe, on the contrary, that learning isn't a removal or a replacement process, but rather an additive one which introduces new conceptual constructs leading to the expansion of the learners' understanding. The learner receives new material (or we should rather say rediscovers it in the case of the workshops given the learning technique that is applied) which needs to be related and added to the learners' current knowledge base. The original knowledge doesn't disappear; it may be reframed with new constraints and conditions, rendering some pieces of it unused which then gradually fade away, but this time through a natural process of forgetting. Indeed, the knowledge that isn't regularly used in a person's daily activities will gradually lose sharpness and eventually be forgotten; this is a natural memory management process that allows the mind to focus on what really matters at any given time. Interestingly, forgotten knowledge can be recalled easily with refresher training (or by going over one's own work notes) if need be. Nobody can claim to have the ability to consciously remove knowledge from his or her mind; one could also call this ability intentionally forgetting something. Ironically, just thinking about the very thing to forget reinforces its memory.

From an epistemological perspective, knowledge is a system of beliefs that are generally considered as being true or that a person singularly holds as being true. This means that these beliefs must be supported by justifications which in turn must be supported by their own justifications in a potentially open-ended regression process. For simple belief propositions, there will be a simple chain of justifications, while for complex ones, they may branch out in multiple directions forming either a tree or a network. The justifications may in fact be patterns of considerations with each component of a given pattern having justifications of its own. Some justifications may be shared, thus the possibility that they form an intricate network.

Therefore, the learners who resist change should be brought to identify what the current and the new knowledge have in common and how they differ. The complementarities represent clear distinctions that offer efficacious opportunities to add the new knowledge without challenging the validity of the current knowledge or revoking it. In the workshop, it is highly advisable, as a general practice, for the trainer to engage the learners pre-emptively in this exercise irrespective of concerns being expressed or not. Indeed, the naysayers in an innovation endeavor may keep their doubts for themselves and covertly denigrate the novelty or the new knowledge points; therefore, it is highly preferable to probe their thoughts to uncover any reservations that they may have in order to address their doubts constructively and openly.

Because the human mind is rationally bounded (Simon 1979, 1991), this potentially infinite regression process is eventually resolved by subjective justifications, which often may be based on one's personal interpretation of the subject matter or experience. The subjectivity of these personal interpretations is what causes most of the resistance to change, since presumably the proposed change isn't put forward for irrational reasons. However, since people tend to prefer what they know over what they don't, connecting justifications for the novelty to what they already know and accept as fact goes a long way towards opening their minds. At these subjective points, there is an internal relationship between knowledge and the knower, requiring the beholder of the beliefs to be satisfied with the network of justifications. This state of satisfaction is mostly an emotional state of mind; it may even occur in the domain of subconsciousness. If this is the case, one needs to bring it into the domain of conscious reasoning. Feelings of self-efficacy come into play, that is to say that one's confidence in being able to complete a task with gratifying performance, or convictions of doing things the right way are common perceptions that ultimately support one's belief system. For example, the notion that a technique is the best way of resolving a particular type of problem may be supported by the memory of repeated successful experiences with it or more vaguely feelings of self-efficacy; the trade practices that one learned from a mentor that one holds in high esteem may also support this notion. Resistance to change comes into play when two bodies of knowledge overlap or contradict one another, that is to say when there is redundancy or discrepancies.

Therefore, in order to make the learners more able and willing to consider change, the trainer needs to add new beliefs that introduce variance in their existing belief systems. He or she must take care to relate them to the existing knowledge base with distinctions and justifications. For example, this could mean presenting supporting evidence that a current piece of knowledge that was believed to be true, may in fact not always be true. Subjective elements are prime focus points for such variances to assemble convincing evidence to be presented to the learners. This mental process based on purposefully cultivating doubt and skepticism about a given assumption facilitates the formation of new justification branches on which the new pieces of knowledge may be connected; this is a process of critical thinking about the justifications that form one's belief system. This may also be achieved by involving the learners in practical exercises that makes them experience the limits of the current knowledge. Since knowledge is usually situated in context, there may also be contextual circumstances that shed doubt on the current body of knowledge. For example, there could be a new technique, technology or paradigm that addresses more efficiently a need than the current ones do. The areas of doubt provide clues about how to integrate the new knowledge in the existing belief systems. Thus, viewed from the angle of this splicing approach, change may not be as radical as initially perceived by those who resist it.

More often than not, an organization remains true to its core competencies and the pivoting-induced knowledge variations relates to new market knowledge; this new knowledge relates to the flexible market "touch downs" that are key to an organization's sustainability, as we previously mentioned. Market opportunities may be circumstantial. A current body of knowledge may have originally been organically developed because of such circumstantial opportunities. Thus, path dependency is a concept that is likely to have influenced the way that one's knowledge base came about. An opportunity that disappears on one market may render specific market knowledge obsolete, while the development of a new opportunity for one's organization's core competencies on another market may require developing new complementary market-related knowledge. For example, a technology firm that may have provided customer account payment-processing technologies in the retail point-of-sales market space may suddenly find itself pushed by shifting conditions to seek new opportunities on other markets, such as online-web transactions payment processing. Its beliefs in the retail payment processing would need to be adapted to integrate considerations relating to online payments. There are common areas, and there are differences. Although, transaction security and validation processes would need to be adapted, the underlying payments processes remain roughly the same.

How can dialectics be explorative and creative?

In the Framework, the term 'deliberation' was used to describe a collaborative discursive act. Mansbridge (2009) defines a deliberation as "a communication that induces reflection on preferences, [values and interests] in a non-coercive fashion", which supports this premise. Her definition supports the notion that a group of people willing to put their minds together can cooperatively find the best way to resolve a problem or to design something new. They seek the common good for their constituents, that we relate in the context of innovation to finding optimal solutions that integrate the stakeholders' preferences in a tangible manner. It is an act of what she calls "collective agency" that requires clear communications, frank and mutual disclosure and joint fact-finding; justifications put forward must be based on evidence or on expert testimony. The participants must also exhibit "reciprocal empathy" in understanding the other party's individual perspectives, and they must seek to explore deeper in keeping with the principles of integrative negotiation. Critical reflection takes place throughout the process. They explore the possibilities by going beyond what is known and commonplace through the power of their combined mental abilities and imaginations. In addition to coming up with creative ideas, each participant must also seek to induce creative thinking in the other protagonists who act not only as their sounding boards, but also as their partners in a co-creation process. The outcome must address the stakeholders' preferences fairly; upon agreeing on an outcome, the participants must be committed to it even if concessions and trade-offs were made along the way. Indeed, optimality is a relative concept that is based on the satisfaction of a constituency's requirements. In other words, an optimal solution is the best possible solution that reflects the plurality of preferences.

Argumentation is a notion that is often associated with deliberations and negotiation; arguments and counterarguments are fundamental components of its dynamics. The online version of Merriam-Webster defines argumentation as "the act or process of forming reasons, and of drawing conclusions and applying them to a case in discussion", which relates to our cooperative interpretation of the notion of deliberation. In addition, Merriam-Webster defines an argument as "a cohesive series of reasons, statements or facts intended to support or to establish a view". We purposefully excluded connotations that refer to any form of quarreling. Although respectful disagreements or conflicting ideas are often useful to stimulate creativity, this should be the most antagonism that is justifiable in present-day workplaces. Van Eemeren and Grootendorst (1984) highlight the "articulated differences of opinion" and the "exchange of views" that characterizes argumentation. It follows an iterative process of information-seeking questions, propositions, rational justifications, requests for clarifications and explanations leading to acceptances or refutations. The goal is to convince someone to view something differently or to persuade someone to do something. They conceive argumentation as a "bilateral dialogue" comprising what they call "speech acts" occurring between a speaker and one or more listeners who interactively exchange roles as a deliberation unfolds. The shared reflections and the mindful exchanges on the subject being investigated seek to reach clarity, shared understanding and agreement. Interestingly, Van Eemeren and Grootendorst (1984) acknowledge that the process is what they qualify as being an "imperfect imitation of logicians". We subscribe to this qualification, since we believe that people engaged in an exploratory and creative deliberation are unlikely to rigorously follow rules of logic; but a best-effort approach in this regard works well enough. Searles (1975) identified five functions of speech acts. Amongst them, "bringing about the changes in reality" is the one that relates the most to creativity. We added a leading function of 'perceiving or understanding reality' which applies when understanding the premises of a problem or conducting critical thinking, and when rediscovering knowledge in the instructional use of dialectics. Van Eemeren and Grootendorst (1984) explain that an argumentation is both a process and a product that "externalizes" the argumentation. We adopted this distinction as well to devise a classification of the exploratory and creative dialectic transformations. We distinguished between those that make the deliberations as an activity more constructive and insightful from those that transform the shared understanding as the tangible outcome of the deliberations. The latter relates to our concept of negotiated innovation that we defined as the optimized outcome produced by the creative deliberations that satisfies the stakeholders' preferences.

In the Framework, as the deliberations progress, the statements exchanged incrementally transform the participants' shared understanding up to a point of agreement. The dialectics may support a creative purpose and an instructional one. The deliberation's traditional purpose also comes into play when resolving disagreements that may also occur when negotiating one's innovation or while conducting critical thinking activities. These are explorative and creative dialectics that focus on creativity, learning, negotiation and critical thinking while always upholding the objective of seeking more value.

Dialectics involve verbal interactions and group reasoning. Through a discursive process, the proponents coherently investigate how to solve a problem, how to design a novelty or, more generally, how to interactively figure out something that is unknown; jointly they seek an optimal outcome. The process can be launched or stimulated by an open question to which a provisional answer (that we shall call a proposition) may be put forward. Arguments in favor and against the propositions are usually voiced. The evidence is collected. The deliberations progress towards finding an optimal outcome. This process may be iterative with nested questions that are recursively stacked and unstacked as complex questions are broken down into more manageable sub-questions or as discussions lead to new previously unforeseen considerations. The discussion meanders through a developing thread of collaborative exchanges of views, inquiries and critical reflections. Like fog concealing the details of a landscape, the vagueness of an original starting point is gradually clarified. The characteristics of the problem to address come into sharper view. The disorganization of confusion is progressively cleared; confused conceptual considerations and their relationships are disentangled. Facts and evidence are weighed. The plurality of perspectives, interests and preferences is duly noted and accommodated. The visions for its resolution are iteratively imagined, validated, and transformed. All these processes seek to convert the initial ambiguity into a structured understanding shared by all, by deliberating openly, rationally and cooperatively, while relentlessly seeking to find the coveted value that will produce innovation.

Ideas are sparked or learning points are inferred along the way, and they are transformed through the discourse between the participants in a process of sublation. It is the process that involves preserving the useful portions of a proposition or of an idea while working out its limitations that may have been drawn out by the reservations expressed by some of the participants. Original concepts, daring visions and creative ideas emerge as they are being subjected to a set of conceptual transformations incrementally applied as the deliberations unfold. These transformations are already available in our common, yet semantically rich, language. The thoughts brought forward get clarified, organized, reorganized, validated and possibly even tested; finally, an "aha!" moment of collective enlightenment is reached. As we previously stated, this discursive process can be used in different ways: to stimulate group creativity, to investigate and to rediscover new areas of knowledge, to seek consensuses on decisions to be made and to overcome resistance to change through critical thinking.

Exploratory and creative dialectics involve a set of conceptual transformations that are applied to intermediate propositions or constructs through discourse. They come into play to facilitate the developing reasoning process and to feed the evolving shared understanding that progresses toward an outcome. Dialectics traditionally involve negation-affirmation dynamics; a proposition, a concept or a construct is transformed when confronted with different perspectives. A proposition brought forward by a proponent who is challenged to expand or to clarify his or her thoughts or to justify them is also part of dialectics. Therefore, there are two aspects to exploratory dialectics, namely transformations that lead directly to the development of the product of what is being discussed and activities that are part of the deliberation process. Fusing and adapting the definitions provided by Merriam-Webster's online version for the noun 'product' and for the verb 'produce', we suggest that, in this situation, an outcome is "something that is produced by intellectual effort which emphasizes the coupling of product and process". The deliberation process comprises various activities designed to generate insights that will hopefully lead to better outcomes. Interestingly, deriving a definition again from Merriam-Webster online dictionary, an activity is a process involving a mental function which, moreover, in the case of education can stimulate learning through firsthand experience that we will approximate to practice.

Tab. 9.1: Process-oriented extended sublations for exploratory and creative dialectics.

Sublation Name	Description of the Effect
Affirm	To confirm to be valid[2]
Analyze	To undertake a detailed examination of anything complex in order to understand its nature or to determine its essential features
Challenge	To arouse interest in a demanding undertaking with a thought-provoking angle to stimulate the development of original ideas and thinking[1,2]
Classify	To define a systematic arrangement in groups or categories according to established criteria[1]
Contradict	To demonstrate that something is inconsistent or incompatible with another
Contrast	To set in opposition in order to highlight a difference[2]
Decompose	To separate something into its constituent parts or elements which are often basic, or into simpler compounds[1]

Tab. 9.1 (continued)

Sublation Name	Description of the Effect
Dissect	To analyze and interpret the separate components of something minutely[1]
Distinguish	To notice and to understand the difference or differences between two or more things[2]
Epitomise	To serve as a perfect example of a quality or a type of thing[1,3]
Evaluate	To carry out a systematic assessment of something
Exemplify	To illustrate by an example[1]
Expand	To express at length in greater detail[1]
Find a Discrepancy	To find a difference between things that should be the same[3]
Find an Inconsistency	To find facts or claims to be incompatible[1]
Illustrate	To represent a conceptual construct in visual or graphical form
Justify	To demonstrate or prove to be valid[2]
Map	To apply in a one-to-one manner one function or a set of functions to a corresponding set of elements[1]
Negate	To suppress or to supplant a proposition
Oppose	To establish the relation between two propositions having the same subject and predicate but differing in quantity or quality or both[1]
Prioritize	To list or rank according to an order of precedence[1]
Progress	To move forward through a continuous series of improvements
Reframe	To look, present or think about something (e.g. beliefs, ideas etc.) in a different way[1,2]
Sort	To put in a certain place or rank according to kind, class, or nature[1]
Synthesize	To put things together to make a new whole[1,2]

Derived from online versions of (1) Merriam-Webster, (2) TheFreeDictionary, (3) Cambridge.

We called these transformations "extended sublations". In fact, they are derived from common words of the English language; they simply need to be viewed from this new perspective. They are classified in two categories corresponding to 'Product' and 'Process' to reflect whether they directly operate on the concepts at play or they represent an exploratory activity. Tables 9.1 and 9.2 show two illustrative sets of sublations for exploratory and creative dialectics; we don't claim these sets of sublations to be complete and definitive. On the contrary, the reader is

Tab. 9.2: Product-oriented extended sublations for exploratory and creative dialectics.

Sublation Name	Description of the Effect
Abstract	To derive or induce a general conception or principle from particulars
Adapt	To adjust to a particular use, purpose or situation[1]
Adjunct	To associate something to another in a dependent and subordinate position[2]
Alter	To make different without changing into something else[1]
Amalgamate	To unite or combine as a mixture of different elements
Associate	To bring together or into relationship in any of various intangible ways[1]
Categorize	To define a general class of ideas, terms, or things that mark divisions or coordination within a conceptual scheme
Combine	To join together for a common purpose[2]
Commutate	To apply an operation on members of a set that is independent of the order
Convert	To change from one form or function to another; to bring from one belief, view or party to another; to change from one unit of reference to another[1]
Deduce	To infer something by thinking about the known facts[3]
Derive	To generate a construct inspired from an original one
Differentiate	To develop differential or distinguishing characteristics in something
Enlarge	To make something larger or bigger[1]
Evolve	To progess from a simpler form to a more complex one[2]
Exclude	To bar from participation, consideration, acceptance, membership or inclusion[1]
Extend	To stretch out to fullest length or to full capacity[1]
Extrapolate	To project, extend, or expand (known data or experience) into an area not known or experienced so as to arrive at a usually conjectural knowledge of the unknown area[1]
Generalize	To formulate general concepts by abstracting common properties of instances
Improve	To enhance the value or quality of something; to make better[1]
Include	To comprise as part of a whole or a group[1]
Induce	To infer a generalized conclusion from particular instances[1]
Infer	To derive logical conclusions from premises known or assumed to be true[2]
Instantiate	To create an individual representative of a category
Integrate	To form, coordinate or blend into a functioning or unified whole[1]

Tab. 9.2 (continued)

Sublation Name	Description of the Effect
Make an Abduction	To find the simplest explanation for an observed phenomenon[4]
Organize	To cause to have an orderly, functional, or coherent structure[2]
Translate	To transfer or turn from one set of symbols to another[1]
Transmutate	To change or alter in form, appearance or nature especially to a higher form

Derived from online versions of (1) Merriam-Webster, (2) TheFreeDictionary, (3) Cambridge, (4) Wikipedia.

invited to add to these lists according to what works in his or her particular manifestation of the Framework.

How can exploratory dialectics be used for instruction?

In the instructional use of exploratory dialectics, the knowledge is mostly rediscovered and partly revealed in a discursive process that engages the learners' imagination with expressive intensity; they become "conversant" with the knowledge that is unlocked in association with the other participants who in turn become earnest proponents in a collaborative knowledge-seeking deliberation. They are expected to draw on their experience, but especially on their ability to reason; the new beliefs are necessarily confronted with their prior knowledge and beliefs that may both help them and hold them back as we have seen earlier in this chapter. The team members having hopefully different backgrounds, the sets of prior beliefs and experiences allow the members to be exposed to different perspectives even in these early discussions.

These exploratory discussions are characteristic of the discursive investigation technique to be used in team deliberations taking place prior to the plenary sessions in the democratized-innovation workshops. After this initial team-based exercise, the same technique is applied in the plenary part of the workshop session but this time with the trainer acting as an active participant in the knowledge rediscovery process. The trainer will strive to use as many of the points brought forward by the representatives of each team, filling in the gaps when required with astutely leading questions or hints in order to get the participants to find the path to the revelation of the knowledge. The learners must be guided through the reasoning that will lead them to the knowledge. The process is repeated for each study point.

In practice, the exploratory dialectics for instructional purposes used in the workshop should be conducted in the following manner: the nine participants must first split up in three teams of three members, as we described in Chapter 8 to carry out a short exercise of critical reflection (see Fig. 8.1). The length of this exercise may range from fifteen minutes for the simpler points to forty-five minutes for the more complex ones. Let us note that the dynamics of these exercises involving small teams working on their own prior to the plenary workshop sessions relate to those of other tried and tested techniques such as 'process-oriented guided inquiry learning' (POGIL) and 'problem-based learning' (PBL) (Eberlein et al. 2008); thus, this approach of getting the learners to work on a problem, a challenge or a study point prior to reporting their findings to the group at large has been proven effective. The aim sought through this initial team challenge is to sharpen their attention on the subject matter that will improve the effectiveness of the ensuing learning in the plenary sessions. Indeed, they will be more engaged in their learning if they applied some effort in trying to figure out the knowledge by themselves through critical reflections and problem-solving with a couple of their peers, possibly uncovering typical issues or even making errors. A friendly spirit of competition between the teams for simple bragging rights for winning on rediscovering a knowledge point may further stimulate them. However, the trainer should take care that this competition doesn't generate feelings of frustration, which is why the composition of the teams should be changed from session to session. They should even be encouraged to take a stand on propositions related to the knowledge because engagement and passions will foster even more acute learning even if the points defended are later contradicted in the plenary session. Like POGIL and PBL, the approach that we advocate emphasizes extensive communication and interactions between the team members. Hence, the study points must not be too easy otherwise they may not engage in any discussions with one another. A member of any team may simply blurt out the answer aloud, and in doing so preclude any further investigation and original thinking from the other participants. At the end of this period, each group must designate a representative who, with the other two representatives of the other two groups, will then engage in an exercise of exploratory (instructional) dialectics with the trainer (see Fig. 8.2). As mentioned in Chapter 8, the optimal size for discussions involving a debate is four. There will not be any need to vote on propositions, since the instructional aim is to rediscover already codified knowledge – although there is certainly always room for improvement and enhancements in anything; the trainer will arbitrate on the ultimate outcome of the exercise by confirming whether or not the knowledge has indeed been rediscovered. The workshop's subject matter is 'the' reference or the standard to attain. The trainer must skillfully orient the discussions to relate and to integrate the learners' ideas and proposals to this knowledge rediscovery process.

As a fictitious example, let us imagine that a group of workers at an online auction start-up is deliberating on the type of products that should be offered. One participant proposed focusing on high-end cars, while the other brought forward the idea of auctioning artwork. In comparing their proposals, they applied the 'Analyze', 'Abstract', 'Classify' and 'Generalize' transformations, which are respectively, process, product, process and product sublations which made them realize that they were both addressing the same market for high-end items intended for the well-to-do. Upon realizing this, they applied the 'Amalgamate' product sublation that brought the two ideas together as separate parts of an online auction designed for wealthy customers. Their colleague from the marketing department later came back telling them that they had to choose one or the other since the start-up couldn't finance both. They reviewed the concept once again, and they agreed to 'Prioritize' (i.e., a process sublation) on the artwork auction and 'Adjuncted' (i.e., a product sublation) the car auction idea to the artwork auction by offering to anyone who buys a work of art a ride in a fashionable car. In effect, the car-related idea became a buyer-perk feature for the artwork auction. In order to reinforce the uniqueness of the perk, they applied the 'Adapt' product sublation to focus the car-ride perks on vintage cars that are more exclusive. Finally, in reflecting on the connection between the purchased artwork and the car-ride perk, they realized that cars may not have existed at the time many of the artworks were created. For authenticity, they then applied an 'Extend' product sublation to include in the ride buyer-perk feature rides in horse carriages that better reflect the era of the older works of art that the customers may buy. Soon after, they launched the service that quickly became popular with customers.

Summation

In this chapter, we presented advanced topics for the training of the trainers in democratized innovation. We described how critical reflection on the chains or networks of justifications that support deep-held beliefs onto which adult learners may hold allow them to overcome the reservations that otherwise brings them to resist change; this process requires discourse exercising critical thinking. Eliciting the new knowledge in the workshops through active group participation may help alleviate the propensity to resist change since they were involved in rediscovering the learning points. The rediscovery training technique associates learning with a co-creation activity. The learners investing their imagination and reasoning in uncovering this knowledge goes a long way to their appropriating and accepting it. They will have developed a special connection with it. They own the path that led to the knowledge that, we contend, opens their mind to it eventually being extended in a process that we called epistemological learning.

Also, we showed how exploratory and creative dialectics may be applied to foster creativity and learning through subject matter rediscovery. We illustrated the dialectic transformations with what we called extended sublations as a set of functions and activities that transform a concept or a conception that a deliberation group is developing collaboratively. Through these sublations, the discourse will be richer and more effective. The learners may intuitively reproduce these techniques by imitating the trainer; the trainer needs to develop a higher level of mastery in order to reorientate the learning while still ensuring that the learners maintain their perception that they rediscovered the subject matter through the single power of the joint deliberations. These techniques can be used for several purposes in the Framework, namely critical thinking, training and of course innovating democratically.

Conclusion

This concludes our journey of discovery through the precepts and practices of democratized innovation. The reader may have already initiated the innovation process by devising ways to implement democratized innovation in his or her organization. Empowering his or her workers to innovate collaboratively through democratized innovation qualifies as a "management innovation" (Hamel 2006) that can bring lasting benefits to one's organization. Carrying out innovation in an organization involves balancing the activities related to exploration and those that are linked with exploitation. It establishes organizational ambidexterity that allows innovation to thrive both in the short term and the long term. We made a case for creative collaboration, and we showed how deliberations can be used to stimulate creativity. Consensus-seeking decision-making leads to negotiated innovations producing outcomes that optimize the value for all stakeholders. We presented a set of thinkLets that the democratized innovators may apply to facilitate their deliberations. It may become commonplace for democratized innovators to inquire with their colleagues whether they have already "negotiated their innovations" because the clash of opinions represents a fruitful additional cycle of creativity. A step-by-step process was presented to develop one's own manifestation of the democratized-innovation framework that is adapted to one's situation, circumstances and preferences. Reaching out to external contributors was related to an approach for protecting the organization's sensitive information. We reviewed the ambiguity surrounding the concept of innovation by running through a set of common misconceptions about it. A straightforward yet coherent innovation typology centered on learning was presented. Since the literature on innovation is already plentiful, we described useful segues into the subject through practical considerations that are common in workplaces. These topics can be easily further expanded into in-depth explorations of the principles of innovation.

Risk is a fundamental consideration in innovation. We derived the iVortoid risk management strategizing framework that allows the users to devise strategies to gain insights into the ambiguity that is typical of innovation projects and to help manage the risks involved in undertaking them. The notion of value-stream innovation was explored; it means innovating on an organization's capabilities. We made the case that organizations should proactively manage their competencies and capabilities to ensure their sustainability in fluctuating market conditions. When innovating, one of the first steps is to reflect on the strategy to apply. We described the iNuggets framework that allows the democratized innovators to define the components of their innovation strategies that they should then relate to best practices in innovation for guidance. It is iterative and runs through four quadrants defined by contingency-related considerations as well as by resource-based ones. The strategy guides the democratized innovators as they carry out their innovations' iterations; it should be revisited when they need to pivot.

https://doi.org/10.1515/9783110683837-014

Since mastering the precepts of democratized innovation empowers the workers, we reviewed the challenges of training them as experienced adult learners in a workshop setting. A participatory and experiential approach was defined that features the rediscovery of the workshop's subject matter, again, through collaborative deliberations. We reviewed a set of practical points, in particular the optimal size for the workshop groups to ensure effective deliberations. We investigated how to address the propensity that people often exhibit to resist change through a process of critical reflection. Finally, the principles of what we called exploratory and creative dialectics that are designed to enhance deliberations were reviewed. The learners may acquire some familiarity with them by observing how the trainer applies them in the workshop. The trainers need to develop a mastery in them to innocuously orient or reorientate the learners' rediscovery of the workshop's subject matter through deliberations.

Since the format of the workshops is participative and experiential, only a limited number of people can be trained at the same time. In addition, democratized innovation requires that all the workers be trained, which, depending on the size of the organization, may involve a high number of workshops. We recommended a train-the-trainer approach that involves identifying workers who have promising dispositions for a trainer role and who demonstrate particular interest in democratized innovation. Their training could include additional advanced academic training in innovation; given the Framework's workshop's participative learning approach, inverted (or flipped) classroom instructional models would be a compatible option for them, particularly those that are discussion-oriented and group-based (Sherbino, Chan and Schiff 2013). Once fully trained, they would then train their colleagues in the Framework's workshops.

"How about the managers? Do they train in democratized innovation as well?", one could ask. As they gain confidence in the Framework, they may be compelled to delegate more and more of the day-to-day decision-making to the workers, which provides the immediate benefit of freeing them up for other activities, such as reflections on the policies regulating the Framework's processes for example. They may also want to attend the workshop, since management innovation is an important source of competitive advantage for an organization (Hamel 2006). They can be democratized innovators too. Workshops in democratized innovation for managers should comprise only managers since it is to be expected that discussions may turn to the managers' roles in the Framework. The managers' power distance (Hofstede 2003) in the organization is another consideration to take into account. If it is long (meaning that management exercises tight and far-reaching control), it may be preferable to organize workshops comprising only managers who are at the same level in the organization's hierarchy. Otherwise, in a more casual management organizational culture with a shorter power distance, mixing levels should work out fine.

Increasingly, workers are spread out across several locations and work as virtual teams. Castellano, Davidson, Khelladi (2017) made the case that creativity techniques enhance knowledge transfers amongst the members of global virtual teams undertaking a co-creation activity. Our negotiation thinkLets and our exploratory and creative dialectics apply in a virtual team setting just as well as in person. The learners' comfort level with training remotely remains the most significant issue. If they are proficient at using collaborative work tools, then holding the workshops remotely could be tried out. We recommend first attempting it as a pilot project before organizing virtual sessions in greater numbers. The collaborative work tools allow sessions to be recorded which provides for an instant record. However, the trainer should evaluate if these recordings stifle the spontaneity of the creative deliberations. Face-to-face interactions facilitate the interpretation of non-verbal exchanges, since even the best resolution video remains an animated 2D picture; the collaborative-work technologies will likely improve in the future to a point at which the online experience truly becomes telepresence. Latency may also become a disturbing issue when part of the group is online, and the other is assembled in person on the same location. Latency may cause the online learners to view and hear the interactions with a slight yet still noticeable delay or lag as it is called. In this case, the interpersonal exchanges in the workshop should slow down and provide pauses in the discussions to allow them to intervene appropriately. They may otherwise get frustrated because of their always needing to struggle to get their points across. Once finally expressed, their points may already be slightly out of context in relation to the lively discussions of the co-located group; as a result, their points often stray awkwardly away from the co-located group's current discussion. Despite the challenges of video conferencing, the online training format can prove to be a significant time and cost saver in distributed organizations; it may be worthwhile ironing out any issues until all the learners master the medium and the format.

We presented the rationale and inner workings of democratized innovation. For small and medium organizations, a manual technique works fine. For larger organizations, it may be advantageous to consider a computerized collaborative team management software tool. There are several commercially available. One should look for tools that can support the spreading activation of resources. Indeed, in large organizations, identifying who has the expertise that one needs and who is currently available to help can be challenging. Without computerization, one could be prompted to limit one's search to a small subset of workers with whom one is acquainted which would partially defeat the purpose of democratized innovation. In addition, the communities of practice could use computerization to diffuse the information about novelties or improvements that they validated to the right people. Diffusing this information in a selective manner rather than broadcasting it will cut down on the amount of information through which every worker needs to sift. The lesser the amount of information, the better. Finally, in order to encourage workers to readily volunteer their expertise, their time and their contributions on innovation projects should be logged; democratized-innovation project codes should be made available for them to use to justify their time away from their regular work. This information should then be compiled and integrated in each worker's performance evaluation file.

We have presented a framework that enhances the regular workers' engagement in innovation. Each implementation must be adapted to one's organization's particular situation and circumstances. This will define one's organization's particular manifestation of the Framework. The seeds of democratized innovation are for the most part already present in every organization albeit in a latent state; it is a matter of revealing and unleashing it. Starting with one single connection is fine; it will grow quickly. Make the power of the knowledge network work for your organization; the knowledge network is there waiting for you to unleash it. The workers simply need to realize that they were democratized innovators all along without even realizing it. Regular workers turned into democratized innovators can achieve extraordinary things for their organization. As an innovation champion the next step is now up to you.

References

Ashford, Nicholas A., George R. Heaton, and W. Curtis Priest. 1979. "Environmental, Health, and Safety Regulation and Technological Innovation." In *Technological Innovation for a Dynamic Economy*, edited by C.T. Hill and J.M. Utterback, 161–221. New York: Pergamon Press.

Argyris, Chris, and Donald A. Schon. 1974. *Theory in Practice: Increasing Professional Effectiveness*. San Francisco: Jossey Bass.

Aristotle. 2012. *Aristotle's Nicomachean Ethics*. Translated by Robert C. Bartlett, and Susan D. Collins. Chicago: The University of Chicago Press.

Bacon, Francis. 1824. "Meditationes Sacræ." In *The works of Francis Bacon: baron of Verulam, viscount St. Alban, and lord high chancellor of England*, 319–334. London: Printed for J. Johnson.

Bandura, Albert. 1993. "Perceived self-efficacy in cognitive development and functioning." *Educational Psychologist* 28 (2): 117–148.

Barnes, William, Myle Gartland, and Martin Stack. 2004. "Old Habits De Hard: Path Dependency and Behavioral Lock-in." *Journal of Economic Issues* 38 (2): 371–377.

Baron, Xavier and Nicolas Cugier. 2016. "Des services généraux aux aménités des environnements du travail. " *L'Expansion: Management Review Solutions*, February 10, 2016.

Bashwiner, David M., Christopher J. Wertz, Ranee A. Flores, and Rex E. Jung. 2016. "Musical Creativity "Revealed" in Brain Structure: Interplay between Motor, Default Mode and Limbic Networks." *Scientific Reports* 6 (1): 20482. https://doi.org/10.1038/srep20482.

Bashwiner, David M., Donna K. Bacon, Christopher J. Wertz, Ranee A. Flores, Muhammad O. Chohan, and Rex E. Jung. 2020. "Resting state functional connectivity underlying musical creativity." *NeuroImage* 218: 116940. https://doi.org/10.1016/j.neuroimage.2020.116940.

Beckwith, Harry. 2014. *The invisible touch: the four keys to modern marketing*. New York: Grand Central Publishing.

Birkinshaw, Julian, and Cristina B. Gibson. 2004. "Building ambidexterity into an organization." *MIT Sloan Management Review* 45 (4): 47–55.

Bittner, Eva Alice Christiane, and Jan Marco Leimeister. 2014. "Creating Shared Understanding in Heterogeneous Work Groups: Why It Matters and How to Achieve It." *Journal of Management Information Systems* 31 (1): 111–143. https://doi.org/10.2753/MIS0742-1222310106.

Boehm, Barry. 2000. "Spiral Development: Experience, Principles, and Refinements." Edited by Wilfred J. Hansen, Carnegie Mellon University, Software Engineering Institute. https://resources.sei.cmu.edu/asset_files/SpecialReport/2000_003_001_13655.pdf.

Boileau, Nicolas. 1998. *Art poétique*. Paris: Flammarion.

Boud, David, Rosemary Keogh, and David Walker. 1985. *Reflection, Turning Experience into Learning*. London: Kogan Page.

Brandenburger, Adam M. and Barry J. Nalebuff. 1996. *Co-Opetition: A Revolution Mindset that Combines Competition and Cooperation: The Game Theory Strategy That's Changing the Game of Business*. New York: Currency Doubleday.

Branson, Richard. 2014. *The Virgin Way: Everything I Know About Leadership*. London: Virgin Books.

Camarinha-Matos, Luis M., and Hamideh Afsarmanesh. 2006. "Collaborative Networks: Value Creation in a Knowledge Society." In *Knowledge Enterprise: Intelligent Strategies in Product Design, Manufacturing, and Management*, edited by Kesheng Wang, George L. Kovacs, Michael Wozny, and Minglun Fang, Volume 207: 26–40. Boston: Springer. https://doi.org/10.1007/0-387-34403-9_4.

https://doi.org/10.1515/9783110683837-015

Castellano, Sylvaine, Philippe Davidson, and Insaf Khelladi. 2017. "Creativity techniques to enhance knowledge transfer within global virtual teams in the context of knowledge-intensive enterprises." *The Journal of Technology Transfer* 42: 253–266.

Chamberlain, Jon. 2014. "Groupsourcing: Distributed Problem Solving Using Social Networks." *Proceedings of the Second AAAI Conference on Human Computation and Crowdsourcing (HCOMP14)*, Pittsburgh, 2014, 22–29. http://dx.doi.org/10.13140/2.1.3912.9607.

Chandy, Rajesh K., and Gerard J. Tellis. 2000. "The Incumbent's Curse? Incumbency, Size, and Radical Product Innovation." *Journal of Marketing* 64: 1–17.

Chesbrough, Henry. 2004. "Managing Open Innovation." *Research Technology Management* 47 (1): 23–26. https://doi.org/10.1080/08956308.2004.11671604.

Chui, Michael, Brad Johnson, and James Manyika. 2009. "Distributed Problem-Solving Networks: An Introduction and Overview." *Oxford Internet Institute Research Paper Series* No. 18. http://dx.doi.org/10.2139/ssrn.1411739.

Christensen, Clayton M., Michael E. Raynor, and Rory McDonald. 2015. "What Is Disruptive Innovation?" *Harvard Business Review*, December 1, 2015. https://hbr.org/2015/12/what-is-disruptive-innovation.

Christensen, Clayton M. 2016. *The Innovator's Dilemma: When New Technologies Cause Great Firms to Fail*. Boston: Harvard Business Review Press.

Cohen, Wesley M., and Daniel A. Levinthal. 1990. "Absorptive Capacity: A New Perspective on Learning and Innovation." *Administrative Science Quarterly* 35 (1): 128–152. https://doi.org/10.2307/2393553.

Cooper, Robert G. 1999. *Product Leadership: Creating and Launching Superior New Products*. Cambridge: Perseus Books.

Corbel, Pascal. 2009. *Technologie, Innovation, Stratégie – De l'innovation technologique à l'innovation stratégique*. Paris: Gualino, Lextenso éditions.

Dahlstrøm, Camilla. 2017. "Impacts of Gamification on Intrinsic Motivation." https://www.ntnu.edu/documents/139799/1279149990/04+Article+Final_camildah_fors%C3%B8k_2017-12-06-13-53-55_TPD4505.Camilla.Dahlstr%C3%B8m.pdf.

Davidson, Philippe L. 1985. "Computer-Aided Decision Making: An Expert System for the Elaboration of Design Strategies." In *Proceedings of the ASME International Computers in Engineering conference and exhibition, Boston, 1985*, Vol. 1: 509–514. New York: The American Society of Mechanical Engineers.

Davidson, Philippe L., and Olga Ivanova. 2011. "Do Challengers from Emerging Nations and Converging Technology Sectors Manage Innovation Differently?" In *Proceedings of the 7th International Conference on Management of Technological Changes, Alexandroupolis, 2011*, Book 2: 577–580. Alexandroupolis: Democritus University of Thrace.

Davidson, Philippe L., Joël M. Malard, and Olga Ivanova. 2012. "Engineering the Management of Innovation Strategy: the iNuggets Framework." Paper presented at the *XXIII ISPIM Conference – Action for Innovation: Innovating from Experience, Barcelona, June 17–20, 2012*. https://conferencesubmissions.com/ispim/proceedings/individual_papers/389713891_Paper.pdf.

Davidson, Philippe L. 2013. "Why Do Many Firms Still Miss the Competitive Advantage of Virtual Teams?" In *Proceedings of PICMET '13: Technology Management in the IT-Driven Services (PICMET), San José, 2013*, 1697–1708. Portland: PICMET. https://ieeexplore.ieee.org/document/6641734.

Davidson, Philippe L. 2015. "Can Creativity Thrive Within Virtual Teams?" Paper presented at the *1st ARTEM Organizational Creativity International Conference, Nancy, March 26–27, 2015*.

Davidson, Philippe L. 2019a. "Democratizing Innovation Through Worker Training: A Framework Based on Andragogy." Paper presented at the *ISPIM Connects Ottawa conference, Ottawa, April 7–10,2019*. https://conferencesubmissions.com/ispim/proceedings/individual_papers/991839468_Paper.pdf.

Davidson, Philippe L. 2019b. "Consensus-seeking Decision-making for Democratized Innovation in Organizations." Paper presented at the *ISPIM Innovation Conference – Celebrating Innovation: 500 Years Since daVinci, Florence, June 16–19,2019*. https://conferencesubmissions.com/ispim/proceedings/individual_papers/1048440736_Paper.pdf.

de Bono, Edward. 1994. *Parallel Thinking: From Socratic Thinking to de Bono Thinking*. Harmondsworth: Viking Penguin.

de Vreede, Gert-Jan, and Robert O. Briggs. 2005. "Collaboration Engineering: Designing Repeatable Processes for High-Value Collaborative Tasks." *Proceedings of the 38th Hawaii International Conference on System Sciences, Big Island, January 3 –6, 2005, 17c*. https://doi.org/10.1109/HICSS.2005.144.

de Vreede, Gert-Jan, Gwendolyn L. Kolfschoten, and Robert O. Briggs. 2006. "ThinkLets: A collaboration engineering pattern language." *International Journal of Computer Applications in Technology* 25 (2/3): 140–154. https://doi.org/10.1504/IJCAT.2006.009064.

Dewey, John. 1938. *Experience and Education*. New York: Macmillan.

Dewey, John. 1939. *Theory of valuation*. Chicago: University of Chicago Press.

Dicocitations. 2021. "Un homme sérieux a peu d'idées. Un homme à idées n'est jamais sérieux". https://www.dicocitations.com/citations/citation-11686.php.

Dingli, Alexiei, and Daniel Tanti. 2015. "Pervasive Social Network." In *Proceedings of The Ninth International Conference on Mobile Ubiquitous Computing, Systems, Services and Technologies: UBICOMM*, Nice, 2015, 31–37. https://file:///C:/Users/UTILIS~1/AppData/Local/Temp/ubicomm_2015_2_20_10025.pdf.

Dion, Kenneth L., Robert S. Baron, and Norman Miller N. 1970. "Why do Groups Make Riskier Decisions than Individuals?" *Advances in Experimental Social Psychology* 5: 305–377.

Doz, Yves L., and Gary Hamel. 1998. *Alliance Advantage: The Art of Creating Value Through Partnering*. Boston: Harvard Business Review Press.

Dufour, Richard, Rebecca Dufour, Robert Eaker, Thomas W. Many, and Mike Matos. 2016. *Learning by Doing: A Handbook for Professional Learning Communities at Work*. Bloomington: Solution Tree.

Dutton, William H. 2008. "Collaborative Network Organizations: New Technical, Managerial and Social Infrastructures to Capture the Value of Distributed Intelligence." *Oxford Internet Institute DPSN Working Paper Series* No. 5. http://dx.doi.org/10.2139/ssrn.1302893.

Eberlein, Thomas, Jack Kampmeier, Vicky Minderhout, Richard S. Moog, Terry Platt, Pratibha Varma-Nelson, and Harold B. White. 2008. "Pedagogies of Engagement in Science: A Comparison of PBL, POGIL, and PLTL." *Biochemistry and Molecular Biology Education* 36 (4): 262–273. https://doi.org/10.1002/bmb.20204.

Eckardt, Wolf Von. n.d. "Ludwig Mies van der Rohe." *Encyclopedia Britannica*. https://www.britannica.com/biography/Ludwig-Mies-van-der-Rohe.

Farrell, Joseph, and Garth Saloner. 1985. "Standardization, Compatibility, and Innovation." *Rand Journal of Economics* 16 (1): 70–83.

Hamel, Gary. 2006. "The Why, What, and How of Management Innovation." *Harvard Business Review*, February 1, 2006.

Hansen, Morten T., and Julian Birkinshaw. 2007. "The Innovation Value Chain." *Harvard Business Review*, June 1, 2007. https://hbr.org/2007/06/the-innovation-value-chain.

Harris, Paul L. 1991. "The work of the imagination". In *Natural theories of mind: Evolution, development and simulation of everyday mindreading*, edited by Andrew Whiten, 283–304. Oxford: Basil Blackwell.

Haveman, Heather A. 1993. "Follow the Leader: Mimetic Isomorphism and Entry into New Markets." *Administrative Science Quarterly* 38 (4): 593–627.

Henderson, Rebecca M. and Kim B. Clark. 1990. "Architectural Innovation: The Reconfiguration of Existing Product Technologies and the Failure of Established Firms." *Administrative Science Quarterly* 35: 9–30.

Heron, John. 1971. *Experience and Method: An Inquiry into the Concept of Experiential Research*. Guildford: Human Potential Research Project, University of Surrey. http://www.human-inquiry. com/Experience%20And%20Method.pdf.

Hodgkinson, Gerard P., Eugene Sadler-Smith, Lisa A. Burke, Guy Claxton and Paul R. Sparrow. 2009. "Intuition in Organizations: Implications for Strategic Management." *Long Range Planning* 42 (3): 277–297.

Hofstede, Geert. 2003. *Culture's Consequences: Comparing Values, Behaviors, Institutions and Organizations Across Nations*. Thousand Oaks: Sage Publications.

Houghton, David Patrick. 2015. "Understanding Groupthink: The Case of Operation Market Garden." *Parameters* 45 (3): 75–85.

Jakobsen, Krisztina V, and Megan Knetemann. 2017. "Putting Structure to Flipped Classrooms Using Team-Based Learning." *International Journal of Teaching and Learning in Higher Education* 29 (1): 177–185.

Kaufman, Scott Barry. 2013. "The Real Neuroscience of Creativity." *Scientific American, Beautiful mind blog*, August 19, 2013. https://blogs.scientificamerican.com/beautiful-minds/the-real-neuroscience-of-creativity/.

Kirkman, Bradley L. 2017. "Why teams often make riskier decisions than individuals (and what you can do about it)." *NC State Enterprise Risk Management Initiative Newsletter*, May 16, 2017. https://erm.ncsu.edu/library/article/why-teams-often-make-riskier-decisions-than-individuals.

Kolfschoten, Gwendolyn L., Jaco H. Appelman, Robert O. Briggs, and Gert-Jan de Vreede. 2004. "Recurring patterns of facilitation interventions in GSS sessions." *Proceedings of the 37th Annual Hawaii International Conference on System Sciences, Big Island, 2004*, Vol.1: 10019c. https://doi.ieeecomputersociety.org/10.1109/HICSS.2004.10007.

Kolfschoten, Gwendolyn L., Robert. O. Briggs, Gert-Jan de Vreede, Peter H.M. Jacobs, and Jaco H. Appelman. 2006. "A conceptual foundation of the thinkLet concept for Collaboration Engineering." *International Journal of Human-Computer Studies* 64 (7): 611–621. https://doi.org/10.1016/j.ijhcs.2006.02.002.

Kop, Rita, and Fiona Carroll. 2011. "Cloud computing: Learning from a Massive Open Online Course on how to enhance creativity in learning." *European Journal of Open, Distance and E-Learning* 15 (2): 1–11.

Krems, Jaimie Arona, Robin I. M. Dunbar, and Steven L. Neuberg. 2016. "Something to talk about: are conversation sizes constrained by mental modeling abilities?" *Evolution and Human Behavior* 37 (6): 423–428.

Langer, Ellen J. 2000. "Mindful Learning." *American Psychological Society* 9 (6): 220–223.

Lave, Jean and Etienne Wenger. 1996. *Situated Learning: Legitimate Peripheral Participation*. Cambridge: Cambridge University Press.

Le Boterf, Guy. 2002. *Développer la compétence des professionnels : Construire les parcours de professionnalisation*. Paris: Éditions d'organisation.

Lee, Jongseok, Jeho Lee, and Habin Lee. 2003. "Exploration and Exploitation in the presence of Network Externalities." *Management Science* 49 (4): 553–570.

Leibenstein, Harvey. 1950. "Bandwagon, Snob, and Veblen Effects in the Theory of Consumers' Demand." *Quarterly Journal of Economic* 64 (2): 183–207.

Legg, Angela M., and Kate Sweeny. 2014. "Do You Want the Good News or the Bad News First? The Nature and Consequences of News Order Preferences." *Personality and Social Psychology Bulletin* 40 (3): 279–288. https://doi.org/10.1177/0146167213509113.

Lencioni, Patrick. 2002. *The Five Dysfunctions of a TEAM*. San Francisco: Jossey-Bass.

Leonard-Barton, Dorothy. 1992. "Core Capabilities and Core Rigidities: A Paradox in Managing New Product Development." *Strategic Management Journal* 13: 111–125.

Lewin, Kurt. 1958. *Group Decision and Social Change*. New York: Holt, Rinehart and Winston.

Lewis, Zakkoyya H, Maria C. Swartz, and Elizabeth J. Lyons. 2016. "What's the Point?: A Review of Reward Systems Implemented in Gamification Interventions." *Games for health journal* 5 (2): 93–99. https://doi.org/10.1089/g4h.2015.0078.

Liebowitz, Stanley J., and Stephen E. Margolis. 1994. "Network Externality: An Uncommon Tragedy." *Journal of Economic Perspectives* 8 (2): 133–150.

Loss, Leandro, Alexandra A. Pereira-Klen, and Ricardo J. Rabelo. "Value Creation Elements in Learning Collaborative Networked Organizations." In *Pervasive Collaborative Networks*, edited by Luis M. Camarinha-Matos and Willy Picard, 75–84. New York: Springer Science+Business Media.

Mansbridge, Jane. 2009. "Deliberative and Non-Deliberative Negotiations." *HKS Faculty Research Working Paper Series RWP09-010, John F. Kennedy School of Government, Harvard University*, April 6, 2009.

McKinley, Jim. 2015. "Critical Argument and Writer Identity: Social Constructivism as a Theoretical Framework for EFL Academic Writing." *Critical Inquiry in Language Studies* 12 (3): 184–207. DOI: 10.1080/15427587.2015.1060558.

Mezirow, Jack. 2000. "Learning to think like an adult: Core concept of transformation theory." In *Learning as transformation. Critical perspectives on a theory in progress*, edited by Jack Mezirow et al., 3–33. San Francisco: Jossey Bass.

Miller, C.Chet, and R.Duane Ireland. 2005. "Intuition in Strategic Decision Making: Friend or Foe in the Fast-Paced 21st Century?" *Academy of Management Executive* 19 (1): 19–30.

Moore, Geoffrey. A. 2002. *Crossing the Chasm: Marketing and Selling High-Tech Products to Mainstream Customers*. New York: Harper Business Essentials.

Morris, Edmund. 2019. *Edison*. New York: Random House.

Müller, Ergon, Sebastian Horbach, and Jörg Ackermann. 2008. "Decentralised Decision Making in Non-Hierarchical Networks." In *Pervasive Collaborative Networks*, edited by Luis M. Camarinha-Matos and Willy Picard, 277–284. New York: Springer Science+Business Media.

Osborn, Alex. F. 1988. *Créativité: l'imagination constructive*. Paris: Bordas.

Owens, William A. 1996. *The Emerging U.S. System-of-Systems*. Washington: National Defense University, Institute for National Strategic Studies. https://apps.dtic.mil/sti/pdfs/ADA394313.pdf.

Plato, and Allan David Bloom. 1991. *The Republic of Plato: Transl. with Notes and an Interpretative Essay by Allan Bloom*. New York: Basic Books.

Porter, Michael E. 1985. *Competitive Advantage: Creating and Sustaining Superior Performance*. New York: Simon and Schuster.

Reason, Peter, and John Heron. 1995. "Co-operative Inquiry." In *Rethinking Methods in Psychology*, edited by R. Harre, J. Smith, and L. Van Langenhove, 122–142. London: Sage.

Reason, Peter, and John Heron. 1997. "A Layperson's Guide to Co-operative Inquiry." https://wag ner.nyu.edu/files/leadership/avina_heron_reason2.pdf.

Ries, Eric. 2011. *The lean Startup: How today's entrepreneurs use continuous innovation to create radically successful businesses*. New York: Crown Business.

Sawyer, Keith. 2007. *Group Genius: The Creative Power of Collaboration*. New York: Basic Books.

Schank, Roger C. and Robert P. Abelson. 1975. "Scripts, Plans and Knowledge." *IJCAI* 1: 151–157.

Schumpeter, Joseph A. 1939. *Business Cycles: A Theoretical, Historical, and Statistical Analysis of the Capitalist Process*. New York and London: McGraw-Hill.

Schumpeter, Joseph A. 1942. *Capitalism, Socialism and Democracy*. London: Routledge.

Searle, John R. 1975. "A Taxonomy of Illocutionary Acts." In *Language, Mind and Knowledge*, edited by K. Gunderson, 344–369. Minneapolis: University of Minnesota Press.

Senge, Peter M. 1990. *The Fifth Discipline: The Art and Practice of the Learning Organization*. New York: Currency Doubleday.

Sherbino, Jonathan, Teresa Chan, and Karen L. Schiff. 2013. "The reverse classroom: lectures on your own and homework with faculty." *CJEM* 15 (3): 178–180.

Simon, Herbert A. 1979. *Models of Thought*, Vol. 1. New Haven: Yale University Press.

Simon, Herbert A. 1991. "Bounded Rationality and Organizational Learning." *Organization Science* 2 (1): 125–134.

Twain, Mark. 2010. *The Adventures of Tom Sawyer*. New York: Library of America.

Utterback, James M. 1996. *Mastering the dynamics of innovation*. Boston: Harvard Business School Press.

Utterback, James M. and William J. Abernathy. 1975. "A Dynamic Model of Process and Product Innovation." *Omega* 3 (6): 639–656.

Van Den Bossche, Piet, Wim Gijselaers, Mien Segers, Geert Woltjer, and Paul Kirschner. 2011. "Team Learning: Building Shared Mental Models." *Instructional Science* 39 (3): 283–301. https://doi.org/10.1007/s11251-010-9128-3.

van Eemeren, Frans H. and Rob Grootendorst. 1984. *Speech Acts in Argumentative Discussions: A Theoretical Model for the Analysis of Discussions Directed towards Solving Conflicts of Opinion*. Dordrecht/Cinnaminson: Foris Publications.

von Hippel, Eric. 2005. *Democratizing Innovation*. Cambridge: MIT Press.

Vygotsky, Lev Semenovich. 1978. *Mind in society: The development of higher psychological processes*. Cambridge/London: Harvard University Press.

Wallach, Michael A., Nathan Kogan, and Daryl J. Bem. 1964. "Diffusion of responsibility and level of risk taking in groups." *The Journal of Abnormal and Social Psychology* 68 (3): 263–274.

Womack, James P, and Daniel T Jones. 1997. "Lean Thinking: Banish Waste and Create Wealth in Your Corporation." *Journal of the Operational Research Society* 48 (11): 1148.

Yin, Chengjiu, Yoshiyuki Tabata, Hiroaki Ogata, and Yoneo Yano. 2009. "Building a participation simulation mobile learning environment through scaffolding technique." *Proceedings of the 17th International Conference on Computers in Education*, ICCE, *Hong Kong, 2009*, 569–573. Hong Kong: Asia-Pacific Society for Computers in Education.

List of Figures

https://doi.org/10.1515/9783110683837-016

List of Tables

https://doi.org/10.1515/9783110683837-017

Index

https://doi.org/10.1515/9783110683837-018

www.ingramcontent.com/pod-product-compliance
Lightning Source LLC
Chambersburg PA
CBHW061814210326
41599CB00034B/6994

* 9 7 8 3 1 1 0 6 8 3 7 8 3 *